All-New
The Book of Lists for Kids

The $\overset{\text{All-New}}{\wedge}$ Book of Lists for Kids

Sandra and Harry Choron

HOUGHTON MIFFLIN COMPANY

Boston · New York

2002

For information about permission to reproduce selections from this book,
write to Permissions, Houghton Mifflin Company, 215 Park Avenue South,
New York, New York 10003.

Visit our Web site: www.houghtonmifflinbooks.com.

Library of Congress Cataloging-in-Publication Data is available.
ISBN 0-618-19135-6

To Annie Leeds,
for her special way of
communicating with the world

Acknowledgments

We are the luckiest writers in the world—we get to try out games and toys, we sit around and think up stuff that will make people laugh (and we are paid to do this!), plus we get to hang out with kids who are our friends and our inspiration. We send out a great big "Hey, thanks!" to these cool people: Tammy Hull Awtry, the Amazing Gabriella Baer, Jake Baer, Noah Baer, Max Cherry, Olivia "the Cupcake" Cherry, Colev Glick, Tony Goldmark (a big kid), Annie Leeds, Katie Leeds, Sophie Leeds, Zach Leeds, Jah Jah, Alexis Stern, John Stern, Grace Townley, Amy Wuhl, and Grace Yang.

We're also grateful to our grownup friends at Houghton Mifflin for caring enough about this book to publish a third edition, especially Susan Canavan and Brandy Vickers. Thanks also to Luise Erdmann, master copy editor.

Contents

1

Making It in a Kid's World

CARL SAGAN LISTS 12 THINGS
HE WISHES THEY TAUGHT AT SCHOOL

In 1985, when we published the first edition of this book, Dr. Sagan was kind enough to share some of his ideas with us, and they are still as useful and important today as they were when he wrote them.

You may already know that Dr. Sagan played a leading role in the Mariner, Viking, and Voyager expeditions to the planets. His scientific research has enhanced our understanding of the greenhouse effect on Venus, dust storms on Mars, the origin of life, and the search for life elsewhere. His award-winning TV series *Cosmos* was the most widely watched series in the history of American public television. The accompanying book, also called *Cosmos,* is the best-selling science book ever published in the English language.

1. Baloney detection. A baloney detector helps tell us when we're being lied to. If you're after the truth, it's usually a good thing to separate out the baloney first. Fallacies (baloney) are everywhere—in schools, in the mass media, and in government. Sometimes the error is unintentional, sometimes it's not. High school algebra and geometry, by the way, are subjects that teach you how to separate the baloney from everything else.

2. Pick a difficult thing and learn it well. This is one of the greatest of human joys. While you learn a little about many subjects, make sure you learn a great deal about one or two. It hardly matters what the subject is, as long as it deeply interests you, and you place it in its broader human context. After you teach yourself one subject, you become more confident about your ability to teach yourself another. Gradually you find you've acquired a key skill. The world is changing so rapidly that you must continue to teach yourself throughout your life. But don't get trapped by the first subject that interests you, or the first thing you find yourself good at. The

All-New
The Book of Lists for Kids

world is full of wonders, and some of them we don't discover until we're all grown up. Most of them, sadly, we never discover.

3. Don't be afraid to ask "dumb" questions. Many simple questions — like why grass is green, or why the sun is round, or why we need 55,000 nuclear weapons in the world — are really deep questions. The answers can be a gateway to real insights. It's also important to know, and asking questions is the way. To ask "dumb" questions requires courage on the part of the asker and knowledge and patience on the part of the answerer. And don't confine your learning to schoolwork. Discuss ideas in depth with friends.

4. Listen carefully. Many conversations are a kind of competition that rarely leads to discovery on either side. When people are talking, don't spend the time thinking about what you're going to say next. Instead, try to understand what they're saying and what you can learn from or about them. Older people have grown up in a world very different from yours, one you may not know very well. They, and people from other parts of the country and from other nations, have important ideas that can enrich your life.

5. Everybody makes mistakes. Everybody's understanding is incomplete. Be open to correction, and learn to correct your own mistakes. The only embarrassment is in not learning from your mistakes. (Governments almost never admit mistakes. What can we learn from this fact?)

6. Know your planet. It's the only one we have. Learn how it works. We're changing the atmosphere, the surface, the waters of the Earth, often for some short-term advantage when the long-term consequences are unknown. Especially in a democracy, the citizens should have at least something to say about the direction in which we're going. If we don't understand the issues, we abandon the future.

7. Science and technology. You can't know your planet unless you know something about science and technology. School science courses, I remember, concentrated on the trivia of science but left out many important ideas. The great discoveries in modern science are also great discoveries of the human spirit. For example, Copernicus showed that—far from the Earth being the center of the universe—the Earth is just one of many small worlds. This may make "us Earthlings" feel less important but it also opens us up to our view of how vast and awesome our universe really is.

8. Nuclear war. This is the most immediate and most dangerous threat to our species and our world. Learn enough about nuclear weapons to be able to understand the threat they pose and how to help resolve the growing crisis. If you can make a contribution to this subject, you will have done something for all generations that are and ever will be.

9. Don't spend your life watching TV. You know what I'm talking about.

10. Culture. Gain some exposure to the great works of literature, art and music. If such a work is hundreds or thousands of years old and is still admired, there is probably something to it. Like all deep experiences, it may take a little work on your part to discover what all the fuss is about. But once you make the effort, your life has changed; you've acquired a source of enjoyment and excitement for the rest of your days. In a world as tightly connected as ours is, don't limit your attention to American or Western culture. Learn how and what people elsewhere think. Learn something of their history, their religions, their viewpoints.

11. Politics. A basic part of American democracy, and one of the principles on which the nation was founded, is the protection and encouragement of unpopular beliefs. (Think again about Copernicus.) No nation, sect or political party speaks the *whole* truth. So consider unpopular ideas and see if any of them make sense to you. Why, exactly, are they unpopular? Learn something about practical politics. Involve yourself in a local political campaign. Understand how political power is used. There are many evils—slavery, say, or smallpox—that were overcome worldwide, through the combination of new insights and political power. Understanding these advances can help us to deal with other evils in our time.

12. Compassion. Many people believe that we live in a very selfish time. But there is a loneliness that comes from living only for yourself. Humans are capable of great compassion, love and tenderness. These feelings, however, need encouragement to grow.

Look at the delight a 1- or 2-year-old takes in learning, and you see how powerful is the human will to learn. Our passion to understand the universe and our compassion for others jointly provide the chief hope of the human species.

20 EARLY WARNING SIGNS OF MATURITY

You are on a sinking ship. The captain calls out to the crew, "Save the women and children first!" but no one comes to your rescue. Here are some other signs that you are reaching maturity.

1. Your parents stop sounding stupid.

2. You start remembering to do your chores without being reminded.

3. You've stopped bullying your little brother or sister and you don't know why.

4. All your homework gets done, all the time.

5. You read a book, and it made you think.

6. You've made friends with a geek.

7. You can sit through one hour of educational television without falling asleep or wanting to.

8. You've asked for a raise in your allowance, explained why, and your parents agreed.

9. Your body starts changing so fast that your best friend doesn't recognize you. In fact, *you* don't recognize you!

10. You stop complaining about getting pinched on the cheek by your grandmother.

11. A cute member of the opposite sex says hello and you don't wonder what they meant by that.

12. You've realized that you probably will never become a cowboy/astronaut/fireman.

13. You stop being embarrassed by your zits.

14. You realize that your dad's 1997 Ford station wagon can take you anywhere your neighbor's new BMW can.

15. Someone calls you "mister" or "miss," "sir" or "ms."

16. You'd rather read *Jurassic Park* than watch the movie.

17. You can sip through a straw without being tempted to blow bubbles out the other end.

18. Candy doesn't taste as good anymore, and you find yourself ordering salads in restaurants.

19. You find what the sitter and her boyfriend are doing on the couch more interesting than the video game you are playing.

20. You've walked away from a fight because the argument was stupid.

9 FAMOUS PEOPLE WHO HAD HEALTH PROBLEMS WHEN THEY WERE KIDS

1. Wilma Rudolph, the black Olympic sprinter who won three medals in 1960, had polio when she was a child and couldn't walk without a brace until she was 8.

2. Al Capp, who created the "Li'l Abner" comics, was hit by a streetcar when he was 12 and had to have his leg amputated.

3. Newscaster Dan Rather had rheumatic fever when he was young and had to spend five years in bed.

4. Aesop, whose fables you've probably read, was a dwarf.

5. Sidney Poitier, the actor, weighed less than three pounds when he was born.

6. When Sylvester Stallone was born, one side of his face became paralyzed. This accounts for his unusual smile. But in school the kids made fun of his deformity, calling him "Slant Mouth."

7. Actor Richard Thomas grew up partially deaf.

8. When comedienne Lucille Ball was little, she was paralyzed in a car accident. No one expected her to walk again.

9. Mr. Rogers is colorblind!

A FEW OF ROSIE O'DONNELL'S FAVORITE THINGS

Rosie O'Donnell is a great role model: She's America's number-one talk show host (she's tossed over 20,000 Koosh balls at audiences worldwide), a champion of kids and their causes, a writer, a Broadway star, and a talented actress who has had memorable roles in movies like *Harriet the Spy, The Flintstones,* and *A Very Brady Sequel*. Plus, she's a devoted mom. All that keeps her pretty busy, but her thoughts tell us who the real Rosie O'Donnell is: "When kids say you're all right, that means you're doing something right in your life." Most important of all, Rosie O'Donnell is a kid at heart.

1. Kickball
2. Softball
3. Skateboarding
4. Basketball
5. Singing
6. Telling jokes
7. Kids
8. Reading books (She started a club called Rosie's Readers.)
9. Watching TV (Her favorite shows on Nickelodeon, which is her favorite channel, are *The Nanny and the Professor* and *My Three Sons.*)
10. Being loved (Do you know that no adult ever told Rosie they loved her until she was in junior high school?)
11. Playing video games, especially Pacman, Tetris, Asteroids, and the Legend of Zelda.
12. Elmo
13. Barbra Streisand
14. Tom Cruise
15. Collecting toys and dolls (But when the Mattel toy company told her they wanted to make a Rosie Barbie Doll, she said she would let them only if it could be a plump doll, just like her. So that's what they did!)

HOW TO PROTECT YOURSELF WHEN YOU'RE OUT IN PUBLIC

1. Stay alert! Always be aware of where you are and the people around you.
2. Watch where you're going and appear confident.
3. Stay on busy streets where there are people. Stay out of dark alleys, woods, and other shortcuts. Avoid being alone.

The All-New Book of Lists for Kids

4. Keep valuable items in your pockets or in a fanny pack.

5. If you have something valuable, keep it out of sight and don't talk about it. Resist the temptation to show off.

6. Don't play in deserted areas where you probably won't be able to get help if you need it.

7. Don't hang around public bathrooms.

8. If you have a locker at school, don't tell anyone the combination to the lock.

9. If you must stay in the building after school has let out, stay only in the area that's under supervision. If you need to go to another part of the building for any reason, get someone else, preferably an adult, to go with you.

10. If other kids tell you that you must give them money or they will beat you up, tell your parents, and make sure they call the police and the school. *Your parents can do this without giving your name.* Gangs of kids who demand "protection money" can be found in all parts of the country. You can't stop them, but the police and the school system can.

11. Don't talk to strangers. That may sound like something you've been hearing since you were a baby, but it's good advice. Don't give any information about yourself to people you don't know. Even saying something simple, like where your mother works, can lead to trouble.

12. Don't get on or off an elevator with a stranger if you are alone.

13. If someone or something scares you, look for bright lights and people and run for help, screaming all the way.

14. Say no — loudly — to anyone who bothers you.

15. Do not agree to keep a secret from your parents.

16. If someone threatens to attack you unless you give them your money, give them the money. In most cases, muggers are after your money, not you. Since you probably won't be able to overpower them, and since your life is more important than your money, give them what they want and then get away as soon as possible. Immediately report what happened to the police.

17. Never hitchhike! Getting into a car with a stranger is asking for trouble. If you must do this because you are stranded somewhere or need help, don't accept a ride from a car that has been circling the area, and try to remember as many details about the person who gives you the ride as you can: the model, color, and license plate of the car; the color of the driver's hair and eyes; what the driver is wearing; and any other distinct characteristics.

18. If a stranger asks you for help with a problem, such as finding a lost dog or carrying packages, suggest that another adult will help them. If these people have really good intentions, they will understand your refusal to help.

19. If someone wearing a uniform approaches you and tells you to cooperate with them, ask to see some identification. Make sure the person is really who they say they are!

20. When you work at other people's homes or go on job interviews, even if you're just at a friend's house, be sure to tell your parents exactly where you are and when you plan to come home.

21. If you witness a crime, call 911 and calmly, clearly, tell what you saw. You do not have to give your name.

HOME ALONE!
How to Stay Safe

1. Always make sure that the doors and windows are locked.

2. Don't open the door for anyone you don't know well. If the person who knocks on the door has real business in the house—for example, if they've come to repair something—they can come back another time. If they claim they need help, say you won't open the door, but you will call the police for them.

3. Pick a password that only you and your parents know.

That way, if someone wants to get into your house when you are alone and claims to have been sent by your parents, you can ask for the password.

4. If someone bothers you at the door and won't go away, make them think that you're not really alone. Tell them your father is sleeping and that you're going to wake him up. Instead, call the police.

5. If you get a phone call from a stranger who asks you personal questions or says weird things, hang up immediately, no matter how tempted you are to tell that person off. If you get a few of these calls, see that your parents report them to the police and to the telephone company.

6. Be careful what you tell other people about your plans. Your friends obviously are not interested in harming you, but they could repeat things in front of strangers. Avoid discussing things like your family's plans to go on vacation, the times when you are alone at home, where you're planning to babysit, where your family hides valuable items, where your family hides an extra house key.

8 THINGS YOU CAN DO IF YOU'RE AFRAID OF THE DARK

Thomas Edison, who invented the light bulb, was afraid of the dark! So don't let anyone tell you that nightlights are for babies. Here are some ways to handle the fear.

1. Use your imagination to create nice, pleasant things from the shapes you see in the shadows. It's just like pretending that clouds are real objects. For instance, if that huge ball of darkness on your ceiling looks like a monster at first, turn it into a big fluffy kitten or a circus balloon.

2. Sing. Noise helps to scare away fear. Practice your very favorite songs out loud.

3. Keep a flashlight next to your bed. If something scares you, shine the light directly on it. You'll see that nothing's there.

4. Keep a notepad next to your bed. If something scares you, write it down on the paper and then rip the paper—and the fear—into shreds.

5. Try to put yourself into a trance that will help you fall asleep. Here's one technique: First, think about the scary shapes in the room that are bothering you. Introduce yourself to these "monsters" out loud. Once you've made friends with them, ask them to leave. As they start to go out the door, concentrate on your own breathing. Count slowly. Before you reach 100, chances are you'll be asleep.

6. If you see shadows that scare you, try to find out what's really creating them. Maybe the "monster" you're imagining is really the shadow of your favorite tree.

7. Read a book, listen to music, or write a letter to a friend to take your mind off your fears.

8. Ask someone to check your room to make sure everything's all right. Say, "This may seem silly, but I'll get to sleep a lot faster if you do this for me."

7 THINGS TO DO IF YOU THINK YOU'RE GOING TO THROW UP

1. RUN to the nearest bathroom. Don't wait to see if you really do need to throw up!

2. Drink ginger ale.

3. Eat a few crackers.

4. If you become nauseated in a moving vehicle, like a car or a boat, stare at something that isn't moving, like the horizon or a building in the distance. You get nauseated because your brain forgets that you are moving but your stomach doesn't.

All-New
The Book of Lists for Kids

5. Breathe through your nose.

6. Don't get scared or embarrassed. Everyone throws up at some point. And if you make a mess—well, that's what you get for being human.

7. Try to breathe in some fresh air.

WHEN A PET DIES

Pet Haven Cemetery in Gardena, California, is one of the most famous pet cemeteries in the world. Jerry Lewis, Tina Turner, Michael Landon, and Nat "King" Cole are just a few of the celebrities whose pets are buried there. The people at Pet Haven know that losing a pet can be an awful time for anyone. Here are some ideas they have that may help you feel better.

1. Take the time to think about your emotions. You may find yourself feeling angry (at whatever caused your pet to die), sad (because you have lost a friend), guilty (if the pet died because of something you did), or even jealous (of other kids who still have their pets). Or you may be feeling a combination of all of them. All these feelings are normal.

2. Share your feelings with others. If you have a brother or sister you don't get along with, here's a time when you may get closer. Even if you think you have nothing in common, the fact is that you both knew the pet and you both miss him. So you *do* have something to talk about! Remember that people who have never had pets may not understand what you're going through. Don't get mad at them.

3. Have a ceremony to say good-bye to your pet, whether it's an actual burial or just a time to think about your pet. Invite others who loved your pet to be part of this ceremony. It's also a good time to decide what you want to do with your pet's belongings.

4. Keep a remembrance of your pet. Even though you are sad now, the pet was your friend. Maybe you can place a picture of the pet in your room. You can write a poem that others might enjoy reading, or you can plant something—like a tree—as a memorial.

5. Continue your normal activities. Some things may have changed but not all of them.

6. Be extra nice to your other pets—they may be sad, too.

7. Think about other pets that might need your care. You may not want to adopt another one right away, but keep in mind that you can sometimes make yourself feel better by being nice to others. There are plenty of people and pets out there who need your love.

8. Say thank you to people who were nice to your pet. Let them know that their caring made a difference in the life of your pet.

9. Say a prayer. Albert Schweitzer, the great philosopher and doctor, wrote this poem when his own pet died:

> *Hear our humble prayer, O God,*
> *For our friends the animals.*
> *Especially for animals who are suffering;*
> *For any that are hunted or lost*
> *Or deserted or frightened or hungry;*
> *For all that must be put to sleep.*
> *We entreat for them all*
> *Thy mercy and pity,*
> *And for those who deal with them*
> *We ask a heart of compassion*
> *And gentle hands and kindly words.*
> *Make us be true friends to animals*
> *And so to share*
> *The blessings of the merciful.*

13 RUDE THINGS THAT PARENTS DO

Parents who are otherwise polite and conscious of the rules of etiquette sometimes violate these rules when it comes to their own kids. Here are just a few things they do that are annoying, embarrassing, or just plain rude.

1. They criticize you in front of your friends.
2. They open your mail.
3. They tell your secrets to other members of the family.
4. They ask you to "perform" for company.
5. They invite your friends to dinner without asking you first.
6. They ask you to be friends with certain kids just because they're friends with the kids' parents.
7. They invite their friends to your birthday party.
8. They hang around when your friends come over.
9. They ignore you when their friends come over.
10. They call your friends by the wrong name.
11. They invade your privacy by entering your room without knocking.
12. They ask your friends rude questions, like what their parents do for a living.
13. They correct your grammar and manners in front of other people.

11 LIES PARENTS TELL

1. Punishing you hurts them more than it hurts you.
2. Eating chocolate causes acne.
3. Lightning never strikes twice.
4. You shouldn't go swimming for an hour after you eat or you'll get stomach cramps.
5. If you cut your hair, it'll grow faster.

6. Tattoos are permanent. (Some are, but not all. Still, this is a decision you want to make when you're older.)

7. You can't get too many vitamins.

8. If you go outside in the winter with wet hair, you'll automatically catch a cold.

9. Eating green apples will give you a stomachache.

10. No one knows which came first, the chicken or the egg. (Of course the egg came first; dinosaurs were laying them for millions of years before the first chicken clucked its way into the world!)

11. "It tastes like chicken."

14 PEOPLE YOU CAN TALK TO IF YOU CAN'T TALK TO YOUR PARENTS

1. An older brother, sister, or friend

2. An aunt, uncle, grandparent, or other relative

3. A teacher you trust

4. The school's guidance counselor

5. A friend's parent

6. The family doctor

7. A religious leader

8. A school social worker

9. The school nurse

10. The school principal or assistant principal

11. Your godparent

12. A public health or social worker. You can find such a person by checking the Yellow Pages under any of these listings: Social Service Organizations, Social Workers, Mental Health Services, Clinics, or Human Service Organizations.

13. A social leader, such as the head of a Scout troop (even if you're not a member)

14. A member of the Alanon/Alateen organization, which helps people with alcohol and drug problems. Look in the

Yellow Pages under Alcoholism Information and Treatment Centers to find one of them. (See also "41 Organizations That Work with and for Kids," page 86.)

15 THINGS EVERY BABYSITTER SHOULD KNOW

This list may seem long, but babysitting is serious business, and you really do need to know a lot more than just what you'll be doing with the child. You need to know what to do in case of an emergency, what to do if someone calls, and how to handle any unexpected circumstance, such as a pet scratching at the door to be let in or out, or how to handle a child's claim that his parents always let him stay up to see *Saturday Night Live*. It may be a good idea to make copies of this list and keep the information in a notebook so that if you babysit for the same people again, you won't have to ask them all the details. Always remember to keep the doors locked at all times, to check on the children every half hour or so once they're in bed, and to stay awake until the parents return.

1. The name of the family and the child's name
2. Their address and phone number (which you should also leave at your own home)
3. How the telephone works (if it's a complicated system)
4. Whom to call in an emergency
5. Where the parents can be reached
6. When they will return
7. Instructions for handling phone calls and visitors
8. The location of clothing, bed linen, food, and first aid supplies
9. Where you can find a house key in case you have to leave with the child in an emergency

10. What games the child may play and TV programs he or she may watch; what Internet and computer privileges are allowed

11. The child's bedtime and eating habits (and if there are any allergies or illnesses you should be aware of)

12. The child's bedtime routine, such as brushing teeth, taking medicine, and getting cleaned up

13. How to handle any pets that may be present

14. Instructions for operating the burglar alarm if they have one

15. Whether it's OK to invite a friend to sit with you. *Never* allow anyone else in the house without getting permission first.

10 DOOR-TO-DOOR SAFETY TIPS

Whether you are raising money for charity, getting a petition signed, or selling candy, always be extra careful when you approach the homes of strangers. Be sure you understand these rules before you start out.

1. Never go alone. Always take a friend.

2. Always let your parents or another adult know the area you will be in and when they should expect you home.

3. Don't leave this area without letting someone know your plans have changed.

4. If you feel uncomfortable going to an unfamiliar area, don't go there.

5. Never enter anyone's home under any circumstances. Don't accept their food or a beverage.

6. If you need to use a bathroom or make a telephone call, go to a well-lighted public area or a store.

7. Always carry some change for an emergency phone call.

8. If you feel uncomfortable about any situation, leave at once. Don't worry about appearing rude.

9. Be aware of what is going on around you.

10. If you are collecting money and expect to handle cash, try to have someone with you.

8 HALLOWEEN SAFETY TIPS

All of the above safety rules should be followed, in addition to these:

1. Do not go trick-or-treating alone. Older children should go with friends; younger kids should be accompanied by an adult.

2. Be sure to carry a flashlight or a glow stick and to wear reflective clothing.

3. Make sure you can breathe easily through your mask and that you can see where you're going. If your costume has a tail, keep it short so you don't trip over it.

4. Only wear costumes and masks that are flame-resistant.

5. Do not approach a dark house or one that looks like the people are not welcoming.

6. If anything weird happens, tell your parents.

7. Don't sample any of your goodies until you get home and an adult examines your collection. Don't eat candy that looks like someone has been fooling around with the wrapping or that doesn't have any wrapping.

8. A good alternative to trick-or-treating is to organize parties at home, in school, or in a community center where everyone can show off their costumes safely.

8 PUNISHMENTS THAT ARE FORMS OF CHILD ABUSE

More than 1.5 million children are abused by an adult each year. Kids who are abused are either physically or emotionally hurt by an adult. This adult can be a parent, step-parent, aunt or uncle, grandparent, teacher, or neighbor—even another kid. Many kids who have been abused believe that they somehow deserved the punishment they received and that the abuser has a right to hurt them. So it's important for you to know what kinds of punishment are considered abuse and to remember that child abuse is a crime. The following punishments are examples of child abuse and should be reported to a teacher, doctor, religious leader, or a friend.

1. Beatings
2. Being tied or locked up
3. Being burned
4. Being cut
5. Any action that causes bleeding or bruising
6. Being denied shelter or food for long periods of time
7. Being constantly screamed at or insulted in a way that scares you. Words *can* hurt.
8. Any action by an adult including any sexual behavior that scares you

5 PUNISHMENTS THAT ARE NOT CONSIDERED ABUSE

You may not want to be punished or disciplined by your parents, but it is their responsibility to do so when they feel it is necessary or appropriate. The following are examples of normal punishments.

1. Being grounded for not doing your homework or some other responsibility
2. Being sent to your room without dinner
3. Having a privilege like watching TV taken away
4. Having your allowance taken away
5. Being scolded in a nonviolent manner

9 THINGS TO DO IF YOU OR A FRIEND IS BEING ABUSED

If you or a friend is being abused you must seek help. The only person responsible for child abuse is the person committing the abuse, not you and not your friend. Here are some ways of getting help.

1. Talk to the parent who is not committing the abuse.
2. Talk to another adult member of your family you love and trust.
3. Talk to a teacher.
4. Talk to a religious leader.
5. Call the police.
6. Talk to your family doctor.
7. Get the phone number of a Child Abuse, Family Services, or Mental Health agency from your telephone book and call them.
8. Get in touch with the National Council on Child Abuse and Family Violence, 1155 Connecticut Ave. NW, Washington, DC 20036 (858-623-2777) or send an e-mail to WCFV@aol.com.
9. Go to a hospital emergency room and report the abuse.

4 HOTLINES FOR KIDS WHO HAVE RUN AWAY FROM HOME

These people help kids find shelter someplace where they can work out their problems *safely* and *sanely*. They also provide a service that lets runaways get messages to their families without revealing their whereabouts. These services are *confidential* and *free*. The call is free, too.

1. 800-621-4000
2. 800-448-4663
3. 800-843-5678
4. 800-411-UWAY

9 WAYS TO RIDE A SCHOOL BUS SAFELY

1. Leave home early enough so that you'll arrive at the bus stop five minutes early—but no earlier.

2. Wait for your bus well off the road. Do not try to board the bus until it has come to a complete stop.

3. Enter the bus in an orderly manner. Pay attention to any instructions the driver gives you.

4. Stay in your seat while the bus is in motion and use the seatbelt if one is provided.

5. Never take large objects (anything larger than a small musical instrument) on the bus with you. And never take pets, especially small ones. They can cause the kind of turmoil that leads to accidents. If you must take something large or weird to school, try to get someone to drive you that day.

6. Keep the aisles clear at all times.

7. Never eat or smoke on the bus.

8. When you get off the bus, leave the bus stop immediately. If you must cross the street, do so in front of the bus (the driver cannot see you if you're at the side or behind the bus), but wait until the driver signals you to do so. Even then, once you're out in the street a few feet, look both ways. Never attempt to get back on the bus unless the driver tells you to do so.

9. If you've dropped something after you've gotten off and need to retrieve it, make sure the bus driver knows what you're doing. Even if the bus seems about to run over it and ruin the object, stay clear of the bus. (Two-thirds of all deaths related to school buses occur *outside* the bus.)

9 REASONS KIDS TAKE DRUGS

Drug use is one of our most serious problems, and drug use among kids becomes more widespread every year. Here is a list of reasons that some kids take drugs in the first place.

1. They are pressured or bullied into taking them.
2. They want to fit in.
3. They think it's cool.
4. They didn't realize that what they took was a drug.
5. They didn't realize that they could become addicted.
6. They're having a serious problem at home or at school and think that using drugs will somehow help.
7. They can't stop because they are afraid to get help or speak with their parents.
8. They are in a lot of pain over something, and they think this will make them feel better.
9. They are too stupid to think of another way to have fun.

8 WAYS TO TELL IF YOUR FRIEND IS TAKING DRUGS

These symptoms don't necessarily mean that the person is taking drugs; they are just things that many drug-users experience. Don't jump to conclusions about other kids just because they may have some of the following problems. If you are suspicious about someone, confront the person and let them know you're concerned.

1. They're tired a lot.
2. They don't seem to have much appetite.
3. Your friend doesn't seem to be himself.
4. Frequent changes in mood—one moment she's happy; the next moment she's sad.

5. Your friend no longer seems to enjoy hobbies or sports that he once liked a lot.

6. She seems angry all the time.

7. The person seems to be stealing money (perhaps to buy drugs).

8. You smell strange odors in their room or on their clothing.

8 REASONS WHY KIDS SMOKE

Smoking is extremely addictive and bad for your health. Some kids who begin smoking will find that it is very difficult to stop and that even two to three cigarettes a day can lead to addiction. For more information on the subject or for tips on how to stop smoking, contact the Foundation for a Smokefree America, P.O. Box 492028, Los Angeles, CA 90049-8028 (310-471-4270); www.tobaccofree.org. These are some of the reasons kids start to smoke cigarettes:

1. Tobacco ads can be very appealing. Did you know that Joe Camel ads are not allowed in publications for kids?

2. Their friends do it.

3. They think it looks cool, when in fact most people look down on smokers.

4. It makes them feel tough. (Actually, it makes them look like kids who are scared but are trying to look tough.)

5. It makes them feel older.

6. They don't know that one out of every five deaths in the U.S. is the result of smoking. (That's 420,000 people a year!)

7. Their parents smoke and they think it's OK.

8. Plain stupidity.

MICHAEL JORDAN'S WORST CHILDHOOD EXPERIENCES

One of the all-time stars of professional basketball had problems when he was a kid, too.

1. Michael was not popular in grade school and had very few friends.

2. He usually felt awkward and embarrassed around other people.

3. He thought he was so ugly that he would never get married. He was so convinced of this that he learned how to cook, do laundry, and clean house so he would be able to take care of himself alone.

4. Kids in school made fun of him.

5. He didn't date when all the other kids did.

5 CAUSES THAT PRO WRESTLER GOLDBERG WORKS FOR

Goldberg loves kids and is dedicated to making a difference in their lives. His advice is, "By working hard, you can accomplish anything." And he stresses: "Don't do anything you see on the WWF; it will only lead to trouble!"

1. The Make-A-Wish Foundation, which grants the wishes of kids who have cancer

2. The Starlight Foundation, for terminally ill children

3. Toys for Tots drives

4. He is a spokesman for the Humane Society, a position that led to his testifying before Congress in 1999.

5. He frequently appears at Wolfson's Children's Hospital, in Jacksonville, Florida, and speaks with young patients there. (Goldberg is a descendant of Louis Wolfson, for whom the hospital is named.)

10 WAYS TO AVOID MOTION SICKNESS

On a boat it's called seasickness, on land carsickness, and on a plane airsickness. Whatever it's called, the feelings of dizziness and nausea are something you want to avoid. Here are some hints that will help.

1. If you think you are going to throw up, you probably will. Try to think about feeling well instead.

2. If you are with other people who are feeling sick, try to stay away from them. We know this doesn't sound very nice, but if you try to help them, you may only wind up becoming sick yourself.

3. Avoid unpleasant odors, and try to get some fresh air as soon as possible.

4. If you travel at night, you are less likely to get sick because you can't see motion as well as during the day.

5. Being well rested before a trip can help. You will be stronger and more resistant to motion sickness.

6. In a car, sit in the front seat and face front.

7. On a boat or in a car, keep your eyes on an object that is not moving. Watching the horizon is a good idea.

8. Don't read on a plane if it's a bumpy flight. Reading in a moving vehicle makes a lot of people feel nauseated.

9. Drinking a carbonated cola drink can help settle your stomach if you feel nauseated.

10. Eating soda crackers can help your stomach feel better.

10 WAYS TO WIN THE BATTLE AGAINST ZITS

Acne is not caused by eating too much chocolate or having dirty hair or skin. Acne is genetic: It's a condition you have inherited from your parents. Here are some facts and hints about acne and pimples (zits) that can help you.

1. Acne can be made worse by sun exposure and changes in the seasons and climate. Stress can also make matters worse.

2. Some doctors believe that foods containing iodine can bring on an acne attack. Some fish contain high levels of iodine.

3. Simple acne can result in just a few blackheads and whiteheads. Serious cases will have many blackheads, whiteheads, pimples, and cysts. The serious version is not as common, but if you have it, you should be treated by a doctor.

4. Never squeeze a pimple. This can lead to an infection and will make things worse.

5. Never squeeze a whitehead. The fluid inside may spread and thus cause pimples.

6. Blackheads can be squeezed. This will not cause a pimple.

7. Some helpful medications and creams can be applied to your skin. But you need to have your parents ask for a doctor's advice.

8. When you use any kind of acne medicine, stay out of the sun, and remember always to clean your skin extremely well.

9. Never use more than one medication at a time, especially if it is a drug prescribed by your doctor.

10. Acne can be a serious condition and sometimes requires a doctor's care. If you think you have a serious problem, ask your parents for help.

6 MAKEUP TIPS FOR GIRLS WHO DON'T WEAR MAKEUP

Girls who aren't ready for makeup but want to look their very best for a special occasion can try these tips.

1. Dab a bit of petroleum jelly on your eyebrows and eyelashes to make them shine.

2. Use clear lip gloss or petroleum jelly on your lips for a special shine. This will also protect them from the cold, wind, and sun.

3. Petroleum jelly will give your cheeks a healthy glow.

4. Comb or brush your eyebrows with a small comb sold just for this purpose. It will give them a neat appearance.

5. Use an eyelash curler to add accent to your lashes. Carefully follow the instructions that come with the package.

6. For a special night out, especially if you're tired and need to get the red out of your eyes, apply any of the following to your eyes (while they're closed) for ten minutes while you lie down: an ice pack; slices of cold cucumber; cold, wet tea bags.

7 THINGS YOU CAN DO ABOUT FRECKLES

People who don't have freckles often wish they did, and some consider them a sign of good luck. If you're determined to do something about them, you should know that you won't be able to eliminate them entirely and chances are they'll disappear by the time you are an adult. Whatever you do, check with your doctor before you try anything, since skin can be very sensitive to anything you put on it, and blotches caused by an irritation are going to look a lot worse than freckles ever could.

1. Once a day, apply plain yogurt to your freckles. Leave it on for one minute, then rinse with cold water.

2. Apply fresh lemon juice to your freckles. Rinse with cool water, then apply a light coat of vegetable oil. If your skin becomes irritated, stop the treatment immediately.

3. Rub the juice of fresh cranberries on your freckles. Rinse with cool water and apply a light coat of vegetable oil.

All-New
^

Again, if your skin becomes irritated, discontinue the treatment.

4. An old folk remedy suggests rubbing your freckles with a penny and then throwing the penny away. Whoever finds the penny gets your freckles!

5. Learn to love them.

6. This one is based entirely on superstition. Squeeze some lemon juice into a cup of rain water and add ten raisins. Stir the mixture every day for nine days and wash your freckles with it on the tenth day.

7. Don't even think about trying this folk cure. It was said that if you mixed buttermilk with some lemon juice and applied this to your freckles *with a live frog,* your freckles would disappear.

4 THINGS TO DO IF YOUR SKIN TOUCHES ITCHY-SCRATCHY POISONOUS PLANTS

Poison ivy, poison oak, and poison sumac can ruin your summer. Learn what they look like and avoid them. Here's what to do if you've been exposed.

1. If you wash the affected area with cold water immediately after making contact, you may be able to prevent the poison from seeping into your skin. Don't use soap with the water.

2. Wash everything that may have touched the poisonous plant, including your clothes, your backpack, your pet, and anything you touched.

3. Don't scratch. Scratching will spread the rash and make things a lot worse. Clean your hands and fingernails if you've already scratched to help prevent the rash from spreading even further.

4. Some medications can help you. Calamine lotion will stop the itching. It also keeps the poison from sticking to your clothes. Follow the instructions on the bottle.

9 WAYS TO STOP THE HICCUPS

Charles Osborne, of Anthon, Iowa, got the hiccups in 1922 and didn't stop for the next 22 years, hiccuping just over 400 million times. That's the worst case of the hiccups ever. Most doctors say that hiccups will usually go away by themselves after a few minutes even if you don't do anything. But if you want faster results:

1. Swallow a teaspoon of dry sugar.
2. Chew and swallow a piece of dry bread.
3. Pull your knees up to your chest.
4. Rinse your mouth with salt water.
5. Suck on crushed ice.
6. Hold your breath; then swallow when you feel a hiccup coming on.
7. Ask someone to tickle you or surprise you.
8. Breathe rapidly into a brown paper bag about ten times.
9. Suck on a lemon.

5 FBI TIPS ON INTERNET SAFETY

While the Internet is a wonderful tool that gives kids access to people and information that were not available a few years ago, it also poses many dangers, including mean and dishonest people who roam chat rooms in search of innocent prey. You need to remember some very important things when you're on your computer either at home or school. Please discuss the dangers of the Internet with your parents.

It's extremely important that you all understand the basics of Internet safety.

1. Never give out personal information such as your name, home address, school, or telephone number in a chat room or on bulletin boards. Also, never send a picture of yourself to someone you chat with without your parents' permission.

2. Never write to someone who has made you feel uncomfortable or scared.

3. Do not meet someone or let them visit you without your parents' permission.

4. Tell your parents right away if you read anything online that you think is weird.

5. Remember that people may not be who they say they are. Someone who says that "she" is "a 12-year-old girl" could really be an older man.

6 WAYS TO TELL IF YOU SHOULD REPORT A STRANGER TO THE POLICE

The police recommend that you call them if you come into contact with anyone who seems suspicious to you. Here are some things to watch for.

1. Any stranger who asks you weird questions, such as where you live, who your parents are, or anything about your friends

2. Any adult who tries to join you while you are playing

3. Any stranger who asks you to go with him or her

4. Any stranger who tries to have a conversation with you at the movies

5. Anyone who tries to touch you

6. Anyone who tries to get you to disobey the rules of safety you have learned

FRED ROGERS LISTS 8 THINGS TO MAKE STARTING A NEW SCHOOL EASIER

Can you say "ter-ri-fy-ing"? That's how the first day at a new school may seem. Here are some things that might help.

1. Try to get together with kids in the neighborhood who will be going to your school.

2. Visit the building before the first day of school to get an idea of what it's like.

3. Try to find someone to walk with to and from school (or the bus if you take one).

4. Try to have a calm routine in the morning before you leave for school.

5. Take a small object from home with you so it won't seem as if home is so far away.

6. Keep a photograph of your old school friends in your notebook.

7. Remember that everybody isn't staring at you. If they are curious about you, you can take it as a compliment.

8. Think of it as a new beginning.

7 THINGS YOU CAN DO IF YOU THINK YOUR TEACHER DOESN'T LIKE YOU

1. Stop talking, fidgeting, throwing spitballs, or passing notes in class. Behave!

2. Ask to speak with your teacher privately and explain your feelings. Say how bad you feel and ask if you did something wrong or annoying. If so, apologize and ask for another chance.

3. Write a note saying something like, "I'm sorry if I did anything wrong. It makes me sad to think you don't like me. Can we start again?"

4. Talk to your parents and let them know how frustrated you are. Perhaps you and your parents can speak with the teacher about these feelings.

5. Say hello to your teacher in the halls. Try to start a conversation. See what kind of response you get.

6. Remember that teachers are there to teach, not to be your friends or pay extra attention to you. Some teachers just aren't that friendly. If they are really being fair and teaching you what you need to know, that's all you can expect.

7. If you try talking with the teacher and it doesn't help, you can talk to the guidance counselor, school principal, or assistant principal and ask what they think you should do.

THE 10 WORST THINGS ABOUT SKIPPING A GRADE

If you're smart enough to be skipping a grade, be proud of yourself, but know that it's not always easy, even though the other kids all wish they were you. Some kids who have a chance to skip a grade decide not to. This is definitely something to discuss with your parents and teachers.

Thanks for this list to Alexa Hamilton, who's been there and done that.

1. The older kids in the new grade think you are "cute" because you're smaller than they are. They may pinch your cheeks and treat you like a baby.

2. You don't get to see your old friends in the grade below.

3. Your friends still have the same experiences together, so you don't have as much in common with them anymore.

4. You don't get invited to all the same parties as your friends.

5. Teachers forget that even though you're smart enough

to be in an advanced grade, you're still not as mature as every-one else, and they expect too much of you.

6. You leave the school a whole year before your friends, so you never get to see them.

7. Some people treat you like you're stuck up, even though skipping wasn't even your idea.

8. You get scared that maybe you won't be able to do the work and they'll put you back in your old class and you'll be embarrassed.

9. Since everyone in the class is older than you, they have more privileges—such as staying up late and going to the movies without a grownup—than you do, so you feel left out.

10. You get more homework than you used to.

JOHN GLENN LISTS 3 THINGS HE WISHES KIDS WOULD THINK ABOUT

On February 20, 1962, John Glenn became the first American and the third man to be put into orbital space flight. But Glenn is much more than an astronaut. Back on earth, he became involved in politics and was elected as a U.S. senator from Ohio in 1974. In 1998 he made headlines again when he was chosen, at the age of 76, to be a member of the Space Shuttle Discovery Mission.

When we asked Glenn to share some of his thoughts about growing up, he offered many useful and thoughtful comments, including some excellent advice about school: "While you have the chance, go to school, study and learn as much as you can, use that knowledge to help yourself today and to-morrow," he wrote. "While I can't promise you that this task will be an easy one, I can guarantee you that it will be chal-lenging, rewarding, and well worth it."

1. Realize that school isn't just a chore. It's also the key that will open the door to your future. I know it often means

All-New
^

spending time doing tough homework problems and not watching part of that favorite TV show. It means studying history and geography and practicing your multiplication when playing outside would be more fun. It means giving just a little bit more time to solving that word problem or writing that report before going over to a friend's house. But it's worth it. Keep your mind open to learning.

2. Remember that in school you have the chance to shine. Here's your chance to use your talents and gifts, to be somebody. Always try—try to work just a little harder and study a little more to understand, not just because you have to or because somebody said to but because you want to.

3. Realize that education goes on forever. This may be the hardest thing of all to understand. You will always be learning new skills and developing new ideas. We are always "in school." Throughout your life you must never close the door, for it is only through learning that you will continue to grow.

10 TIPS FOR LOOKING GOOD IN YOUR SCHOOL PICTURE

1. Wear comfortable clothing. (A battle with one of your parents may be necessary here. Explain that you'll look better if you're relaxed. Promise to smile; that usually works.)

2. Wear a solid color, but not white.

3. Don't wear jewelry or things in your hair.

4. Wear your hair the way you normally do.

5. Stand (or sit) up straight.

6. Don't fidget.

7. If you wear braces, practice your smile.

8. Be yourself.

9. Avoid blinking during the flash. (If you can—it's hard.)

10. If you get a zit, don't panic and don't try to cover it up —you just wind up looking as if you have a zit you're trying to disguise. A big smile will overpower any zit. If you're determined to cover up something really gross, get someone who's experienced with makeup to help you. (And don't use anyone else's makeup without permission.)

HOW TO MAKE IT APPEAR AS THOUGH YOU HAVE CLEANED YOUR ROOM IN ONLY 27 MINUTES—NO MATTER HOW MESSY IT IS

If your room looks like they used it to shoot the last *Star Wars* sequel, it's probably because you don't clean it a little each day—you wait until it's a complete disaster area and then feel overwhelmed when your parents finally threaten to ground you if you don't do something about the mess. Here's a way to get it all started.

1. Get a huge trash bag and walk around the room with it, throwing into it everything you don't need: candy wrappers, ticket stubs, the styrofoam that came with your new DVD player, the broken crayons, and the pen that doesn't work. It's a good time to even think about throwing out stuff you don't *really* need: pieces of toys you know you won't ever play with again, stuff you sent away for that was free but not even worth the $1 you had to include for postage and handling. The more stuff you get rid of now, the less chance there is for a future mess. Do this in 10 minutes.

2. Put dirty clothes in the hamper. Put clean clothes back in drawers or in the closet. Do this in 3 minutes.

3. You'll still have a mess. You need to sort the rest of it into the following piles:
- stuff that belongs outside your room (the scissors you borrowed, the book that has to go back to the library)
- school stuff

- computer and music disks, electronic game cartridges
- pencils, pens, and other writing and drawing tools (stick these in an empty jar)
- toy parts
- loose change
- everything else

Make neat piles. In the next few days, tackle each of these piles *one at a time*. Do this in 10 minutes.

4. Make the bed. Do this in 3 minutes.

5. Open a window to air out the place. Do this in 1 minute.

6. For extra credit, vacuum the room.

JAMES MICHENER EXPLAINS HOW TO USE A LIBRARY

It's no wonder that Pulitzer Prize–winning novelist James A. Michener is such a great believer in libraries. His books, which are counted among the great fiction of our time, required lots of research, in addition to his own talent. You may have heard of some of his books: *Hawaii, Chesapeake, Alaska, Texas, Tales of the South Pacific.*

"It's hard for me to imagine what I would be doing today if I had not fallen in love, at the ripe old age of 7, with the Melinda Cox Library in my hometown of Doylestown, Pennsylvania," says Michener. "At our house, we just could not afford books. The books in that free library would change my life dramatically. Who knows what your library can open up for you?

"My first suggestion for making the most of your library is to do what I did: read and read and read. For pleasure—and for understanding." Here are Michener's tips.

1. First, kick the TV habit. Here's how: Go to the library and take out a stack of books that look interesting. Pile them on the TV set. The next time you're tempted to turn on a program you don't really want to see, reach for a book instead.

2. Learn to use the card catalog in the library. The card catalog lists every book in the library by author, title, and subject. Some libraries have actual card catalogues; others have the information on computers. If you don't understand your library's setup, ask the librarian to explain it to you. Always have a pencil and paper handy when you use the card catalogue so that you can jot down the numbers of the books you want.

3. Learn to use the "stacks" — or shelves. Browse through and find out which books are located in certain areas. But feel free to explore and to pick up books on subjects you're unfamiliar with. You never know what's going to grab your attention. If you take a book from the stacks, do not try to return it to its proper place. That's work for the experts. If you replace it incorrectly, the next seeker won't be able to find it.

4. Learn to know the reference librarian. Introduce yourself. State your problem. And be amazed at how much help you will receive. But don't waste the librarian's time by asking silly questions you ought to solve yourself. Save the reference librarian for the really big ones.

5. Learn to use *The Reader's Guide to Periodical Literature.* This reference book, organized by subject, enables you to find magazine and newspaper articles on the subject you're researching and provides a guide to the very latest expert information on any subject that interests you. When you use this wonderful tool effectively, you show the mark of a real scholar.

6. Take notes when you use magazine articles, since you usually can't take these home. Or find out if your library has a photocopy machine and copy the pages you might have to refer to later.

7. If you are working on a project that will require repeated library visits, keep a small notebook in which you record the numbers of the books you will be using frequently. This will save you valuable time, because you won't have to consult the card catalog or search aimlessly through the stacks each time.

8. Practice using the library by taking up projects that can be both fun and rewarding. For instance, try tracing your roots. Find out who your ancestors are by consulting books on genealogy. Or use the local history books in your library to find out if George Washington ever spent time in your neighborhood. Or plan a Polynesian feast using the cookbooks you find. You name it—your library has it all!

TONY RANDALL LISTS 4 WAYS TO IMPROVE YOUR VOCABULARY

Tony Randall loves words almost as much as he loves acting. "The better command you have of words," he says, "the better chance you have of saying exactly what you mean, of understanding what others mean, and of getting what you want in the world." Here are some ways in which to achieve all that.

1. Try to guess the meaning of a word from the way it's used. You can often get at least part of a word's meaning just from how it's used in a sentence. And a good way to get better at this guessing game is to read different kinds of magazines, books, and newspapers. Of course, to find out exactly what a word means, you need to consult a dictionary.

2. Learn about root words and their meanings. The root is the basic part of a word—its heritage, its origin. Most roots come from Latin or Greek words. For instance, the root word of manacle is *manus,* which is Latin for "hand." Other words using the same root word are manual, which means to do something by hand; manage, which means to handle something; and manufacture, which means to make something. (Originally all things were made by hand!) Learning these roots will help you to remember words better, to understand the meanings of more words, and to learn the meanings of groups of words all at once. Think of the root as a clue to what the word means.

3. Learn prefixes and their meanings; these give you further clues to the meanings of words. A prefix is a word part that attaches at the front of a word and affects its meaning. Prefixes are usually Greek and have meanings all their own. For instance, the prefix *con*, which means "with," is found in the word "conform," meaning to "form with." And the prefix *contra*, meaning "against," is used in the word contradict, which means to "say something against." Since there are only about a hundred important prefixes in the English language, it shouldn't take all that long to familiarize yourself with all of them and thereby learn the meanings of many more words than you already know.

4. Use the new words you learn right away. This is really the best way to remember them. Say them out loud; write them in sentences; you'll impress your friends and expand your vocabulary at the same time.

12 TIPS ON HOW TO MAKE A SPEECH— AND LIVE THROUGH THE EXPERIENCE

Speaking in front of a large group of people is the number-one social fear, not only for kids, but also for grownups. If this is a problem for you, you can get over it now and avoid a lifetime of being scared.

1. Plan your speech first.

2. Don't read from big, messy pages. Write your ideas on index cards. Try just to write a few words about each idea and then talk about the ideas instead of reading from notes.

3. If you're nervous, try to imagine that you're only talking to your little brother.

4. Talk to everyone in the room. Make eye contact with as many people as you can while you're talking.

5. Don't speak too quickly. Take your time.

6. Keep your talk short and to the point.

7. Believe what you say.

8. Don't be afraid to be funny, especially at the end.

9. Ask questions of your audience to get them more involved, even if you don't expect them to answer. For instance, you can start by saying, "How do you think it feels to be the first person to walk on the moon?"

10. If you're intimidated by someone in the audience, try to imagine the person wearing pink furry bunny pajamas—the kind with feet. It's hard to be scared of a big pink bunny!

11. Think about what you're saying, not about the faces staring back at you, the grade you want to get, or whether your socks match. If *you* seem interested in your subject, the audience will want to listen.

12. If you screw up, take a deep breath, smile, apologize to your audience, and then go on with the speech. Remember that you're not the first person in the world to be in this position; *everyone* goes through this.

19 TIPS FOR GETTING GOOD GRADES ON TESTS

Nobody likes taking tests, but there they are, just the same. Even when you're out of school, there are tests to take, whether they're driving tests, tests for getting jobs, or tests to get into other schools. So it's best to develop good studying and test-taking skills early. Here are some tips from experts.

1. When studying, read all the material straight through first. Then go back and read it again. This time, underline the important points.

2. Never wait until the last minute to study for a test; it will make you panic. The best time to study is two days before a test. The night before should be used for reviewing the most important points.

3. Have all your reference materials right in front of you when studying so you don't have to go hunting for anything. Keep a dictionary, encyclopedia, and any other things you need close by.

4. Two heads are better than one! Studying with a friend is a good idea as long as you really study. Give each other quizzes. Tutor your friend in the parts you understand well and let him or her do the same for you.

5. Rehearse for your test. Have someone give you a practice test. This does more than help you learn the answer; it also helps you get used to the test, so you're less nervous.

6. Keep old tests. Review the earlier tests, even those you didn't do well on. Most teachers have certain kinds of questions that they ask, and you'll be ahead of the game if you come to know what to expect. If you have a friend or older sibling who had the same teacher, see if they have tests you can look at.

7. A good way really to get to know something is to talk about it out loud. Pretend you're teaching it to someone else (the mirror?), or try discussing the material with your family at the dinner table.

8. Get a good night's sleep before a test. You'll be able to relax better if you're well rested.

9. The night before the test, right before you fall asleep, picture the important material in your mind. This is the time when your brain is most open to learning. You'll be surprised how much memorizing you can do this way.

10. Your brain needs proper food before a test. Make sure to eat a good breakfast if the test is in the morning. If the test is in the afternoon, don't eat too much sugar or junk food for lunch. Scientists have proved that this kind of food clouds your mind and makes it harder for you to think.

11. Bring all the things you'll need to the test—sharp pencils with erasers, working pens, ruler, etc.

12. Wear comfortable clothes on the day of the exam. You'll have an easier time concentrating if you don't feel restricted in any way.

13. Before arriving in the classroom, find a quiet corner, and review the important material right before the test. If you've got it written down, this is your last chance to go over it.

14. If you can, get to the classroom a few minutes early and get seated so you'll definitely be ready when the test begins.

15. When taking the test, always make sure you give yourself enough time to understand the material fully, especially the specific question that is being asked. If you have trouble with the instructions, get the teacher to help you.

16. Take your time; use all the time allotted for the test. Don't try to rush, or you're likely to forget the material and may even miss some of the questions.

17. Don't panic. If you can't answer a question, skip it and go on to the next. After you've done the last question, if you still have time, go back and see if you can get some of those you missed. If you *really* don't know the answer, take a guess. Sometimes it's better to guess than to leave a question unanswered.

18. During test-taking time listen carefully to your teacher's instructions. *This is extremely important!*

19. Remember to do the best you can and that the world won't come to an end no matter what grade you get (although your parents might not want you to know this). Relax during an exam and you will think more clearly.

19 EXERCISES FOR YOUR BRAIN

Try doing three of these exercises (pick different ones each day) to keep your brain in gear. It's like calisthenics for your head. Before you do any of these, take a moment to relax so that you can really concentrate on what you're doing and get the most out of the exercise.

1. Picture your bedroom. Create a mental map of the room and of where everything is. Now imagine rearranging the furniture. Make sure that each piece of furniture changes position.

2. Read a newspaper and memorize 10 facts.

3. Recite 3 tongue-twisters.

4. Think of an important event in history. Now think of how history would have been different if one part of your event changed. For instance, "What if . . . the South had won the Civil War? . . . computers had not been invented? . . . there was no such thing as school?"

5. During a trip, make a mental map of the route you are taking.

6. Write down a word that has more than 12 letters and see how many smaller words you can make from it.

7. Doodle.

8. Play a video game. Just one.

9. Stare at a cloud and try to imagine that it's different objects. Look for faces in the clouds.

10. Do a crossword puzzle as fast as you can.

11. Read 10 pages of a novel.

12. Play Scrabble or another word game.

13. Think about something you really believe is true. Now try to prove that you're wrong.

14. Think about being in a perfect place. Look at everything around you and make a list of 20 things you see in your perfect place.

15. Do a jigsaw puzzle.

16. Memorize a list of the first 10 objects you see when you wake up in the morning.

17. Think about how many windows there are in your house. How many doors? How many chairs? Closets?

18. Imagine that you are the main character in a book you just read. What would you have done differently?

19. Use your instruction manual to learn something new on your computer.

9 WAYS TO IMPROVE YOUR MEMORY

These suggestions will help you remember names, important dates, and chores you're supposed to do, find that missing toy you want, and may even help you on tests.

1. When you meet someone whose name you want to remember, find one feature about that person and connect it to the name. For example, if the person's name is Armstrong, you may visualize that person with big muscles.

2. If you have an important errand to do and you don't want to forget it, put a rubber band around your wrist as a reminder.

3. If you have a list of things to remember, make up a story about them. For instance, if you are going to the store for your mom and she wants you to pick up some milk, eggs, bread, and a newspaper, your story can be about a *cow* that is eating an *egg* sandwich on white *bread* while reading a *newspaper*.

4. If you are trying to remember the name of an explorer during a history exam and can't think of it, try to remember the name of the country he came from, which may help you to remember the language spoken, which may help you to remember his name.

5. If it's hard for you to remember words, it's because you're not using them often enough. Whenever you learn a new word, try to use it in a sentence during normal conversation. Reading as much as you can is also a good way to learn and remember words.

6. If you've lost something, a good way to find it is to close your eyes and retrace your steps after you last used the item.

7. Sometimes making a mental picture is not enough. If you talk to yourself and say, "I'm leaving this toy under my bed," it will help you later. Don't be embarrassed about talking to yourself. This method will really help you.

8. It is much easier to remember something when you are relaxed. If you panic, it will be much harder if not impossible to recall what you want.

9. The only way to really learn how to spell properly is to use the words in your everyday vocabulary, unless the word is something like antidisestablishmentarianism.

16 ALTERNATIVES TO "THE DOG ATE MY HOMEWORK"

Don't use these; they don't work.

1. "I left it in my pocket and then my mom put my shirt in the washing machine and it got ruined."

2. "I did the assignment, but I used invisible ink by mistake."

3. "It flew out the car window on the way to school."

4. "My father took it to work by mistake."

5. "I didn't know you were going to collect it."

6. "The cat had kittens on it, and it's still wet."

7. "I thought it was optional."

8. "You said you don't give homework on weekends" (if the problem occurs on a Monday).

9. "I got it mixed up with the homework from two nights ago that I forgot to do, so I did the wrong assignment."

10. "I had to babysit until really late last night and there weren't any pencils."

11. "We went to the car wash on the way to school this morning, and my mother, genius that she is, left the windows open, so all my homework dissolved."

12. "The maid threw it out."

13. "Don't you remember? I came in early this morning to give it to you, but you were busy. You told me to leave it on your desk."

14. "It's in my locker, but someone jammed the locker up with bubble gum, so I can't open it."

15. "You already *gave* us that assignment."

16. "Whoops!"

8 STATISTICS ABOUT STUTTERING

You can get help with a stuttering problem by contacting the National Center for Stuttering, 200 E. 33rd St., New York, NY 10016. If you enclose $3 for handling and postage, it will send you a whole book on the subject. If you stutter, talk to your parents or your school's guidance counselor about getting help.

1. Two and a half million Americans stutter.

2. Five times more men than women stutter.

3. The I.Q. of the average stutterer is 14 points higher than that of the general population.

4. While stuttering begins in childhood, 75% can expect to shed the problem by adolescence.

5. Stuttering usually begins between the ages of 2 and 7.

6. Stuttering affects self-esteem, job and school performance, and social development.

7. Stuttering has a physical cause (a spasm of the vocal cords).

8. New techniques for treating stuttering show extremely high success rates.

6 WAYS TO BUY SCHOOL SUPPLIES THAT LAST

Neatness counts! One way to make sure that your school supplies always look like you take care of them is to buy top-quality stuff in the first place. (As with toys or anything you buy, it makes sense to shop around for the best price.) Here are some basic things to look for when considering quality.

1. When the metal spirals on notebooks unwind, they can get caught in your clothing and even cause injuries. To avoid the problem, get notebooks with double rather than single spirals. (Double spirals stay wound better.) If the ends of the wires still look as if they will unwind at some point, try turning the ends up with a pair of pliers. Plastic spirals will not solve the problem; they don't unwind, but they do tend to break.

2. Look for notebooks with heavy covers; they will last longer. There are lots of notebooks with colorful pictures of TV and film stars on the covers, but most of them are printed on cardboard that's likely to rip after just a few weeks of school. Also, look for a stiff back on a notebook so you won't need anything to lean on when you write in it if you're not at a desk.

3. Try to stay away from plastic-covered ring binders. The trouble is that if the plastic winds up in a very hot or very cold place, it gets brittle and starts to tear. Those blue canvas binders that have been around forever are really your best buy —which is why they've been around forever. They're also the cheapest. If you think they look boring, decorate them with stickers.

4. When shopping for a ring binder, open and close the rings to test them before you buy it. They should open and close easily (but not too easily), and the two halves of the ring should come together evenly.

5. Stay away from erasable pens. Kids like them for the obvious reason—you can get rid of your mistakes faster than you can say "whoops"—but they don't necessarily write as smoothly as the regular kind. They tend to skip, and because the ink isn't all that permanent, you can smear your writing if you touch the page.

6. Get the sturdiest bookbag or backpack you can find. This means double-sewn seams that won't rip if you're carrying a lot of books and straps and handles made from a strong fabric, like woven nylon. Since you'll want to use the bag or pack for at least one school year, it pays to look for the following additional features:

- Lots of pockets or compartments for holding smaller items, like money or pencils, so you don't have to hunt through the whole bag each time you need them.
- Machine washability, so you don't have to throw it out if it gets dirty.
- Room enough to hold everything—your books, your lunch, and anything else you may want to take to school.

PETER PIPER PICKED A PACK
11 Things to Look For When You Buy a Backpack

1. It should be made of woven nylon. Nylon is strong and weighs very little.

2. The straps should be adjustable and should have foam pads so they don't cut into your shoulders.

3. There should be plenty of small compartments for special items like keys and money, but not so many pockets that you have to stand there and open them all just to find a pencil.

4. Make sure all the zippers, clasps, and snaps open and close easily.

5. All the stitching should be reinforced, especially where the straps are sewn to the bag. All seams should be double-sewn.

6. The fabric around the zippers should not be so close to the zipper that it gets stuck when you zip and unzip.

7. Make sure that when the bag is closed, rain can't get in through the openings. (You may not always get credit for wet homework!)

8. Try the bag on and walk around with it before you buy it to make sure it's a good fit.

9. It should be roomy enough to carry *all* your stuff. Sometimes the cheaper backpacks are a bit smaller, and you don't realize it until you try to fit all your books into it.

10. It should be machine washable so you don't have to throw it out if your lunch leaks.

11. If you get the kind of backpack with wheels, be sure the wheels are sturdy and made out of metal.

7 THINGS YOU CAN DO IF YOU GET RIPPED OFF

If the toy you got for your birthday doesn't work the way it's supposed to, if something you bought doesn't do what the ad said it would, or if something breaks after you've used it only a few times and you're sure it's because it was badly made (and not because your little brother ran over it with his Barney Big Wheel), you don't always have to just throw the thing out and chalk it up to experience. Here are some ways to get your money back.

1. Take the item back to the store (even if you don't have the receipt) and politely explain the problem. Small neighborhood stores and even some large chains are likely to be helpful, since they do generally value you as a customer. Always ask to speak to the manager. It's a good idea to bring an adult with you if you think you'll have trouble explaining your problem.

2. Call your state or local consumer protection agency. These organizations exist to help people with consumer problems and make trouble for those who run unfair businesses. To find out if your state has an agency to protect consumers, call the state capitol (listed in your phone book under "Government"). If it's hard to do, ask a librarian or a telephone operator to help you.

3. Complain to the manufacturer. Make sure you find the manufacturer, not just the trademark name of the item. The manufacturer's name should appear on the item's packaging. Or you can call the store where the toy was purchased and ask for the proper address. Follow the same procedure for other types of items.

4. Call the Better Business Bureau. The Directory Assistance operator will help you find the office nearest you. (There's usually one in the state capitol, if not in your immediate area.) The Better Business Bureau helps consumers who have complaints. It also tells you how reliable a company is and keeps an eye on advertising to make sure that products live up to the promises that are made about them. Sometimes the Bureau will help you settle your problem; sometimes it will send you to a different agency.

5. If your problem concerns the safety of an item and you feel that someone's health or well-being is endangered, get in touch with the Consumer Products Safety Commission. It has the power to ban products or to regulate their sale to reduce the risk of injury. To find the office nearest you, call the national toll-free number: 800-638-2772.

6. If you believe that your gripe is really aimed at an industry rather than a specific product, you can file a complaint with the trade association that represents that industry. Ask your reference librarian for help in finding the appropriate address. To complain about practices in the toy industry, write to the Toy Manufacturers of America, which keeps an eye on the toy people. Its address is 200 Fifth Ave., New York, NY 10010.

7. Go to court. If you've tried everything else and you still aren't satisfied—and you're in the mood for a fight—you can sue the company or store that's cheated you by contacting the small-claims court in your state. You won't need a lawyer, but you'll probably need an adult to help you fill out some forms. You'll be given a court date, when the person you're suing will be told to appear and answer your charge. You will be asked to explain your case, produce receipts and any letters you have written or received on the case, and explain why the court should decide in your favor. If you call any courthouse, someone there will tell you how to contact the proper small-claims court in your area.

4 WAYS TO MAKE SURE YOU GET TREATED RIGHT WHEN YOU GO SHOPPING

Some kids complain that they have problems when they go shopping. They feel they are being watched closely for shoplifting, even if they would never dream of doing such a thing. They say that salespeople often ignore them and that they are sometimes cheated out of the right amount of change. Here are some things you can do to make sure you get the respect you deserve.

1. If you act like an adult, you'll have a better chance of being treated like one. When you enter a store, be polite at all times, and don't go around the store picking up items you have no intention of buying. Tell the salesperson exactly what you are looking for so they can help you find it.

2. Don't be afraid to speak up if you are mistreated, but do it in a polite way. If someone tries to get ahead of you in line, if someone gives you the wrong amount of change, or if you have any other complaints, ask to speak to a manager.

3. Shop with an adult for really expensive items or for things that are complicated to buy, like clothing that needs to be tried on. If you're buying something for a parent and you want it to be a surprise, ask someone older to go with you.

4. Keep all the receipts for the things you buy in case you need to return them. But if you need to return something and you *don't* have the receipt, ask to speak to the manager and politely explain your problem. If you speak confidently, most managers will help you.

4 THINGS YOU AND YOUR PARENTS SHOULD CONSIDER ABOUT YOUR ALLOWANCE

Your allowance is something *you're* going to spend, but your *parents* have to supply it. That makes it a good subject to talk about together. Don't get discouraged if your parents don't see things your way at first. Perhaps by acting responsibly and living up to whatever bargain you make, you will get them to look at things differently. Here are some of the things you should discuss.

1. How much allowance you get. Probably the best way to decide on the right amount is to keep an account of the money you spend—and how much you really need—for a few weeks. Then show the list to your parents and decide together which purchases make sense.

2. Decide when you will get your allowance. Once a week is best, and it should always be on the same day. If you need more money before that day comes around, you're going to have to wait until that day comes around. Or make a rule so that you can get some money sooner if you can prove that you need it for something really important.

3. Keep track of how much money you spend. When you

eventually ask for a raise, you'll be able to show where your money has gone and why you need more. For instance, if you've been paying for your school lunches and the price goes up, you'll be able to explain why it's time for a raise.

4. Agree on what items your allowance is supposed to cover. If it's supposed to cover the cost of school supplies, you need to know that so you can plan ahead. Also, are you allowed to spend money on whatever you choose, or will you need permission to buy certain things?

15 THINGS YOU SHOULD KNOW IF YOU WANT TO START YOUR OWN BUSINESS

It's great to have an allowance and get gifts of money, but you can't always depend on this money to help you buy the things you want or save for the future. You may be too young to get a job, but you're not too young to start your own business. First, speak with your parents, to get both permission and advice. They may even lend you the money you need to get your business started. Here are some important things to consider before you begin.

1. There are opportunities to make money all around you, but you must look for them. Use your imagination! If you have a specific talent or interest, try to find jobs related to it.

2. List all your hobbies, sports activities, special talents, and any work experience you may already have. This list may give you some job ideas.

3. Consider whether you want to work indoors or outside, provide a service, or make money selling things, or whether you want to do something that may lead to an adult career.

4. Keep a list of all your job ideas. Your jobs may change from month to month, depending on the season. Be ready for any changes in job opportunities.

5. Any work you choose should be right for your age, appropriate for the time of year, and something you know you can handle. You should also consider how much money you need to start this business.

6. You will succeed only in a business that you're excited about. If you have a business idea but it doesn't excite you, don't waste your time.

7. You *must* write down a plan of action. Name your business, state what your business does, when you plan to work, how to get customers and who they will be, and what you need to do to get started.

8. It is extremely important to have *goals* planned. Decide how much money you want to earn each week, how many hours you think you will have to work, and how much money you plan on saving. Write these goals down. Always keep your goals in mind when making business decisions.

9. Getting customers for your business is going to involve telling people about your services. You'll need to sell yourself and your product or services. You will also have to advertise your business.

10. Make a list of potential customers—people you think may want your services (neighbors, relatives, store owners, senior citizens, etc.).

11. Write down what you will say to a potential customer about your business. When you explain what you are doing, always have a positive attitude, be friendly and courteous, explain to the customer why they need your service and why they should buy that service or product now.

12. There are three inexpensive tools you can use to help you advertise. You can use signs and posters, flyers, and business cards. You will have to distribute your ads yourself, so be sure you know exactly where you want to put them. Remember, if you do your job well, you will get what is called word-of-mouth advertising, when satisfied customers tell their friends about you.

13. You can also advertise by wearing a T-shirt with the name of your business on it. Put a sign on your bike or in front of your house. You may even be able to get your school newspaper to do an article about your business. Advertising involves a lot of creativity. Go for it!

14. Keep records of all the money you collect, including the name of the customer and the date you were paid. Keep records of all your expenses, including supplies, advertising costs, phone bills, and transportation costs. All this information will allow you to calculate how much money you're earning. The money you have collected minus your expenses will be your profit, or actual income. See if your income has equaled your goal. If it hasn't, you'll have to decide if you can continue this service or if you should try something that may be more profitable.

15. Doing a great job is the most important ingredient in making a business successful. If your customers are happy, you will succeed.

7 JOBS FOR KIDS WHO LIKE ANIMALS

If you like animals, consider one of the jobs listed here as a great way of making some money and getting some good experience.

1. Dog walker. Dog owners sometimes aren't able to walk their dogs. Let your neighbors know you are available and ask them to spread the word.

2. Pet sitting. Be sure you have seen the pet you are going to care for to be sure you can handle the animal and feel comfortable with it.

3. Bait service. If your home has fishing facilities nearby, consider digging up worms and selling them to a bait shop or at a fishing area.

4. Find-a-pet-a-home service. Look out for free kitten or puppy signs or ads and call the owners to offer your services.

5. Pet grooming. You should get advice from a veterinarian or pet shop owner about flea and tick sprays.

6. Horse care. You can feed or exercise horses or clean out stables.

7. Volunteer at a veterinary office, kennel, or pet shop. You may not get paid, but you'll learn a great deal about animals, and the experience will help you get a paying job in the future.

25 WAYS TO MAKE LIFE BETTER FOR SENIORS

Don't just think about your grandparents. Do you know other elderly people who need a friend?

1. Take your pet to visit them.

2. Read a book aloud.

3. Ask them to teach you how to do something or for advice with a problem you have. Maybe they can help you with your homework.

4. Get large-type books out of the library for people who have trouble reading.

5. Take a friend along when you visit them.

6. Send them a copy of your report card if it's a good one.

7. Draw a picture of your family and include them in it.

8. Tell them a joke.

9. Watch a movie with them.

10. Sing a song.

11. Call them on the telephone.

12. Take them a photograph of yourself.

13. If you say you're going to visit, don't cancel just because something else you'd rather do comes up.

14. Help them in the garden.

15. Offer to help them clean a part of the house that's difficult for them, like the yard or a closet.

16. Play board games with them.

17. If they are forgetful or have difficulty with something like walking or talking, be *very* patient.

18. Bake cookies together.

19. Help them to organize their photo album if it's a mess, and ask them to tell you about the pictures when you work on them together. On the back of each picture, ask them to help you write the date and where it was taken.

20. Help them go shopping.

21. Tape record or videotape a message saying how you feel about them.

22. If they can't attend a family event, take pictures of it for them.

23. If the person walks with a cane, ask if you can decorate it with ribbons and cute stickers. (Be sure to ask for permission!)

24. Let them know they are needed.

25. Just cuddle.

10 JOBS YOU'LL ENJOY IF YOU LIKE BEING OUTDOORS

If the great outdoors appeals to you, the following jobs may be for you:

1. Pool and driveway cleaning. You'll need some instruction about the chemicals used in water maintenance and other details.

2. Shoveling snow. You'll need a good shovel and a lot of muscle.

3. Mowing lawns.

4. Yard upkeep. This can include raking leaves, removing fallen sticks and branches, possibly some weeding, and trimming shrubbery.

5. Car washing. You'll need a bucket, an appropriate soap, clean towels or rags, and perhaps some auto wax (you can charge extra for waxing).

6. Outdoor painting. Decks, outdoor furniture, fences, porches, and doghouses need to be painted from time to time.

7. Firewood supply. If your neighbors have fireplaces, offer to stack their woodpiles.

8. Flyer distribution. Many businesses and organizations need people to distribute their ads. If your bike has a basket or you have a backpack, you should be able to do this job.

9. Messenger or delivery service. Check with the stores and businesses in your neighborhood for these opportunities.

10. Walking dogs.

6 JOBS YOU'LL ENJOY IF YOU LIKE TO SELL THINGS

If you have a way with words and are comfortable speaking with the public, you may enjoy a job that involves selling a product.

1. Sell baseball cards. If you are a collector and have extra cards, set up a stand.

2. Open a refreshment stand. You can set yourself up at a park, a baseball field, or even in front of your house and sell things like slush, iced tea, and homemade cookies.

3. Hold a yard sale. Offer to run a yard sale for a neighbor or group of neighbors and charge a percentage of the money you collect. Or set up your own yard sale and sell toys you don't play with anymore.

4. Run a babysitter referral service. Find kids who want to baby-sit and match them up with customers. You can collect a small fee from any sitter who wants to be part of your service as well as a small fee from the parent customers.

5. Sell used books. Collect old books and sell them at garage sales or to a flea market dealer.

6. Take pictures. If you have a camera, you can take pictures of people during special moments at special events (like baseball games and picnics) and sell them to the people you have photographed. (Who wouldn't want a photo of their kid sliding into third?) You can also take pictures of kids in their Halloween costumes or at special school performances.

9 WAYS TO MAKE MONEY GROW

You can't. But you can do some things to make sure you put some of it away for special stuff.

1. Keep your money in a piggy bank that has a key. Give the key to your parents and tell them not to return it to you until you've saved enough money to buy the thing you want.

2. When you get your allowance, make up a list of the things you need to spend it on. Be sure to set aside a portion for savings. This is called budgeting yourself.

3. Decide that you're going to save only pennies or nickels. Each time you get these coins in change from a purchase, put them aside in a special jar or bank.

4. Ask your parents to help you with a "matching fund." That means they will give you, say, a dollar for every five dollars you save. Your parents are more likely to do this if you agree on how the money will eventually be spent.

5. Make a chart that allows you to mark off a box for every dollar you save. At the top of the chart, paste a photograph of the thing you want. There should be one box for each dollar it will take to buy your "prize."

6. Charge yourself a small fine every time a certain thing happens. For instance, each time you don't get a good grade on a test, add 50 cents to your savings. Or you can reward yourself by putting away a dollar each time you get an *A*. Be creative with your rules: 10 cents every time you hiccup; 25 cents each time you hear the word *aardvark;* 50 cents if you see a green truck with red lettering. You can set money aside every time you finish reading a book or make a phone call or bite your nails. Ask your parents for more suggestions. (If they know you're serious about saving up for something, they may help you.)

7. Ask your parents to put part of your allowance aside for you toward something special.

8. When you go shopping, don't take *all* your money with you, just take as much as you think you'll need.

9. Don't spend money impulsively. If you see something you think you really want, wait a day before you buy it and think about it again. Will you really enjoy it? Will it wind up in the back of your closet within a week?

YOUNG AMERICANS BANK OFFERS 6 TIPS FOR CONTROLLING YOUR MONEY

Bill Daniels got the idea for a bank for kids when he read a newspaper article about some fifth-grade students who were laughed at when they went into a bank and asked for a loan. Today the Young Americans Bank is the first bank set up especially for young people — under 22. It specializes in small savings accounts, loans, investments, and even credit cards and checking accounts for kids over 12. To learn more, contact the bank at 311 Steele St., Denver, CO 80206 (303-321-2265) or visit its Web site, which has lots more information about kids and money: www.young americans.org. We are grateful to the Young Americans Bank for taking kids seriously and for the two lists that follow here.

1. Open your own bank account. When you go to the bank to do this, politely ask the person at the bank to explain everything you need to know. If you still don't understand and they are being impatient, say, "Excuse me, but I plan to be very rich some day, so this information is really important to me. Please help me to understand this."

2. Ask your parents to let you be responsible for part of the family budget.

3. Design a personal budget—and stick to it!

4. Talk to financially successful people to find out how they did it.

5. Find out if there are any programs or classes in your community to help you learn about money.

6. Get a job or find a way to make extra money to help buy the things you want.

8 TOP MISCONCEPTIONS KIDS HAVE ABOUT MONEY AND BANKS

1. Banks put customers' money in a shoebox with their name on it.

2. Banks are owned by the government.

3. Banks print money.

4. If we just printed more money, everyone would be richer.

5. Credit cards and checks are free money.

6. Our bills and coins belong to us (actually, it all belongs to the government).

7. It's OK to write on or change money.

8. If you deposit your favorite silver dollar in the bank, you will get the same silver dollar back if you ask for it.

HOW TO CHANGE THE WORLD

1. Define the problem you want to solve. Homeless people, drug abuse, sex education, dangerous traffic situations, and child abuse are all different issues. Pick one and try to aim all your efforts in this one direction. (Don't try to take on too much or you'll be overwhelmed and *nothing* will get done.)

2. Learn all you can about the problem. Go to the library or use your online resources. Talk to people in your neighborhood and at school. Find out if someone has already tried to solve the problem, what obstacles they faced, and why they may have failed.

3. Consider different solutions. Encourage people around you to contribute their ideas and don't be afraid to consider even the "craziest" proposals. Sometimes you have to listen to lots of bad ideas before you can find one that will work.

4. Find out who opposes your ideas. Meet with these people and try to win them over. Find out why they feel the way they do and see if you can find a solution to the problem that takes their views into account. Remember that nobody wins unless everyone wins!

5. Spread the word. Kids should be seen *and* heard: Call your TV and radio stations in your town and ask to speak to a reporter. Explain what you're doing. Invite the person to visit you and your friends and, if possible, to film your activities. And be a big mouth—tell everyone what you're doing. You never know who will be able to help.

6. Develop a network. Do everything you can (through school, local media, and online forums) to find others who feel the same way you do and combine forces. No matter how much you care, you can't change the world all by yourself. *Important:* Even if you find yourself working with people you don't like, learn to get along with them in order to accomplish your goal.

7. Choose a plan and make it happen. You can solve big problems by breaking them up into groups of smaller problems. Make a list and tackle them one by one.

8. Hang in there! Don't give up if things don't go your way. If your solution fails, find out why and use what you've learned to develop a new solution. Maybe you'll need more people to help you the second time around. Maybe you didn't tell enough people. Maybe you should try to raise money to advertise and get the word out. Whatever the problem was, try to correct it. Remember that sometimes *trying* to accomplish something may be more rewarding than arriving at your ultimate goal. You learn so much along the way! Try to learn from everything that happens, especially your mistakes.

9. Get a copy of a book called *The Kid's Guide to Social Action,* by Barbara Lewis (Free Spirit Publishing, 424 Washington Ave. S., Minneapolis, MN 55401; 800-735-7323). It describes everything from how to raise money for your cause and give a speech to getting laws changed. Free Spirit Publishing has many similar, excellent books for kids. Call or write and ask for its catalog.

19 GOVERNMENT OFFICES YOU CAN WRITE TO

1. The President of the United States
White House Office
1600 Pennsylvania Ave.
Washington, DC 20500
202-456-1414
The "Chief"

2. The Vice President of the United States
Old Executive Office Bldg.
Washington, DC 20501

202-456-2326
Works with the president in leading the country

3. Office of Management and Budget
Executive Office Bldg.
Washington, DC 20503
202-395-3080
Helps decide how the government's money will be spent

4. Council of Economic Advisers
Old Executive Office Bldg.
Washington, DC 20502
202-395-3000
Analyzes the national economy and reports to the president

5. National Security Council
Old Executive Office Bldg.
Washington, DC 20506
202-395-4974
In charge of military and national security

6. Office of Policy Development
1600 Pennsylvania Ave., NW
Washington, DC 20500
202-456-1414
Advises the president on foreign and domestic issues

7. Office of the U.S. Trade Representative
600 Seventeenth St., NW
Washington, DC 20506
202-395-3230
Deals with how the U.S. will do business with other countries

8. Council on Environmental Quality
722 Jackson Pl., NW
Washington, DC 20503

202-395-5750
Advises the president on environmental issues

9. Office of National Drug Control Policy
Executive Office of the President
Washington, DC 20500
202-727-9472
Advises the president on how to control illegal drugs

10. Office of Administration
Old Executive Office Bldg.
Washington, DC 20500
202-456-7052
Handles the president's mail and helps get things done

11. Office of Science and Technology Policy
New Executive Office Bldg.
Washington, DC 20506
202-456-7116
Advises the president on scientific and technological issues

12. Department of Defense
The Pentagon
Washington, DC 20301

13. Department of Education
400 Maryland Ave., SW
Washington, DC 20202

14. Department of Energy
1000 Independence Ave., SW
Washington, DC 20585

15. Department of Health and Human Services
200 Independence Ave., SW
Washington, DC 20201

16. Department of Housing and Urban Development
451 7th St., SW
Washington, DC 20410

17. Department of Labor
200 Constitution Ave., NW
Washington, DC 20210

18. Department of Transportation
400 7th St., SW
Washington, DC 20590

19. Department of the Treasury
1500 Pennsylvania Ave., NW
Washington, DC 20220

HOW TO SOUND LIKE A GROWNUP WHEN YOU MAKE A PHONE CALL

Whether you're calling a radio station with information about your school event or asking an organization about its activities, these tips will help you to get a good response.

1. Before you call, write down what you want to say so that if you get nervous, you won't forget something important. If you are inviting someone to an event, be sure to give them all the information they'll need.

2. When your call is answered, state your name and give the person a *short* explanation of what you're doing: "Hello, my name is William Clinton and I'm working with a group of kids to clean up the garbage on Seventh St.." Then tell them why you're calling ("I would like to know if your company can donate cleaning supplies") and ask to speak with the right person ("Can you help me or should I be speaking with someone else?").

3. If you get an answering machine, leave your name, phone number, a short explanation of why you're calling, and when you would like your call to be returned ("after school," "evenings," etc.) If your call is not returned, keep trying at different times of the day.

4. If a person asks you to leave a message, offer the same information but also ask when would be a good time for you to call back. Keep trying if your call is not returned.

5. Never be rude, even if you are treated badly. Let's face it: A lot of adults are too stupid to take kids seriously. Convince them that they are wrong by keeping your cool and then following up with a letter that makes your point.

6. When you finally reach someone, be sure to write down everything they tell you. If you don't understand what they are telling you, *say so* and ask them to say it slowly. If you don't understand some of the words, don't pretend you do. And ask the person to spell names for you so that you'll get them right.

7. *Always* thank the person for taking the time to listen to you, even if they have turned down your request. This makes it easier for the next kid who tries to call that person.

THE GIRLS' BILL OF RIGHTS

Girls Incorporated helps over a quarter of a million girls between the ages of 6 and 18 by promoting education, awareness, communications, sportsmanship, and pregnancy prevention. You can contact this organization at 120 Wall St., New York, NY 10005 (800-374-4475); or type "Girls Incorporated" into the keyword box on an Internet search engine.

1. Girls have a right to be themselves—people first and females second—and to resist pressure to behave in sex-stereotyped ways.

2. Girls have a right to express themselves with originality and enthusiasm.

3. Girls have a right to take risks, to strive freely, and to take pride in success.

4. Girls have a right to accept and enjoy the bodies they were born with and not to feel pressured to compromise their health in order to satisfy the dictates of an "ideal" physical image.

5. Girls have a right to be free of vulnerability and self-doubt and to develop as mentally and emotionally sound individuals.

6. Girls have a right to prepare for interesting work and economic independence.

15 WAYS TO FIGHT RACISM

Racism refers to any action or idea, whether carried out intentionally or not, that puts down people because of their skin color or race. Ending racism does not mean pretending that we're all the same. It means learning to live together peacefully *because* of our differences and even to celebrate those differences. *Many* colors make up a rainbow.

1. Find out what cultures are represented in your community. Look around you; how many different ethnic groups can you identify?

2. Learn about each of these cultures. Get to know people of other backgrounds at school and online.

3. Discuss racism with your friends and on computer forums.

4. If people make racist remarks, tell them you are offended.

5. If you see something on TV that's racist, e-mail or write to the station and object.

6. If you have certain racist impressions—if there's a group of people you find yourself disliking for no real reason—think about how you came to feel this way. When did you first see a person from that group? What did you think? Why?

7. If your parents have racist attitudes, talk to them about it. Tell them how you feel.

8. Participate in a student exchange program. See "How to Join a Student Exchange Program," page 95.

9. Get a pen pal in another country.

10. When you celebrate your own cultural holidays, include members of other groups so that they can learn more about you.

11. Attend someone else's religious or cultural celebration.

12. Organize an art show with racism as the central theme.

13. If someone tells a racist joke, don't laugh.

14. Tell an *anti*racist joke: For instance, Why are all racist jokes so short? So racists will understand them!

15. Join Amnesty International, a worldwide organization that helps people fight for certain basic human rights. You can find out which of their programs involve kids by writing to Amnesty International USA, 322 Eighth Ave., New York, NY 10001 (212-807-8400).

8 WAYS TO PROTECT WILDLIFE

Many plants and animals are in danger of becoming extinct, which means that the plant or animal is lost forever. Plants and animals can't help themselves. We must all help them so that we can prevent their loss. For more information, write to: Education Coordinator, Defenders of Wildlife, 1101 14th St., NW, Suite 1400, Washington, DC 20005.

1. Learn about your own ecosystem. An ecosystem is a group of animals and plants living in the same area or environment. Look around you and list all the animals, insects, trees, and plants in your neighborhood. Then go to the nearest park, woods, or any natural setting and record what you see. Compare the two lists.

2. Ask your teacher to contact Project Wild through your state's environmental department. Project Wild will tell you how to build a schoolyard habitat or ecosystem.

3. Express your concern about protecting the environment for wildlife. Write to your state's senators, representatives, and the mayor of your own town and explain why you think that they should also be concerned.

4. Volunteer your services at a park or wildlife refuge. You can help by cleaning up litter, maintaining trails, or teaching visitors about the importance of respecting wildlife.

5. Ask the owner of a nearby pet store not to sell animals that have been taken from the wild. Many of these animals die from stress or disease soon after they are captured. Ask an adult to go with you. Starting a petition is also a good idea.

6. Get your friends involved by throwing a costume party. Ask everyone to come dressed as a plant or animal and to explain who they are and what they need.

7. Write an article for your school newspaper about some of the things you have learned about wildlife.

8. Read the science section of your newspaper to learn about the wildlife issues in your area.

18 THINGS KIDS CAN DO TO END HUNGER

Each night 600 million people go to bed hungry. Each day 40,000 children die of hunger. We *can* end hunger, but it's going to take increased awareness, commitment, and hard work. Here are some things that kids can do that can make a difference.

1. Learn about hunger throughout the world by reading newspapers and books and asking questions. Then talk to other people about what you have learned. If you have to give a speech to any of your classes or write an essay, make hunger your subject.

2. Send a chicken to a poor family in a foreign country. It costs only a dollar! The Heifer Project sends animals such as cows, goats, pigs, and even bees to families who must feed themselves. Contact: Heifer Project International, P.O. Box 8085, Little Rock, AR 72203 (800-422-0474); www.heiferproject.org.

3. Adopt a foster child in another country. Here is one group that organizes such activities: International Children's Aid Foundation, 10 Fox Ave., Medford, NJ 08055; www.icafkids.org.

4. Publicize your efforts. If you are involved in an activity to end hunger, contact the newspapers and radio and TV stations, as well as online services to tell everyone what you're doing. Maybe you'll inspire others to help.

5. Instead of giving presents on birthdays and holidays, donate the money you were going to spend to a hunger project. Then decorate a gift card to read: "Because you are so special, we are celebrating your special day in a special way. A donation has been made in your name to [name of the organization] so that your spirit will help end hunger in the world." Don't *ever* send a card like this without sending a donation. You don't have to tell your friend how much money you donated.

6. Enlist other people. Write to politicians, religious leaders in your community, and celebrities and tell them how you feel about the hunger problem. Ask what they are doing to help.

7. Find out what efforts are being made in your community to feed the hungry and volunteer to work for these groups. Maybe you'll hand out flyers or help cook food to be served at a homeless shelter. To learn about the groups in your area, call the local United Way office.

8. Feed someone who is hungry. If you're aware of hungry people in your neighborhood, get your parents' permission to share your food with them. Think of them when you leave a restaurant with a "doggy bag" of leftovers.

9. Talk to managers in the restaurants your family visits

and make sure they have arranged to donate their leftovers to homeless people in the neighborhood.

10. Support World Food Day, October 16. Groups all over the country do something special each year on this day to make people aware of the problem of hunger. Contact the U.S. National Committee for World Food Day, 2175 K St., NW, Washington, DC 20437 (202-653-2404); www.gsu.edu.

11. Skip a meal and feed the hungry! Each year, on the Thursday before Thanksgiving, many people skip a meal or fast for the whole day and donate the money they would have spent on food to Oxfam America, 26 West St., Boston, MA 02111 (800-597-FAST); www.oxfamamerica.org. Contact them for more information.

12. Trick or treat for UNICEF on Halloween. You can do this on your own or you can organize a group—and *no one* is too old for this one! For information and collection boxes contact UNICEF, 3 UN Plaza, New York, NY 10017 (212-326-7000); www.unicef.org.

13. Organize a supermarket food drive. Get your market to urge shoppers to buy one or two extra items every time they shop and donate them to nearby shelters. Talk to the store manager and offer to help by making signs explaining the program. Get your parents to help transport the donated food.

14. Start your own chapter of Youth Ending Hunger (YEH). Contact this group at 15 E. 26th St., New York, NY 10010 (212-251-9100); www.thp.org, to get a starter kit. It will tell you how to organize the kids in your area.

15. Hold a CROP WALK. This is a national effort in which people walk for 10 miles (or more or less) and get people to donate money for each mile they walk. People of all ages can participate. To learn more about organizing such a walk, contact Church World Service, 475 Riverside Drive, New York, NY 10115 (212-870-2257).

16. Support Africare. This group tries to feed people in more than twenty African countries. For $10, you and your friends can provide 100 pounds of fertilizer for crops, feed two people for a month, or buy enough seeds to plant an entire field. Contact Africare, Box 66415, Houston, TX 77266 (713-521-1420); prores@insync.net.

17. Support the American Jewish World Service. This foundation organizes health and agricultural projects for people of all religions in Africa, Asia, and Latin America. Contact the American Jewish World Service, 989 Ave. of the Americas, New York, NY 10018 (800-889-7146); www.ajws.org.

18. Help hungry people start projects to end their own hunger. To find such efforts, contact IDEX (International Development Exchange), 827 Valencia St., San Francisco, CA 94110 (415-824-8384); idex.org.

13 THINGS YOU CAN DONATE TO HOMELESS PEOPLE

Call United Way (see the White pages of your phone book) to find out what efforts are being made to help homeless people in your area. You can participate in many of the following activities through these local groups.

1. Food, including "doggy bags," that you have taken home from a restaurant

2. Clothing

3. Shelter

4. Money

5. Kindness

6. Gift certificates from fast-food restaurants

7. Recyclable materials, especially bottles, which poor people can collect for money

8. The money you make from a garage sale or another fund-raising event

9. Toys, if they're in good condition. (The next time you get a lot of presents, like for a birthday or Christmas, think about giving away one thing before you even open it.)

10. Your time, which you can spend working at a homeless shelter or a soup kitchen

11. Your brain. You can tutor homeless children or just visit with them. Many shelters have such programs.

12. Your energy. Use it to inform everyone around you— parents, friends, the media, and community leaders—that you *demand* that attention be given to the problem of homelessness.

13. Your respect

10 WAYS TO HELP SAVE THE PLANET

1. Start a carpool. To combat the smog and acid rain caused by our cars' exhaust, the best thing to do is carpool or use mass transit. Fewer cars on the road means less exhaust. And it's more fun to ride with a friend!

2. Get involved. It's up to us to save our planet, so get involved in an environmental organization. Check with your zoo, chamber of commerce, or an environmental publication to find a job that's right for you.

3. Be an environmentally conscious consumer. You can cast your vote to save the environment each time you shop. Buy products that use recycled materials and less packaging. Buy products in bulk. And try never to buy single use or disposable items.

4. Check your bulbs. Don't waste energy by using a light bulb that has a higher wattage than you need. You can also save energy and money by installing more efficient, compact fluorescent bulbs and turning them off when you're not in the room.

5. Get rid of hazardous waste safely. Batteries, antifreeze, pesticides, paint, paint thinner, drain cleaner, mothballs, and many other household products are considered hazardous waste, so don't pour them down the drain or throw them in the trash. Contact your city's waste facility or government information center to find out how to dispose of these substances properly.

6. Recycle, recycle, recycle. From newspaper to egg cartons to organic materials such as leaves and yard clippings, lots of things can be recycled. Even coffee grounds can be used to fertilize some plants. Don't throw away what you can use again!

7. Save water by checking the location of your sprinklers. Save water by not watering your driveways or sidewalks. Make sure sprinklers are properly located and are turned to a moderate level.

8. Avoid single-serving and multipack food items. Their excessive packaging is extremely wasteful. Buy food in bulk and store it in resealable containers. And of course, bring your own reusable bag to carry home your groceries.

9. Camp safely. If you go camping or hiking in the wilderness, pay attention to how you clean up. Try washing with soapless hot water and sand—even the mildest soap puts a strain on the environment. If you must use soap, use one that is biodegradable. Since there are no bathrooms, be sure to dig your latrine as far as possible from any water sources to avoid contamination.

10. Use nontoxic cleaners to unclog drains. Instead of using a commercial drain cleaner, which is highly toxic, simply pour a handful of baking soda down the drain followed by half a cup of vinegar. Cover the drain with a heavy pot or stopper; this will force the pressure down and clear the clog instead of allowing the mixture to fizz up out of the drain.

21 POLLUTION PROJECTS

You can help make the world a cleaner place. One way to start is by performing simple projects at home and at school. Here are some suggestions. You can probably think of others. For more information, write to Keep America Beautiful, 9 W. Broad St., Stamford, CT 06902.

1. Hold a "litter art show." Make a display of mobiles, collages, or sculptures made from pieces of litter. Give awards for the prettiest and most unusual.

2. Fancy cans. Decorate the litter barrels that have been placed in your community. Used drums may also be available at supermarkets, car washes, schools, and manufacturing plants. Decorate them and place them where they can be easily seen.

3. Walk. Have an adult walk with you to nearby activities instead of asking for a ride. Have your friends go with you when you do ride. The less a car is used, the more your family contributes to clean air and saves energy.

4. Make a booklet. Describe the environment with stories and illustrate them with drawings. Make a list of things to do to keep it clean.

5. Paper is precious, so use it wisely. Write on both sides of the page. Don't use a fresh sheet for scratch paper. Ask your teacher to start a paper recycling project.

6. Save electricity. Turn off the lights, the TV, and the radio when no one is in the room. Don't leave the refrigerator door open.

7. Share your ideas. Describe three littered places in your community. How do you think they got this way? List the reasons that you think people litter. Talk about how to prevent littering.

8. Create quiet. If you carry a radio, keep the volume low. It's all the louder-than-necessary sounds that create noise pollution.

9. Dump it all. When you take out the garbage, be sure that it all goes into the garbage can. Put the lid on tightly. Loose trash becomes litter.

10. Start a forest. You may be able to get tree seedlings from a garden center or state agricultural office. Plant them in your yard or at school. Be sure to get the advice of an expert, because new trees need special care.

11. Hold a contest. Award prizes for the best poster, poem, song, or skit about the environment. Arrange to show the posters at school or in store windows.

12. Be kind to trees. Carving your initials on trees allows bugs and diseases to get under the bark and expose it to disease and rot. Peeling the bark off a tree will hurt it.

13. Take a field trip. Ask your family or teacher to take you and your friends to a center where recyclable items are collected or visit a sanitary landfill. List all of the equipment you see and the types of jobs people are doing.

14. Name those tunes. Make a list of all the songs you know about our land, such as "America the Beautiful," or write your own lyrics to the tunes.

15. Make litter bags. Give them to your teachers and friends.

16. Use litter bags. Put them on your bicycle and in your desk or locker. Ask your parents to put a litter bag in the car.

17. Recycle at home. If there's a recycling center in your community, collect recyclable items yourself and turn them in. Ask your family to help.

18. Write a play about pollution. Present it at a school assembly or for your family and neighbors.

19. Make bookmarks. Write DON'T LITTER on them and give them to students and teachers.

20. Pollution pin-ups. Start an ecology bulletin board. Display pictures that show both clean, well-kept areas and those spoiled by litter and debris. Select a title for your project, such as, "You Choose."

21. Do a "litter bit" more. If you see a piece of litter on the ground, pick it up and throw it away properly. If everyone picked up one piece of litter each day, think how much cleaner our streets and parks would be!

5 THINGS YOU CAN DO ABOUT WORLD HUNGER

Over 34,000 children from all over the world die every day from causes related to hunger and poverty. In places like Africa and India, many people can't grow their own food. But hunger is also a problem in our powerful, wealthy United States. Hunger, homelessness, and poverty should not be considered a normal part of our society. Here's how you can make a difference.

1. Learn about hunger and poverty and talk to your family, friends, and teachers about the real causes and about the practical solutions.

2. Find the programs in your community that are effective and ask how you can help. Students from the sixth grade at a private school in New York City spent a weekend raising funds for World Hunger Year. Some of them answered phones during the annual Hungerthon radio show.

3. Write to government officials, newspaper editors, business leaders, and producers of television news programs to let them know how you feel about the problem. In Concord, New Hampshire, two sixth-grade students wrote to all 100 U.S. senators about a bill before them dealing with the homeless. The students researched everything they said and presented their ideas in a mature way. They received responses from nearly every senator.

5. Hold a fund-raising event and collect donations for a nearby food bank or homeless shelter.

14 FUND-RAISING IDEAS

1. Hold a bake sale. It's everyone's favorite—it always seems to work.

2. Sponsor a neighborhood flea market. Kids and their families can sell their books, used clothes, tapes or handmade crafts. Ask them to donate part or all of their profits to a particular cause.

3. Hold a costume ball, ideally around Halloween. Give it an international theme. Charge admission and donate the money.

4. Read-, dance-, or walkathon. Collect pledges from family, friends, and neighbors for each hour or mile students walk or dance or for each book read.

5. Student-faculty playoff. Compete for the benefit of others. Choose a sport like volleyball or basketball and invite the rest of the school as well as parents to watch and cheer. Charge admission at the door.

6. Hold a student-faculty talent show. Advertise and sell tickets. Donate the proceeds to your cause.

7. Hold a raffle. Get the stores in your area to donate things to offer, like a bike or even a coupon good for free dry cleaning. Then sell tickets and raffle off the prizes.

8. Hold a community auction. Ask families, friends, and businesses to donate their specialties—including skills—to be auctioned off. Think of things you've never tried. Some teachers and students have offered a day of baby-sitting or tutoring. Teachers have made videos of their classroom over the course of the year and auctioned them off to parents. Restaurant and theater owners can donate dinners and tickets. This takes some organizing, but you can raise lots of money for your cause. Students can create posters and canvass the neighborhood for donations.

9. Fast. Give up one meal a week or give up junk food for one week and donate the money to a cause. Get the school involved by talking to other classes and explaining where their money will go.

10. Be creative. Think of something that hasn't been done. Seventh-grade students in South Portland, Maine, conducted a program at the Portland Museum of Art called Celebrating the Arts in Honor of World Hunger Education. The same class "adopted" a single-parent family living in a shelter and provided them "with a Christmas they will never forget." How about a poetry reading or something that relates to an upcoming holiday?

11. Have a community car wash. Students can hold a weekend car wash or they can make themselves available to run errands, do yard work, walk dogs, etc. Make up fliers to advertise these services and explain where the money earned will go.

12. Birthday donations. On birthdays you can ask parents, other relatives, and friends to make a donation to a special organization instead of buying you a gift. You can do the same thing for other people's birthdays. Make a card explaining that a donation was made in his or her honor to a specific organization. Explain how the organization works.

13. Hold a food drive. Ask people to bring canned foods to a specific area. The people at the local food bank will be happy to pick them up.

14. Contact Amazing Kids! This is a project of Community Partners, a nonprofit educational and charitable organization. Their mission is to help new nonprofit organizations. For further information on the program and how you can become involved, e-mail them at kids@kidscanmakeadifference.org.

14 CHARACTERISTICS OF YOUNG INVENTORS

1. They enjoy solving problems.
2. They're creative.
3. They are interested in many different subjects.
4. They have a lot of positive energy.
5. They're good at getting other people to help them.
6. They're generally curious.
7. They're resourceful.
8. They like to explore new ideas.
9. They don't mind working hard.
10. They're willing to learn from others.
11. They won't quit until they succeed.
12. They're not afraid to make a mistake.
13. They can look at a problem from different viewpoints.
14. They are often lazy! One guy invented the wheel because he was too lazy to carry stuff from one place to another. Six-year-old Suzanna Goodin, tired of cleaning the cat food spoon, came up with the idea of an edible spoon-shaped cracker. She won a grand prize for her invention in the Weekly Reader National Invention Contest.

5 PEOPLE WHO NEVER FAILED AT ANYTHING

1.
2.
3.
4.
5.

2

Getting It Together with Other Kids

60 GOOD DEEDS

1. Write a letter to an elderly person.

2. Teach someone younger than you how to do something.

3. Go to the library after school and volunteer for two hours.

4. Call someone who's sick.

5. Plant something for someone.

6. Help someone clean his or her room.

7. Apologize to someone for something bad you might have done.

8. Look through your closet and drawers for three pieces of nice clothing you don't wear anymore. Get permission to donate these to a clothing drive.

9. Make a toy for your pet.

10. Tell someone you love that you *really* love them.

11. Talk to the shyest person at school.

12. Try to think of three nice things about someone you don't like.

13. Write a funny poem for someone.

14. Read a story to a person who can't read.

15. When you're on vacation and you see one person in a family taking a picture of the rest of the family, offer to take a picture of all of them together using their camera.

16. Let someone get ahead of you in line.

17. Forgive someone you're mad at.

18. Clean up a mess that somebody else made.

19. Do the dishes when it's not your turn.

20. Fix something for someone.

21. Let someone win an argument, even if he or she is wrong.

22. Tell your favorite teacher how you feel about him or her.

23. Collect three toys you don't play with anymore and give them to a younger child.

24. Do something nice for someone and don't let them know it was you who did it.

25. Keep a secret.

26. Draw a picture of a relative and send it to the person.

27. Return something you borrowed.

28. Offer to loan your favorite book to a person you think will enjoy it.

29. If you find money in the street, give it to the person you're with. (There's an old superstition that it's bad luck to spend money you've found.)

30. Donate a whole week's allowance to a charity.

31. If you find something that someone lost, try to locate the owner.

32. Smile at someone.

33. Read a story to a small child.

34. If you have videotapes of movies that you don't watch anymore, donate them to the library.

35. Borrow a videotape from the library and arrange to show it at a nearby home for the elderly.

36. Pass along your old magazines.

37. Stick up for someone.

38. If there's only one piece of cake left, let someone else have it.

39. If you have a video camera, offer to tape a special event for someone who can't attend.

40. If you're going trick-or-treating, do it for UNICEF, a homeless shelter, or some other special cause.

41. Teach a little kid how to do something.

42. In the autumn, plant one red tulip where no one would expect to find it. (Someone will be *very* surprised in the spring.)

43. Write a song for someone.

44. Draw a picture of you and a friend doing an activity together. Send the picture to your friend.

45. Offer to copy the homework assignment for someone who's absent from school.

46. Donate blood.

47. Volunteer at a community event.

48. Write a letter to a newspaper editor about an issue that is important to you.

49. Write a letter to someone's boss telling them what a good job the employee did.

50. When you win a prize, give it to someone who wanted it more than you did. (Wasn't it nice just to win?)

51. Encourage other people to do good deeds.

52. Make breakfast for someone.

53. Help someone on your block clean up the mess from a storm or another disaster.

54. Clean someone else's room.

55. Write a fan letter to someone you admire.

56. Make someone laugh.

57. Fix a broken toy for a small child.

58. Draw a picture for someone who is deaf.

59. Let someone watch whatever they want on TV, even if it's your turn to choose the program.

60. Don't get mad the next time you have a right to get mad.

41 ORGANIZATIONS THAT WORK WITH AND FOR KIDS

1. ABA Center on Children and the Law
750 15th St., NW
Washington, DC 20005
202-662-1000
www.abanet.org
Finds lawyers for kids and offers scholarships for kids who want to be lawyers

2. Al-Anon/Alateen
Family Groups
1600 Corporate Landing Hwy.
Virginia Beach, VA 23454
888-4AL-ANON

wso@al-anon.org
Help for family and friends of alcoholics

3. Alpha Club
Optimist International
4494 Lindell Blvd.
St. Louis, MO 63108
314-371-6000
Organization for elementary school kids stressing self-discovery, service to the community, and spiritual values

4. American Anorexic/Bulemia Association (AABA)
165 W. 46th St.
New York, NY 10036
212-575-6200
aabaine.org
Helps kids with eating disorders

5. American Federation of Riders
P.O. Box 53301
Cincinnati, OH 45253
513-661-6080
www.afr1982.org
An organization made up entirely of motorcyclists who help kids with education and social issues

6. American Student Council Association
National Association of Elementary School Principals
1615 Duke St.
Alexandria, VA 22314
703-684-3345
Helps elementary and middle schools set up student councils in their schools

7. Amnesty International Children's Human Rights
Network
322 Eighth Ave.
New York, NY 10001

212-807-8400
www.amnesty-usa.org
Organizes kids in grades 4–8 to write to political leaders around the world asking for fair and humane treatment for all human beings

8. Artists Against Racism
P.O. Box 54511
Toronto, Canada M5M 4NF
416-410-5631
artistsagainstracism.org
Popular artists such as Céline Dion, Mike Myers, Aerosmith, Ani DiFranco, and Raffi, among many others, work with young people to end racism, homophobia (look it up), and sexism

9. Big Brothers/Big Sisters of America
230 N. 13th St.
Philadelphia, PA 19108
215-567-7000
Connects underprivileged kids with adults who can help them

10. Boy Scouts of America
P.O. Box 152079
Irving, TX 75015
214-580-2000
scouting.org
Activities, character development, and citizenship for boys

11. Boys Clubs of America
1230 W. Peachtree St.
Atlanta, GA 30309
404-487-5700
tuesday@bgca.org
For kids from 7 to 18, organized recreational, athletic, and social activities

12. Camp Fire
4601 Madison Ave.
Kansas City, MO 64112
816-756-1950
info@campfire.org
*Camping skills, responsible citizenship, and self-reliance
for boys and girls*

13. Cancer Kids
P.O. Box 2715
Waxahachie, TX 75168
Staff@cancerkids.org
Questions and answers for kids about cancer

14. Childhelp USA
15757 N. 78th St.
Scottsdale, AZ 85260
480-922-8212
childhelpusa.org
Research, prevention, and treatment of child abuse

15. Common Sense About Kids and Guns
418 C St., NE
Washington, DC 20002
www.kidsandguns.org
*Educates kids and adults about the dangers of keeping
firearms in the home*

16. 4-H Youth Development
U.S. Dept. of Agriculture
Washington, DC 20250
202-720-3029
*Agricultural, technological, and interpersonal skills
for ages 9–19. Camping and international exchange
programs*

17. Girl Scouts of the USA
420 Fifth Ave.

New York, NY 10018
212-852-8000
Activities, character development, and citizenship for girls; international programs, too

18. Girls Clubs of America
30 E. 33rd St.
New York, NY 10016
212-509-2000
Athletic activities and health and education programs, including AIDS awareness and substance abuse prevention, for girls

19. Guardian Angels
982 E. 89th St.
Brooklyn, NY 11236
718-649-2607
www.ai.mit.edu/people/ericldab/ga.html
Local programs of this national organization encourage kids to aid the elderly and others who need their help

20. Hearts and Minds
3074 Broadway
New York, NY 10027
212-280-0333
where@heartsandminds.org
Inspires kids and adults to get involved with issues of racism, poverty, and the environment

21. Hug-A-Tree and Survive
P.O. Box 712739
Santee, CA 92072
Tbt.com/hugatree
Teaches kids what to do if they're lost in the wilderness

22. International Assn. for the Child's Right to Play
c/o Tom Reed
University of South Carolina School of Education

All-New

800 University Way
Spartanburg, SC 29303
864-503-5579
www.ipausa.org
*Believes in kids' right to have fun and educates people
about important things like games and recess*

23. Jack & Jill of America Foundation
P.O. Box 468
Pickerington, OH 43147
jackandjillfoundation.org
*Helps mothers and their children develop community
social, recreational, and cultural programs*

24. Kids at Hope
11811 N. Tatum Blvd.
Phoenix, AZ 85028
866-275-HOPE
kidsathope.org
*Educates adults on helping kids understand that no
matter how bad things get, there is always hope*

25. Kids Eat Here
P.O. Box 64485
Tucson, AZ 85728
www.kidseathere.org
Raises money to feed hungry kids

26. Let's Play to Grow
University of Buffalo
Center for Assistive Technology
515 Kimball Tower
Buffalo, NY 14214
716-829-3141
www.cosmos.buffalo.edu/letsplay
*Helps organize playgroups around the country for kids of
all ages with mental and physical disabilities*

27. National Beta Club
151 Beta Club Way
Spartanburg, SC 29306
803-845-8281
betaclub.org
For kids in grades 5–12 with outstanding leadership and academic abilities

28. National Coalition Against Domestic Violence
P.O. Box 18749
1201 E. Colfax, Suite 385
Denver, CO 80218
800-343-2823
www.givedirect.org
Gives out free information about organizations that help victims of violence

29. National Council on Child Abuse and Family Violence
1155 Connecticut Ave., NW, Suite 400
Washington, DC 20036
202-429-6695
info@NCCAFV.org
Helps people find agencies nearby that offer family counseling

30. National Crime Prevention Council
1000 Connecticut Ave., NW
Washington, DC 20036
202-466-6272
www.ncpc.org
Offers information about starting crime watch programs in your community to prevent vandalism, robberies, drug dealing, and other crimes

31. National Information Center for Children and Youth with Disabilities
P.O. Box 1492

Washington, DC 20013
800-695-0285
nichy@aed.org
Provides information on support groups, individual disabilities, laws that affect kids with special needs, and helpful state agencies

32. National Jewish Council for the Disabled
11 Broadway
New York, NY 10004
212-613-8233
www.ou.org/ncsy/njcd
Provides recreational and informal educational programs for kids with disabilities

33. The National School Safety Center
141 Duesenberg Dr.
Westlake Village, CA 91362
805-373-9977
www.nssc1.org
Helps school groups form violence prevention programs

34. Reading Is Fundamental
2130 E. First St.
Los Angeles, CA 90033
323-268-8755
info@rifsocal.org
Encourages kids to read by setting up school programs and educating people about illiteracy

35. SADD (Students Against Drunk Driving)
P.O. Box 800
Marlboro, MA 01752
508-481-3568
With chapters in thousands of schools, a group devoted to spreading the idea that "friends do not let friends drive drunk"

36. StandUp for Kids
P.O. Box 121
Chula Vista, CA 91912
800-365-4KID
www.standupforkids.org
Volunteers organize others to look for missing and run-away kids

37. Toys for Tots
P.O. Box 1947
Quantico, VA 22134
703-640-9433
www.toysfortots.org
Founded by the marines, this organization gets toys to kids in homeless and needy families

38. Winners on Wheels (WOW)
7477 E. Dry Creek Pkwy.
Longmont, CO 80503
800-WOW-TALK
wowtalk@earthlink.net
A national learning and social program, similar to scouting, for children in wheelchairs

39. Workshop on Nonviolence
The Martin Luther King, Jr., Center for Nonviolent Social Change
449 Auburn Ave., NE
Atlanta, GA 30312
404-526-8900
thekingcenter.org
Promotes nonviolent solutions to problems, mostly through school programs

40. World Federalist Association
420 Seventh St., SE
Washington, DC 20003
800-WFA-0123

www.wfa.org
Promotes a strong, fair-minded United Nations as the means to world peace

41. YMCA of the United States
101 N. Wacker Dr.
Chicago, IL 60606
312-977-0031
800-USA-YMCA (800-872-9622)
www.ymca.net
Chapters offer athletic programs, summer camp, and child care facilities. It has national programs, too.

6 GROUPS YOU CAN CONTACT IF YOU WANT TO BE OR HOST A FOREIGN EXCHANGE STUDENT

Getting to know someone from a foreign country can be like visiting that country yourself, and being lucky enough to travel or study in another country can be one of the most exciting experiences ever. These groups all sponsor exchange programs. Most exchange students have to be in high school, but any family can host someone from abroad.

1. AFS International
71 W. 23rd St.
New York, NY 10010
212-807-8686
www.afsweb.org

2. American Institute for Foreign Study
River Plaza
9 W. Broad St.
Stamford, CT 06902
800-727-2437
www.aifs.com

3. American Intercultural Student Exchange
   7720 Herschel Ave.
   La Jolla, CA 92037
   800-SIBLING
   www.aise.com

4. American International Youth Student Exchange
   Program
   200 Round Hill Rd.
   Tiburon, CA 94920
   800-347-7575
   www.aiysep.org

5. World Heritage Student Exchange Program
   210 N. Lee St.
   Alexandria, VA 22314
   800-785-9040
   www.world-heritage.org

6. Youth for Understanding International Exchange
   YFU International Center
   3501 Newark St., NW
   Washington, DC 20016
   800-787-8000
   www.youthforunderstanding.org

8 ADVANTAGES OF HOME SCHOOLING

Ever want just to stay home and not go to school? If you said no, check your nose in the mirror—it may have just gotten longer! A lot of kids don't go to school, but that doesn't mean they're off the hook. Instead, they are educated at home by either a parent or private teacher, and they often get a better education since they get plenty of attention. Would home schooling be good for you? To get more information, contact the Washington Homeschool Organization, 6632 S. 191st Pl., Suite E100, Kent, WA 98032 (425-

251-0439), or go to AOL keyword: Washington Homeschool.

1. You learn at your own pace, so you never have to worry about competing with other students. But then there aren't other kids around to inspire you, either.

2. You won't experience negative peer pressure. But then you may not be sharing opinions and experiences with other kids.

3. You can stay home with your family. But then you don't get the challenge of putting yourself in a new situation, and if you have bratty siblings, you're stuck with them all the time.

4. You get lots more attention from a teacher at home. But sometimes you may feel like you're getting too much attention and you'd rather blend into a crowd. Also, you miss the influence of many different teachers.

5. Most of your role models are accomplished adults. But then you may miss the fun you can have with kids your own age.

6. Learning at home is less stressful. But then you may not be able to deal with stress when you get older and need that skill.

8. You have all the tools you need for learning, such as your own computer. But then you won't learn much about sharing resources with others.

8 ORGANIZATIONS THAT WORK TO GRANT THE WISHES OF VERY SICK OR DYING CHILDREN

1. Benefit4Kids
P.O. Box 356
Algonac, MI 48001
810-387-0454
www.benefit4kids.com

2. Grant-A-Wish
P.O. Box 21243
Baltimore, MD 21228
800-933-5470
www.grant-a-wish.org

3. Kids Wish Network
160 Scarlet Blvd.
Oldsmar, FL 34677
888-918-9004
www.kidswishnetwork.com

4. Make-A-Wish Foundation
555 Grant St.
Pittsburgh, PA 15219
800-676-WISH
www.wish.org

5. A Special Wish Foundation
436 Valley St.
Dayton, OH 45404
800-611-3232
www.aspecialwish.org

6. Starlight International
5900 Wilshire Blvd.
Los Angeles, CA 90036
323-634-0080

7. Wishing Star Foundation
W. 915 Second Ave.
Spokane, WA 99201
509-744-3411
www.wishingstar.org

8. Wishing Well Foundation
3929 Veterans Memorial Blvd.
Metairie, LA 70002
888-ONE-WISH
www.wishingwellusa.org

7 WAYS YOU CAN'T GET AIDS

1. Touching
2. Ordinary kissing
3. Being sneezed on
4. Sitting on a toilet seat
5. Coming into contact with an AIDS victim's sweat
6. Holding hands
7. Hugging

22 THINGS KIDS FEEL PEER PRESSURE ABOUT

Peer pressure can be tough to deal with. But it will help you to remember that you do have choices. No one has the right to force you to do something you don't believe is right, especially if it's dangerous.

If someone stops being your friend because you didn't join them in a certain activity or won't wear the same clothes or got better grades or don't want to play the same games, maybe it's time to look for new friends. Good, true friends will respect your right to be you. Even best friends can have different feelings and values. Each person is, after all, different. Here are some of the situations in which you may encounter peer pressure.

1. If your friends are smoking, drinking, or using drugs and say they won't be your friends anymore if you don't do it.

2. If someone tries to cheat at school by copying your paper or homework and tells you you're not really a friend if you don't let them.

3. If your friends want to trespass on private property and you know you shouldn't.

4. If other kids are wearing certain kinds of clothing that you're not allowed to wear or don't want to.

5. If you're the only one wearing something that nobody else is wearing.

6. If most of the other kids have a girlfriend or boyfriend and you don't.

7. If other kids in the locker room are more or less developed than you.

8. When you're asked to get into a car with a bunch of kids, and you know that the driver has been drinking.

9. If everyone else is teasing someone or being mean to them, and you don't want to go along with the "joke."

10. If everyone wants to go see a certain movie and you don't want to see it—or if you've chosen one that no one else is interested in.

11. If everyone else likes a certain kind of music that you don't care for.

12. When kids come over to your house when your parents aren't home and you're not allowed to let them in, but they want to come in anyway. Or if they try to break a lot of rules around your house when your parents aren't home.

13. If an unpopular person asks to spend time with you and you really want to but know that all the other kids will make fun of you.

14. When friends dare you to do something you know is wrong (such as stealing something or saying something rotten to someone) and you think they'll call you a baby if you don't do it.

15. When you don't have as much money to spend as everyone else does.

16. When someone wants to get involved in kissing or romantic touching and you don't feel you're ready.

17. When you really want to be nice to a sister or brother, but everyone expects you to be mean to them in public.

18. When everyone wants to goof off the day before a test but you really want to study for a good grade.

19. When friends expect you to misbehave in class and throw spitballs or pass notes and you don't want to.

20. When you want to join a club or team that everyone thinks isn't cool.

21. When other kids can go online without parental supervision and you can't.

22. If you don't have a computer and everyone is always asking for your e-mail address.

KIDS' MOST EMBARRASSING MOMENTS

1. When ice cream falls off your cone onto the street

2. Not having enough money for the pizza you just ordered

3. Finding your friends in town with other friends after they told you they were busy and had to go to a dentist's appointment

4. Not being able to stay out as late as your friends or having your parents pick you up early when everyone is allowed to stay

5. Opening a sandwich in the lunchroom and having everyone around you yell, "Phew!" "Gross!"

6. Receiving an award at an assembly and having the person who's presenting it get your name wrong

7. Having to repeat a grade and hear everyone saying you've been "left back"

8. Having to dress up when everyone else is wearing jeans

9. When your parents won't let you go out with your friends

10. When your parent scolds you in front of your friends

11. When your parent is drunk in front of your friends

12. When your parent dresses differently from all your friends' parents

13. Singing an extra word in a concert when everyone else is silent

14. When your teacher catches you sending a note in class and reads it aloud

15. Being teased about being smaller, taller, or more or less developed than other kids

16. Listening to a joke, having everyone around you laugh hysterically, and not understanding what's so funny

17. When your parents catch you and your date kissing

18. Being caught in a lie

19. When your mother walks in when you and your friends are trying on her bras and stuffing them with socks!

20. When your sister or brother listens in while you and your friend are talking privately and then spreads your secret around the school

21. When your teacher reads the test grades aloud and you failed or got one of the lowest marks

22. Getting sick and having to throw up in public

23. Waking up in the morning and finding out you wet the bed during the night

24. When the kids tell you your haircut looks awful

25. Having the school nerd fall in love with you

26. When you're at a birthday party and they're opening the presents and you realize yours isn't as nice as the others

27. When someone gives you a Christmas present and you didn't get anything to reciprocate

28. When a parent or other relative kisses you and calls you by a pet name in front of your friends

29. When you're "just touching" something at your friend's house and it accidentally breaks

30. When you show up at a party wearing jeans and everyone else is dressed up

31. When someone does something gross in front of you

32. When your friends come to visit and your parents are walking around in their underwear or look *really bad*

33. When your parents criticize your friends

34. When you get a private itch in a public place

8 WAYS TO HANDLE EMBARRASSING MOMENTS

You're not the first person on the planet to be embarrassed—by anything. Somehow, the millions of people who have been in your position managed to survive. You will, too.

1. Make a joke out of it.

2. Quietly ask the person who is embarrassing you to stop.

3. Get angry—privately.

4. Leave the room.

5. If someone is teasing you, tease them back in a friendly way.

6. Write down your feelings.

7. Talk to your parents or a friend for support.

8. Be thankful that all the things on the previous list didn't happen to you!

14 WAYS TO LET SOMEONE KNOW YOU WANT TO BE A FRIEND

1. Smile and act friendly toward them.

2. Say something nice—about the person's appearance or something that happened in class.

3. Ask questions to show that you're interested in them.

4. If you notice that someone seems troubled, say that you're concerned and that you care enough to listen to the problem.

5. Walk up to them, introduce yourself, and ask if you

can walk to school together or eat lunch at the same table.

6. If you need help with a school subject, ask if you could study together. Or offer to help with something that you know a lot about.

7. Find out if you have any of the same interests (like video games or a favorite rock group) and suggest that the two of you get together.

8. Invite them over to do homework at your house after school.

9. Ask the person over on a weekend for lunch or to a small party.

10. Call them on the phone if you didn't see them in school and tell them you just wanted to check and see if everything is OK. Offer to bring over their books and homework.

11. Talk about yourself—but don't overdo it. That doesn't mean you should brag; you should just say something about yourself that might be of interest.

12. If someone is embarrassed by something, let them know that you're laughing *with* them, not *at* them.

13. Read the list of "60 Good Deeds" (page 84) and try showing someone you want to be their friend.

14. Find out the person's e-mail address and write a short note. Think of a question you can ask that will get a conversation started. Avoid questions that require only a "yes" or "no" response.

HOW TO TELL SOMEONE YOU DON'T WANT TO BE THEIR FRIEND ANYMORE WITHOUT HURTING THEIR FEELINGS

You can't! The best you can do is to try to be as kind and as caring as possible. Say what you have to say in person, speak softly, and don't put the blame on anyone. Say what you have to say honestly but be sensitive about feelings, which will hopefully ease the hurt. But remember that there's no way to take away the hurt altogether. Here are some ways to open the conversation.

1. "I really don't want to hurt you, but I think we should be completely honest with each other."

2. "I know you're not going to be happy hearing this, and I feel awful saying it, but I care about you too much not to be honest."

3. "I care about you a lot, but I feel that we spend too much time together. Why don't we give each other some room and then see how we feel about things."

4. "I like being with you, but I have a lot of other interests and need to have more time to be with other people."

5. "I think we disagree about too many things to be really close all the time."

HOW TO FIGHT FAIR

1. Stick to solving a particular problem. Don't try to change the whole world—or even one person—in one argument.

2. Listen to the other person's side with an open mind. Don't interrupt.

3. Think about how the other guy is feeling.

4. Take responsibility for your actions.

5. Tell the truth.

6. Don't try to bully or scare someone into accepting your point of view.

7. No physical violence.

8. No name-calling. Don't make threats.

9. Don't make excuses.

10. If you're too angry to be fair, take a break to cool off, then get back to the fight.

11. When the fight is settled, live up to your part of the agreement.

17 WAYS TO HANDLE BULLIES

Bullies are people who want control and are willing to hurt other people in order to stay on top. They're tough on the outside, but inside they're scared and feel that they're not as good as everyone else. So they reject rules of fair play and make up their own set of rules, which makes them feel powerful. You can learn a lot more about handling bullies by reading an excellent book, *Why Is Everybody Always Picking on Me?*, by Terrence Webster-Doyle. Or contact the Campaign Against Workplace Bullying, P.O. Box 1886, Benicia, CA 94510; www.bullybusters.org. Here are some ideas that will help.

1. Walk away from the fight. This can be hard to do, especially when you know that you are right. But going through with a fight is not going to settle anything.

2. Make friends with the bully. Offer friendship and try to show some interest in something the two of you may have in common, like an interest in music or a particular sport.

3. Use humor, but make sure to laugh at yourself and not the bully. If someone is threatening you physically you might say, "Well, it looks like I'm going to be roadkill in about three minutes!"

4. Trick the bully into thinking your parents are about to arrive, or that you have a serious illness, or that one of your brothers is on the police force.

5. Show that you're not afraid. Stand up to the bully and say, "I'm not afraid of you!" Bullies will sometimes back down if you show you're not afraid.

6. Agree with the bully. If a bully calls you a wimp, say, "You're right, I'm a wimp. Now leave me alone!"

7. Try reasoning. If you're good at arguing, try talking about the situation.

8. Distract the bully. Raise a subject that will surprise the bully ("Did you know that your father and my father are going fishing together next weekend?"). Or divert his or her attention elsewhere ("Hey, what are all those police cars doing in the parking lot?"). Then RUN!

9. Get someone with authority to help you. This can be a teacher, a parent, or even an older friend. You may feel like this is a cowardly way out, but if you've tried other methods, this may be your only solution. Remember that a bully has no right to hurt you. If *they're* going to change the rules, then so can you.

10. Ignore the bully. This can mean turning your back and walking away, but it can also mean acting like you don't even know that you're being bullied. Act stupid! The bully may think that you aren't worth picking on.

11. Practice confidence. Use language, body movements, and facial expressions to let bullies know that you think highly of yourself and that you're not going to let anyone push you around.

12. To reduce the chances of being bullied, try never to be alone in the halls, yard, or locker room when no adults are around to help you. Don't waste your time trying to understand why you are being bullied.

13. Imagine that you are in a protective force field when the bully is talking to you. Try to walk toward an area where there are people to protect you.

14. Know that nothing the bully does is your fault. No one deserves this kind of treatment.

15. Don't give in to the bully when he or she tries to take something away from you. Hold on to your lunch, your money, your homework. Refuse to help the bully cheat on a test.

16. Rat on the bully. Tell everyone—your friends, teachers, and parents—when you are being threatened, even if the bully specifically said that he will "get you" if you do this. Ask for help.

17. If you were physically hit, shoved, or kicked, have your parents file a police report, tell the school, and if the situation is bad enough, get a restraining order.

THE MANUAL ALPHABET

The following sign language alphabet was kindly supplied by the National Association for the Deaf. If you have questions about signing or would like some materials, write to them at 814 Thayer Ave., Silver Spring, MD 20910-4500 (800-587-1791); www.nad.org.

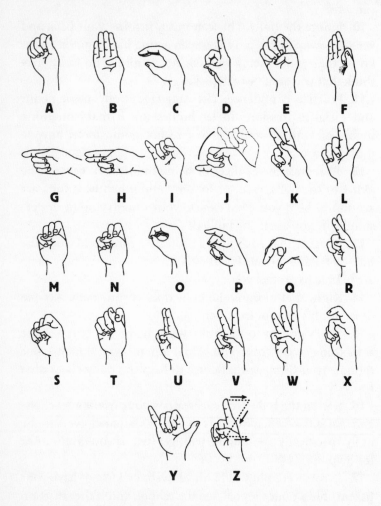

WHEN SOMEONE IN YOUR FAMILY HAS A SERIOUS DISEASE

When someone in the family is very sick, everyone in the family is affected. If you are in this situation, be sure to find someone you can talk to about what *you're* going through. Here are some feelings brothers and sisters may have.

1. You worry about your brother or sister. It's hard to watch someone you love when they're in pain. You may feel strange about feeling good about yourself when your sibling is stuck at home or in the hospital.

2. You feel incredibly sad. You may feel like crying all the time, and you just don't feel like doing much of anything.

3. You feel guilty and wonder if you did something to cause your brother or sister to get cancer. (That's impossible!)

4. You feel jealous and left out. *This is normal!* Your sibling is probably getting lots of attention and presents. It can look like a pretty good deal. It's OK to feel the way you do.

5. You feel angry. One minute everything seems fine, and the next minute everything's a mess. Illness disrupts the family. You never know what to expect.

6. You worry about the treatments your sibling has to have. Some of them sound scary and painful. Ask questions and maybe even go along on some treatment visits to learn how chemotherapy and radiation are given.

7. You worry that you or your parents will get it next. You have to remember that you can't catch diseases like cancer or multiple sclerosis from other people. Learning about the disease will make you feel less scared. Ask the person who is sick to tell you more about it and ask how you can help.

8. You miss your parents because they always seem to be busy taking care of your brother or sister.

9. You worry about what this is doing to your parents. Talk to them. They need you and your love right now just as much as you need theirs.

13 WAYS TO GET COMFORTABLE WITH A DISABLED FRIEND

Unfortunately, when most people meet someone who's disabled, they tend to think about the disability first and the person second. But it doesn't have to be this way. Here are some ways that will ease the path for you and a disabled friend.

1. Try to learn more about the disability so that it isn't a mystery to you. Ask questions if you think your friend won't be self-conscious about answering them (and keep in mind that your friend doesn't *have* to answer), or try to get information from the library or from your parents. Remember that disabilities are not "catching."

2. Try not to let the disability fool you into thinking that the person can't be a good friend. Remember that if someone can't walk or talk or even see or hear the way you do, they can still feel just as much as any other human being.

3. Say what you want to say and talk about whatever you would normally talk about, even if your disabled friend can't do the same things. For instance, if you want to talk about how much fun your soccer game was, go ahead. Your friend will probably be happy to hear about it.

4. Don't act as if the person is not disabled. Disability is not a secret that you have to pretend doesn't exist. If you and your friend can talk about the disability honestly, it will probably bring you closer together.

5. Try not to protect your friend too much. You'd be surprised at what disabled people can do, even if they do it a little differently or more slowly from you. Let your friend do as much for themselves as he or she wants to do. If you're not sure what to do, wait until you are asked for help.

6. If you feel uncomfortable about the disability, talk about it with your friend. It's OK to say "It's really strange to see your legs when you take your braces off. Does it hurt?" Or,

"Sometimes it's hard for me to talk to you because I don't know if it's OK to say certain things." It's perfectly all right to use words like *see, walk,* and *run* around people who can't do those things.

7. When you're talking to someone who's in a wheelchair, sit down near them so they won't have to stretch their necks to look up at you. (If you take a picture of someone in a wheelchair or in bed, take the picture at *that person's* eye level.)

8. It's OK to ask someone with a speech problem to repeat something if you didn't understand them the first time.

9. Don't talk loudly to blind people. They can hear.

10. Never pet or play with Seeing Eye dogs. They're not supposed to ever be distracted from their jobs. Don't feed them, either.

11. Remember that the disability is not the person's fault. Your friend may have been born with the condition or been involved in an accident. If you're really curious, wait until you know the person pretty well and then ask how they got that way.

12. Remember that a disability does not determine who a person is. No matter how your friend may look or talk or

learn new things, don't let the problem get in the way of your finding out what sort of special friend the person can be. You can't tell how nice a person is just by looking at his or her body.

13. Treat a person with a disability exactly as you would like to be treated.

8 THINGS YOU MAY FEEL WHEN A FRIEND DIES

The death of a close friend is an experience that will be part of your life for a very long time, and yes, it will hurt. But things will look better in time, though it may be hard to believe. You can speed up this process by talking to a friend or relative about your feelings. You should also try to get a copy of an excellent book, *When a Friend Dies,* by Marilyn E. Gootman. (Free Spirit, which publishes the book, also has some other great books on the tougher aspects of being a kid. You can ask for a free catalog: Free Spirit Publishing, 424 Washington Ave. S., Minneapolis, MN 55401; 800-735-7323.)

1. It's hard to believe that it really happened. You feel pain, but then you keep expecting your friend to walk through the door. It's hard to believe that you're not always going to feel this way.

2. You feel as though the world has ended and you no longer have the right to enjoy yourself ever again. You feel guilty if you are having a good time and your friend clearly isn't. It's very important for you to continue living your life.

3. You don't know how to act. Sometimes it's hard to know when it's appropriate to smile or cry or which emotion to show. It's important to remember that we are all entitled to express our feelings in our own way.

4. You keep thinking of things you should have said or done before your friend died. Even if the two of you had a big fight, that was part of your friendship, too. You can't change anything that already happened, and your friend didn't die because of your fight.

5. You're angry because you think that someone (doctors, friends, maybe even God) *let* your friend die. You want to blame it on someone. Maybe you're even angry at your friend for dying. Others around you are probably feeling the same way. If you talk with them, maybe you can all turn your feelings of rage into healthy grief.

6. You miss your friend. You're lonely. You feel like you've been left behind, and you don't think anyone can ever replace the friendship that has been lost. You're right. But each of your relationships is unique, and there are many possible friends out there. You will find new ones when the time is right.

7. You feel frustrated because you have so many feelings you can't express. You just don't have the right words. Maybe you don't need them. Maybe this is a good time to try expressing yourself creatively, perhaps with music or painting.

8. You feel like you're going crazy, having weird thoughts or dreams, and you may want to talk to a professional therapist. If you have your parents' cooperation, you can get a good referral by talking to the guidance counselor at your school or your family doctor. If your parents are against the idea, talk to the guidance counselor to find out what you can do.

33 THINGS THAT ARE HARD TO TELL YOUR PARENTS

These problems will be a lot easier to handle once you have your parents' help. They may even get really mad when you first tell them, but in the end you'll be much better off. Also, check out the list called "14 People You Can Talk to If You Can't Talk to Your Parents" (page 16).

1. You got a low grade on a test.

2. You or your friend is drinking or taking drugs.

3. That they embarrass you.

4. That they treat you like a baby and you want more privileges.

5. That you've been hanging out with kids you know they don't approve of.

6. That you've gotten yourself into trouble on the Internet and you don't know how to handle it.

7. That you think you have too many responsibilities and you don't want to do some of them anymore (such as having to babysit for a younger sibling).

8. You're afraid they're thinking about getting a divorce.

9. You don't like your mom or dad's cooking.

10. That they're old-fashioned.

11. You got your period or have started to have wet dreams.

12. They don't understand you.

13. They don't spend enough time with you.

14. They insist on spending time with you when you'd rather be with your friends.

15. You don't think they love you as much as they do your brother or sister.

16. You wish they wouldn't compare you to a brother or sister or friend.

17. Anything about sex.

18. They have bad breath or body odor.

19. That you can't stand it when they chew with their mouth open or talk with food in their mouth.

20. You don't like the present they got you.

21. You don't like the clothes they pick out for you and would like to dress the way *you* want.

22. You're scared they're ill or might die soon.

23. You disagree with some of their religious beliefs.

24. You don't like the way your house looks.

25. You'd like to be friends with someone they might not approve of.

26. You need more money because you spent your allowance or you think you're not getting enough.

27. You think they make fun of you in front of relatives. (They call it "teasing"!)

28. You lied about something or did something dishonest.

29. You are embarrassed at the fact that they don't speak English.

30. That you did something that goes against your principles or religion.

31. That you are afraid of them.

32. That you are involved in something violent.

33. That you don't want to be something they want you to be.

8 PROBLEMS THAT COME UP WHEN YOU HAVE TO SHARE A ROOM WITH SOMEONE
(And What You Can Do About Them)

1. One person wants to do homework and the other wants to sleep. Set up the room so that the light is facing away from your brother's or sister's bed.

2. Both of you want to entertain friends at the same time. Agree on which days of the week you each get to have the room privately. If you want to switch days, you can. Then you'll know which days are yours and you can respect each other's privacy.

3. One of you wants to listen to the radio or watch TV and the other doesn't. Again, work out a fair schedule. Remember that every once in a while you're going to have to compromise and give in to the other's wishes. Also, you can agree on certain "quiet hours," when no music or TV is allowed unless both want it. Those are the times when homework or reading gets done in silence.

4. One person needs privacy to talk on the phone. In a polite way, you can ask if the other person would please leave the room for a while. Remember, it's a two-way bargain, and if you cooperate at such times, your roommate will, too. If this doesn't work out, take the call in another room.

5. One person wants to get up early but the other person doesn't want to be disturbed. The one who wants to get up first can agree to be *verrrry* quiet. They can put out their clothes the night before so they don't make a lot of noise when getting dressed, or they can plan to get dressed in the bathroom. He or she can also keep some books or games near the bed so there's something quiet to do until the other gets up.

6. Both feel they don't have enough room for their things. First, you have to make sure you're really dividing the available space equally. If it's still crowded, ask a parent to help create more room by adding shelves to closets, hanging more hooks for clothes, and getting some storage boxes that can be hidden under the bed. You can also ask other members of the family if you may use some of their drawers or closet space. As a last resort, you can always get rid of some junk.

7. One keeps using the other's things. Set down some rules, such as each one having to ask permission for certain items while other things become common property. Post the rules in the room on a sign. Anyone who breaks a rule has to put a quarter into a special envelope. After a while, the money can be used to buy something nice for the room, like a poster, a plant, or a new game that must be shared.

8. You both want to use the computer at the same time. You'll have to make up a schedule to divide the time, but try using the computer at the same time. That doesn't usually work if you're doing homework, but you can share game time, taking turns at the keyboard. And maybe something your sister is researching might be of interest to you, too.

11 THINGS YOU CAN DO WHEN YOUR PARENTS FIGHT

When parents fight, it doesn't mean they don't love each other. There are lots of reasons for parents' arguing. They may be concerned about money or work and may be taking out their frustrations on each other. If you are seriously worried about their relationship, wait until the battle is over and talk to them honestly about your concern. In the meantime, here are some things you can do to avoid the fight while it's still going on. It's rarely a good idea to get involved.

1. Take a walk.

2. Go outside and do something physical, like running or playing ball, to relieve some of your own anger and frustration.

3. Go into your room, shut your door, and turn up the TV, stereo, or radio so you can't hear them.

4. Call a friend on the telephone to take your mind off the fighting.

5. Take a shower.

6. Escape into the world of a really good book. If it's too noisy to read, get a book on tape and listen to it using your headphones.

7. Go visit someone.

8. Spend the time with a brother or sister who may need help at this time just as much as you do.

9. Give your dog a bath.

10. Write down how the fighting is making you feel. Either keep your notes private or share them with your parents later. After they've read your notes, you can talk with them about your concerns.

11. Log on to a chat room or learn how to do something new on your computer.

KIDS' REACTIONS TO FINDING OUT THAT THEIR PARENTS ARE GETTING SEPARATED OR DIVORCED

If your parents are splitting up or already have, it may help you to know that other kids have felt the same way you do. Or if a friend's parents are separating, this list will help you understand what your friend may be going through.

If the separation is happening in your family, it's very important to talk about your feelings with your parents. If you can't speak to them for any reason, see the list of "14 People You Can Talk to If You Can't Talk to Your Parents" (page 16). They may be able to listen and advise you. Talking can help you understand your feelings better, and it can be a comfort just to know someone cares enough to listen. And since it really can hurt to keep all those bad feelings inside, it's often a great relief to get the feelings out.

1. Anger that a parent has already left before you knew they were leaving, with no time to say good-bye or get used to the idea first.

2. Anger that your parents are splitting up when you want so badly for them to stay together.

3. Frustration at not being able to change the situation.

4. Being confused about how your life will change, whom you will live with, and so on.

5. Confusion, anger, hurt, and sadness at being put in the middle—for instance, when either parent tries to make you think the other is horrible.

6. Not knowing what to do when they compete to win you over to their side—one may buy you lots of toys or give you extra freedom, but you know it's only to win your loyalty.

7. Fear about having your whole life change.

8. Being scared that you won't see one parent as much anymore and that he or she won't love you as much as before.

9. Feeling stupid because the whole thing was a surprise to you; no one even hinted that it was going to happen.

10. Great relief! For many kids, fighting between parents is horrible to hear, and the sadness, strain, and frustration felt when living with parents you know are not happy together are very hard to take. Lots of kids have said they couldn't wait for their parents to separate so they could have a peaceful home again.

11. Confusion over finding yourself behaving in ways you don't understand. For instance, some kids take out their frustration by misbehaving in school or being mean to friends they really like.

10 DIFFERENT KINDS OF FAMILIES

Family life in the U.S. has changed in recent years, and the term "normal family" has taken on new meanings. Many different kinds of families are now considered typical or normal.

1. Dad works and Mom stays home and takes care of the kids and the household.

2. Mom works and Dad stays home and takes care of the kids and the household.

3. Mom and Dad both work and the children have a babysitter or go to a day care center.

4. Mom and Dad are divorced. The children live with one parent and visit the other or take turns living with each parent.

5. One parent raises the children because the other parent is unable to be there.

6. Two men or two women raise children together.

7. The children live with foster parents or parents that have adopted them.

8. The children live with one birth parent and one stepparent.

9. The children live with relatives.

10. The children live with parents sometimes and relatives at other times.

9 TIPS FOR KIDS WHO LIVE IN STEPFAMILIES

Today, more than half the kids in the U.S. live with only one of their real parents. Becoming part of a new family when one parent remarries can be a great adventure. You sometimes get new siblings, new grandparents, and a new place to live. But leaving the old arrangement behind can hurt, too. Here are some ideas that can help.

1. Try to be happy for the parent who is getting married, even if you are sad for yourself. Chances are your parent was lonely, just as you would be if you didn't have friends your own age.

2. Talk about how you feel. If you're afraid your parent doesn't love you the way they used to, tell them, and give them a chance to make things right if they have been ignoring you. Listen to what they have to say.

3. If you have new brothers or sisters, consider yourself lucky! (Perhaps you'll have fewer chores to do.)

4. You may feel funny about getting along with the new stepparent. You may think you are not being loyal to the other parent if you are nice to this one. But that's not how love works. You can be friendly with your stepparent and still let your absent parent know that you love them and that they are not being replaced.

5. Take time to get to know your stepfamily. Maybe they know things you want to learn about. Maybe they would like to learn to do something that you know how to do. Try to use this time to make your world a little bigger.

6. Be patient. Friendships don't happen overnight. It's

going to take time for your new family to adjust to all the changes, especially the new living arrangements.

7. If you've had to move away from your old neighborhood, try to arrange for a friend to come and visit.

8. If you've tried everything and there's still a lot of fighting going on, call a truce. Sit down with the other family members and say, "We're never going to feel the same way about this issue. Let's just come to some sort of agreement so we can stop arguing all the time."

9. Ask yourself this one important question and answer it honestly: "What's it like to live with *me?*"

THE 6 WORST THINGS ABOUT BEING PART OF A LARGE FAMILY

1. It's hard to have privacy.

2. You usually have to wait to use the bathroom.

3. You may have less private time with each parent.

4. You have to share your things with more people.

5. You may have more responsibilities (like having to babysit for a younger brother or sister), which gives you less time to be with friends.

6. You have to wear a lot of hand-me-downs.

THE 9 BEST THINGS ABOUT BEING PART OF A LARGE FAMILY

1. You're hardly ever lonely because someone's usually around.

2. You can get great hand-me-downs and have lots of extra clothes.

3. There's usually someone to help you with your homework.

4. There's usually someone to give you advice when you need it.

5. There's lots of activity in a large family, which makes it fun, and you're rarely bored.

6. You get to meet and have relationships with your sister's or brother's friends.

7. Holiday and birthday celebrations are even more festive with lots of people around.

8. If you get into trouble with your parents, a brother or sister is likely to stick up for you.

9. If something really awful happens, like there's a family crisis, there are lots of people around to share the feelings with.

THE 10 WORST THINGS ABOUT HAVING A YOUNGER BROTHER OR SISTER

1. They get in the way when your friends are around.

2. You have to babysit for them when you'd rather go out with your friends (or babysit for someone else and be paid for it).

3. They get into your drawers, invade your privacy, or use something of yours.

4. Your parents make a big fuss about them every time they do something "cute," and you feel you don't get as much attention.

5. Sometimes they get the same privileges as you even though you're older.

6. Parents expect you to teach them how to behave, so if they get into trouble, you wind up getting part of the blame.

7. They embarrass you in front of your friends.

8. They want to play with your things before they know how to care for them properly.

All-New

9. They're very noisy when you want some quiet.

10. They ask a lot of questions.

THE 8 BEST THINGS ABOUT BEING AN ONLY CHILD

1. You always have your parents' complete attention—you're the star!

2. You don't have to share your things with a sister or brother.

3. You have your own room.

4. You always have more privacy.

5. You don't have to listen to comparisons with a brother or sister.

6. You don't have to babysit for a sibling.

7. Your parents are more likely to take you on vacation with them, since there's only one to pay for and it's a lot less trouble to take just one kid along.

8. All your clothes and toys are bought especially for you.

THE 7 WORST THINGS ABOUT BEING AN ONLY CHILD

1. Being by yourself can be boring and lonely.

2. There's no one around to introduce you to new friends.

3. There's no older child to give you advice.

4. If you get into trouble with your parents, there's no one to defend you.

5. You don't have a sister or brother with whom to share feelings about your parents or other relatives.

6. Parents tend to be overprotective with an only child.

7. There's no one to borrow things from.

10 PROBLEMS TWINS HAVE

If you're a twin, you know that the world usually expects you both to be the same. But like any other kid on this planet, you're an original, even if you look exactly like your twin. Here are some of the problems twins have to live with. (By the way, if you want to meet 3,000 other sets of twins, go to Twinsboro, Ohio, where they hold Twins Day each year. Call 330-425-3652 for more information.)

1. Friends sometimes can't tell you apart.

2. People may expect you always to like the same things.

3. If one twin gets better grades than the other.

4. If one twin gets a girlfriend or boyfriend first.

5. If one twin is more popular.

6. If one twin has a special talent that the other doesn't have.

7. If one twin starts to develop earlier than the other.

8. If the two of you don't like each other, yet everyone always expects you to be close and hang out together.

9. You have to deal with kids who may have trouble being friendly with one of you and not the other.

10. One of you may want to dress the same while the other wants to dress differently.

8 WAYS IN WHICH MARY-KATE AND ASHLEY OLSEN ARE DIFFERENT

TV's famous twins may have a lot in common (their favorite colors are purple, blue, and yellow; their favorite store is the Gap, and they both hate brussels sprouts), but they are *not* identical.

Ashley

Right-handed
Fave film: *Spice World*
Quiet
Fave pastime: horseback
  riding
Likes books
Best subject: reading
Likes to wear jeans and
  T-shirts
Fave book: *The Jungle Book,*
  by Rudyard Kipling

Mary-Kate

Left-handed
Fave film: *Titanic*
Outgoing
Fave pastime: dancing

Likes video games
Best subject: math
Loves dresses, heels, and
  makeup
Fave book: *Oliver Twist,*
  by Charles Dickens

35 THINGS FRIENDS DO FOR EACH OTHER

1. They accept each other just as they are without trying to change things about the other.
2. They understand each other.
3. They spend time together.
4. They make each other laugh.
5. They share stuff.
6. They help each other when they are needed.
7. They tell each other what they really think.
8. They listen to each other.
9. They make each other happy.
10. They enjoy friendly competition.
11. They trust each other.
12. They tell each other things nobody else knows.
13. They dream together.
14. They don't talk behind each other's back.
15. They defend each other.
16. They don't betray each other.

17. They aren't jealous of each other.

18. They fight fair.

19. They do not say things to hurt the other person.

20. They support each other.

21. They laugh at the world together.

22. They teach others about friendship by setting a good example.

23. They keep secrets.

24. They remember each other's birthdays.

25. They promptly return stuff they borrow.

26. They are loyal.

27. They don't ask to borrow money.

28. They compliment each other.

29. They complement each other.

30. They are patient with each other.

31. They respect each other's differences.

32. They give each other space.

33. They are sensitive to each person's special issues.

34. They see talents and qualitites in you that you don't even see in yourself.

35. They pray for each other.

3

Toys, Games, and Hobbies

10 CONTESTS YOU WANT TO ENTER

1. All-American Soap Box Derby, Akron, Ohio. Soap box derby cars are cars that kids build out of boxes, crates, and junk. They were popular throughout most of the 20th century, going back to the Depression, when everyone was poor, so kids built these cars instead of riding the bikes they couldn't afford. To enter this race, you have to win a local Soap Box Derby first. Call 330-733-8723.

2. Big Whopper Liar's Contest, New Harmony, Indiana. If you're good at making up excuses, this one may be for you! Each year in September, about fifteen contestants try to outdo one another by telling the most outrageous tall tales. They win points for exaggeration, humor, and storytelling ability. Call 618-395-8491.

3. Calaveras County Fair and Jumping Frog Jubilee, Calaveras, California. Probably the oldest frog-jumping contest in the country. You can even read about this one in Mark Twain's famous story "The Celebrated Jumping Frog of Calaveras County." Any frog that sets a new world record gets a $1,500 prize. The current record is held by Rosie the Robiter, who jumped a little more than 21 feet in one leap. Call 209-736-2561.

4. Egg-Frying Contest, Oatman, Arizona. Since the sidewalks can get as hot as 106° in July, the citizens of Oatman put their streets to use by holding an annual contest in which entrants have 15 minutes to fry an egg using nothing but the sidewalk and their own ingenuity. One year, one man even managed to cook bacon and potatoes with his eggs! Call 520-763-5885.

5. The Great American Bathtub Race, Nome, Alaska. If you're anywhere near the Arctic during Labor Day, you might want to enter this one. Bring four friends. Each team needs five members, four of whom push the bathtub (wheels are usually attached, but some use horses to pull theirs) while one member sits in the tub, which is filled with bubbly hot water. Call 907-443-2798.

6. International Rotten Sneaker Contest, Montpelier, Vermont. There are now regional Rotten Sneaker contests, and if you win one of them, you can enter the biggest event of all, held every March. You bring your most worn-out, disgusting stinky sneakers, and if they're awful enough, you can win a $500 savings bond. Winning sneakers are kept in the Hall of Fumes, making them a permanent part of dirty-sneaker history. Call 212-371-2200.

7. Nathan's Famous Hot Dog Eating Contest, Brooklyn, New York. If you think you can eat more than 25 hotdogs in less than 12 minutes, enter this one and see if you can break the record. The contest is held every Fourth of July and is so famous, it attracts contestants from other countries. Call 212-627-5766.

8. National Fence-Painting Contest, Hannibal, Missouri. This contest is part of National Tom Sawyer Day, in which boys dress up like Mark Twain's famous character and paint fences to see who can do it the best and fastest. (Girls are not allowed to participate in this contest.) Other contests at this annual celebration include bubble-gum blowing and watermelon-seed spitting. Call 573-221-5052.

9. Spamarama, Austin, Texas. Each May, over 10,000 people get together in Austin to compete in the Spam Toss (how far can you throw the stuff?); the Spam-Eating Contest (you need to be *really* hungry for this one); and the newest event, the Pork Pull, a tug-of-war in which each team tries to drag the other team into a pool of Spam jelly. Call 512-834-1960.

10. World Championship Watermelon Seed Spit, Luling, Texas. The world's record holder for this event is Lee Wheells, who in 1989 spit a watermelon seed more than 68 feet. If you think you can do better, enter this contest and win $1,000 if you succeed. Plus, you'll get your name in *The Guinness Book of World Records.* Call 830-875-3214.

11 TIPS FOR EASIER TOY ASSEMBLY

Before you buy any toy, read the package to see how much assembly is required. If it's clearly something you can't do yourself, make sure you have help lined up before you spend your money. *Always keep the sales receipts and warranties.* Then you can begin.

1. Make sure you have a well-lit, clear space to work in.

2. Open the box carefully so that if the toy has to be returned, it can be replaced just the way you got it. Don't throw away anything!

3. Read through the instructions before you start assembling, just to get an overall idea of what's involved. If anything seems beyond you, get help.

4. The instructions should include a list of parts. Make sure you have all the parts before you begin. If anything is missing, call the store where you bought the toy and ask them how to go about getting a replacement.

5. Go online and see if the manufacturer has a Web site where you can get help.

6. Have all the right tools ready at hand.

7. Keep things organized while you work. Put all small parts together so they don't get lost. Use small dishes or paper cups to sort the pieces.

8. Work slowly and continue to read the instructions as you do each step. Do one step at a time, even if you think you know exactly what comes next. Be patient.

9. Save any spare parts. Store them in a plastic bag together with your receipt, the instructions, and the warranty.

10. Fill out and send in the warranty registration card if the toy came with one.

11. Read the instructions for *using* the toy once you're ready to play with it, even if you think you know exactly what to do.

10 WAYS TO AVOID GETTING
RIPPED OFF AT CARNIVAL GAMES

Winning a prize at a carnival can be an expensive experience. There are some games that are easier to win at than others and there some games that seem easy but are nearly impossible to win. Follow these tips and save yourself some money.

1. Wheel of Fortune. You are probably better off staying at home and watching the TV show. The best way to increase your chance of winning is to increase the number of your bets. But if you lose, you may lose more than you wanted to.

2. Basketball players beware! The ball you will be using will be too large for the hoop. But if you feel like going for the prize anyway, shoot directly at the hoop and not the backboard. Be sure that the ceiling clearance is high enough for this kind of shot. If it isn't, move on to the next booth.

3. Ring a Bottle. Throwing a ring around the neck of a bottle is nearly impossible. Some booth operators will place rings around some bottles to mislead you into thinking it's possible to do. They will also sometimes give you rings that aren't wide enough to fit the neck of the bottle.

4. Razzle-Dazzle. There is only one tip for this game. Don't play it. You can't win, but you can lose a lot.

5. Guess Your Weight. The prize you win if you can fool the person guessing your weight will cost less than what it costs you to play the game. If you want to try your luck anyway, puff up your cheeks, stick out your stomach, and think fat. Good luck!

6. Swinger. This one is impossible to win. A pin or metal bottle is placed directly under a ball that is supposed to swing at the pin and knock it down. If you miss the pin on the first swing, it will never hit the bottle. The game operator will try to fool you by setting up a pin and knocking it down, but he won't place the pin directly under the ball.

7. Plate-Pitch. The idea here is to toss a coin onto a plate and keep it on the plate. This is very difficult but not impossible. Aim for the back rim of the plate and hope the coin bounces back. If the plate doesn't have a rim, don't play; you'll just be throwing your money away.

8. Baseball and Basket. Throwing a baseball into a wooden fruit basket and keeping it from bouncing out is not easy. The bottom of the basket is very springy and will send the ball sailing out. Aim for the side or rim of the basket even if you have to step off to the side a little. Or throw the ball gently so that it just makes it over the bottom rim.

9. Water Balloon Race. This game requires only a steady hand, good eyes, and a little luck. There is always a winner at this one, and it could be you.

10. Stay away from any game that has complicated rules or rules that change.

44 THINGS THAT KIDS COLLECT

1. Action figures
2. Advertising signs
3. Animal figures
4. Autographs of famous people
5. Barbie dolls
6. Baseball cards
7. Beanie Babies
8. Birds' nests
9. Bookmarks
10. Books
11. Bottle caps
12. Buttons, badges, patches, and pins
13. Butterflies
14. Cabbage Patch dolls
15. CDs and cassette tapes
16. Chess sets
17. Comic books
18. Dolls and doll houses
19. Dried flowers
20. Gum wrappers
21. Harry Potter memorabilia
22. Horse figurines
23. Hot Wheels cars
24. Insects
25. Keys
26. Leaves
27. Maps
28. Marbles
29. Matchbox cars
30. Miniatures

31. Models
32. Movies on video
33. Paper dolls
34. Postcards
35. Posters
36. Quarters from each of the 50 states
37. Rocks
38. Seashells
39. Snow globes
40. Stamps
41. Stickers
42. Teddy bears
43. Troll dolls
44. Video games

TOY PRICES, 1897

In 1897, Sears, Roebuck and Company, now known as Sears, called itself "the cheapest supply house on earth." Its hefty catalog listed everything from ladies' underwear to farm equipment, but it didn't have a toy section, since most kids made their own toys back then. But the following appear in the catalog at prices that make us want to turn back the hands of time.

1. A pair of steel blade ice skates: 62 cents (Average price today: $100)
2. The Spaulding Official Boys' League Baseball: 72 cents (Average price today: $25)
3. The Spaulding boys' catcher's mitt: 20 cents (Average price today: $55)
4. Toy wagons, made of solid steel: starting at $1.15 (Average price today: $100)
5. Rocking horses, which were called "shoo-fly horses": 75 cents (Average price today: $70)
6. A deck of Tally-Ho playing cards: 13 cents (Average price today: $2.75)
7. The Brass Band harmonica, advertised as "the king of harmonicas": 22 cents (Average price today: $22)
8. Girls' 20-inch, two-wheel bicycles: $29 (Average price today: $100–$300)
9. Girls' toy brooms: 9 cents (Average price today: $5)

10. A steel toy safe, an ancestor of the piggybank: 25 cents (Average price today: $20)

TOY TRIVIA

1. The teddy bear, which first appeared in 1902, was named after President Theodore Roosevelt.

2. The Raggedy Ann doll was named after the comic strip character Little Orphan Annie.

3. Roller skates were first patented by James Plimpton in 1863, when they first became a fad.

4. Silly Putty was first created by the General Electric Company as a substitute for rubber, but it was found to have no industrial uses, so it was marketed as a toy instead.

5. The Frisbee flying disk was named after the Frisbee Company of Bridgeport, Connecticut, which made pie plates. (The flying disk got its start as a toy when someone noticed that college kids liked tossing the plates to one another for fun.)

6. The hula hoop was the greatest fad in toy history. When it became available in the 1950s, it sold 20 million in the first year.

7. The yo-yo got its start as a weapon, used by the Philippine Island warriors in the 16th century. Theirs was a 4-pound sphere with a 20-foot cord. The first toy version, which appeared in the U.S. in 1929, was developed by Louis Marx, the famous toy manufacturer.

8. Dominoes were created by French monks. They named the game after the first line of Psalm 110 in the Bible, which in Latin reads: "*Dixit Dominus meo*" ("Said my Lord.")

9. Each year the Parker Brothers Company prints more play money than the U.S. mint prints real money.

10. Germany is the largest manufacturer of toys. The U.S. is second.

11. In 1914, poor Charles Pajeau couldn't get anyone to pay attention to his new toy invention. So that Christmas, he had the idea to hire dwarfs in elf costumes to play with the toy in a Chicago department store window. The plan was an instant hit: A year later, over a million sets of Tinker Toys had been sold.

12. Napoleon and his army played with yo-yos before battles in order to relax.

THE 10 MOST EXPENSIVE BEANIE BABIES

In 1994, Ty Warner produced the first Beanie Baby—and the world of collecting hasn't been the same since. Beanie Babies have been the subject of national headlines, they've caused violent fights among obsessed shoppers, and they've been copied by counterfeiters. The thing that makes these valuable is the fact that they came out early, not many were manufactured, and they were "retired" shortly after they appeared. If you haven't played with your Beanie Babies in a long time, check them out—there may be a fortune waiting for you in your toy closet! By the way, remember that prices go up and down all the time; these numbers will change slightly from year to year and dealer to dealer.

1. Peanut (dark blue). About 2,000 of these elephants were made in July 1995 before Warner changed the color to light blue. Price: $5,000.

2. Brownie. One of the original nine Beanie Babies produced in 1994; this bear's name was eventually changed to Cubbie, and he was retired in 1997. Price: $4,000.

3. Nana. This little monkey was issued in 1995 and was retired the same year. He looks just like Bongo, who is still around today. Price: $4,000.

4. Teddy (violet). This one is expensive because it was never sold in stores. The little bear was given only to Warner's employees as a gift for all their hard work. It doesn't even have a tag on it. Price: $4,000.

5. Punchers. This is one of a few lobsters that were made and was also produced as "Pinchers." Punchers is the expensive one, but even a first-generation version of Pinchers goes for up to $350. Price: $3,800.

6. Derby (fine mane). This one is still around but with a coarse mane and tail, making the original horse more valuable. Price: $3,800.

7. Teddy (brown, old face). The older version of this bear had a pointy snout and the eyes were set far apart. Price: $3,000.

8. Chilly. Because Chilly is white, it's almost hard to find a really clean version of him. Even so, the dirty versions of this little polar bear are still valuable. Price: $2,500.

9. Humphrey. This little camel wasn't very popular when he came out because collectors thought he looked weird with his tall skinny legs. If you passed him up, you made a mistake. Price: $2,500.

10. Peking. This panda bear is extremely rare, since it was only produced for one year. It was followed by another panda bear named Fortune, who is also hard to find. Price: $2,300.

HOW TO JUDGE A TOY

If you follow these tips when you go toy shopping, you'll probably wind up with toys that last longer and hold your interest. It really doesn't make sense to spend a lot of money on something that will only last a short time, especially since toy prices have gotten so high. (See "5 Tips for Toy Shoppers," which follows this list.)

1. Toys should be creative. You're better off with a toy that gives you choices about putting it together rather than a toy that does the same thing every time you play with it. For instance, Lego and Construx, two building sets that come in different "editions," let you build things in a variety of ways, and the different pieces challenge your imagination and allow you to make more complicated things as you "grow" with the toy.

2. Toys should be convenient. You probably already know that toys that take a long time to set up get played with far less than toys that are ready when you are. A lot of the racing car sets for sale today look like a lot of fun, but they take up too much space to stay assembled in your play area all the time. Unless you have lots of room, don't spend a lot of money on car sets with huge tracks. Remember that toys that require adult help because they are complicated will only get played with when an adult is available. That may not be as often as you like.

3. Toys should be challenging. Of course, playing isn't supposed to be work, but if a toy is too easy to master—like a video game that only has one screen—you'll probably get bored with it quickly. When you shop, look for things that look a little bit complicated. Chances are, you'll learn something from them.

4. Toys should be original. Watch out for new versions of old toys—you could be buying the same toy you already have, only with a different package and a new name. If you already own a race car set, make sure that the one you're thinking of buying does something that your old one doesn't do. You'll also find a lot of copycats among video games.

5 TIPS FOR TOY SHOPPERS

Toys are a multibillion-dollar industry in America, so there a lot of different companies out there trying to get your attention—and your money. You'll get more for your "moolah" if you keep these pointers in mind when you shop for toys.

1. Compare prices. If you compare prices for the same toy at different stores, you'll find a difference of $5, $10, or even $20, depending on the toy. Call a few stores before you make your purchase or check newspaper ads for sales and bargains. You could save enough money to buy a whole other toy!

2. Test the toy before you buy. This may not always be possible, since stores don't have display models for everything they sell. Ask a friend who already has the toy if you can try it out, or just get other opinions from kids you know or by consulting a computer forum. In the case of home video games, you can try out the arcade version, but be careful: These can often be *very* different from one another.

3. Don't buy something just because it looks great on TV. Toys rarely work in real life the way they do in commercials, which we think is *very* unfair. TV commercials use special effects, and let's face it: The kids in the commercials are being paid to look like they're having a great time. (See "6 Ways in Which Advertisers Try to Get You to Buy Toys," which follows this list.) Pictures on boxes often are also misleading. If you can, try to get a look at the real thing before you buy it.

4. Check warranties. In many cases, if the toy breaks down after you've played with it a few times, you can get your money back—but only on the toys that have warranties and for which you have held onto the warranty (sometimes on the box; sometimes inside). Even if you lose these or throw them out by mistake, large toy stores and department stores will usually try to help you if you are able to show that there was something wrong with the toy when you got it.

5. Find out whether batteries are included with the toy. It's always frustrating to rush home to play with a new toy only to discover that you'll have to make another shopping trip to get the necessary batteries. Read the writing on the box before you head home for the fun.

6 WAYS IN WHICH ADVERTISERS TRY TO GET YOU TO BUY TOYS

According to the law, the stuff you buy at a store is supposed to look just like it did when you saw it in an ad. Unfortunately, that's not the way it always works out. Here are some of the ways in which advertisers cheat. If you wind up being the victim of unfair advertising, do something about it. Start by taking a look at "7 Things You Can Do If You Get Ripped Off" (page 50).

1. They make the product look better on TV than it does in real life. Like when they show you a toy oven "that really bakes," they show perfectly scrumptious-looking golden cookies coming out the oven door. But chances are, those cookies were not baked in that oven but in a real professional oven. Yours won't look like those!

2. With hobby kits, they often make you think that something will take just minutes to finish, but there are many steps involved, and often you have to wait a whole day between steps.

3. They *do* let you know when toys require assembly. What they *don't* tell you is that assembly may be very complicated, involving over 40 parts and badly written instructions.

4. They make you think that the toy makes sounds or creates effects that are really just part of the TV commercial. This is especially true of ads for video games and space toys. More often than not, the sounds you hear are *not* coming out of the toy.

5. They try to make you feel like you're not being loyal to your favorite TV character if you don't rush out and buy the toy with his or her picture all over it. They sometimes do this by showing lots of kids playing with the toy, so you'll feel like the only kid in the world who doesn't have it.

6. They make things look bigger than they really are.

Sometimes they do this by packing small toys in large boxes that are mostly filled with cardboard. (Don't forget to recycle this stuff!) Or they show you a picture of the toy standing by itself, so you're not really sure how large it is.

7 TOY MANUFACTURERS YOU CAN WRITE TO FOR REPLACEMENT PIECES

Has your little brother run off with Mr. Potato Head's nose? Has Barbie lost her shoe again? No problem. These companies will replace parts, sometimes for free, sometimes for a shipping and handling charge.

1. Lego will replace, at no charge, building instructions and missing pieces from models you own. Call 800-233-8756.

2. Erector will also replace, at no charge, building instructions and missing pieces. Call 800-268-1733.

3. Hasbro will replace up to 10 Scrabble tiles free. Either call 800-327-8264 or send an e-mail from its Web site, www.hasbro.com.

4. Bandai, which makes Power Rangers and other action figures, gives away replacement laser guns, swords, and decals. Call 714-816-9561.

5. Need money for Monopoly? For $2 you get it all. The number for Milton Bradley, Parker Brothers is 888-836-7025.

6. If the dog ate Barbie's shoe, a new pair costs 50 cents. Call Mattel, Tyco at 800-524-8697.

7. A bag of Mr. Potato Head pieces (not including the potato) goes for $4. Call Hasbro, Kenner, Tonka at 800-327-8264 or send an e-mail from its Web site, www.hasbro.com.

IMPORTANT DATES IN PINBALL HISTORY

1775. Bagatelle, a pin game, is introduced in Europe. A pin game is basically a box with a bunch of pins, or obstacles, sticking up from the bottom. You drop a ball in the top, then whack and shake the box while trying to get the ball to fall through various holes. Some holes are worth more points than others. Bagatelle (the word means "little thing" or "trifle"; today it's pronounced "bag-uh-telly") was a smash hit in coffee shops and other 18th-century hangouts.

1929. Whoopee, the first copyrighted game of Bagatelle, is marketed in the U.S. by George Deprez and the In and Out Game Company of Chicago. Whoopee doesn't advance the Bagatelle concept very much. It, too, is simply a box covered with glass; you drop the metal ball in and shake the box around. Different versions have different arrangements of pins and holes. There is no art or design on the box, other than the name of the game. In some places the game was used for gambling.

1934. The first Tilt feature appears on an electric pin game, Signal, manufactured by Bally. As every frustrated pinballer knows, tilt mechanisms shut the game off if you get too rough. This innovation added years to the life of a machine, since these games had been subject to lots of abuse.

1947. Humpty Dumpty, created by the D. Gottlieb Company, is the first to use flippers—six of them, to be precise. (Technically, machines without flippers were known as "pin games"; once flippers evolved, they became "pinball" or, to be really accurate, "flipper pinball.")

1954. Super Jumbo, also by Gottlieb, is the first game for more than one player. In this game, two players take turns, and their scores are tallied by separate counters on the back panel.

1966. Capersville, by Bally, is the first game to use multiple balls. Certain targets trap up to three balls and then release them simultaneously.

1975. Spirit of '76, by Micro Games, is the first all-electronic pinball machine. This one uses digital scoring instead of the revolving mechanical reels common up to that time. (Don't confuse this game with the "Spirit of '76" released by Gottlieb the same year.)

1979. Gorgar, the first talking pinball game, is released by Williams. Besides grunting and groaning, the monster taunts players with such phrases as "Me Gorgar—Beat me!" and "Hurt Gorgar!" (Bonus factoid: In 1933, Contact, a battery-operated pin game by Pacific Amusement Manufacturing, introduces sound—bells and buzzers—to the game.)

1980. The Black Knight, by Williams, is the first game to feature a multilevel playing field. (Two years later Gottlieb's Haunted House goes one better and introduces the three-level field.)

1992. The Addams Family, by Bally, becomes the best-selling pinball game in history. The fast, complicated action, the wide variety of targets, and the fidelity to the movie all contribute to the machine's vast popularity.

1995. Sega releases Apollo 13, a game based on the hit movie starring Tom Hanks. It's the first pinball game to offer a 13-ball multiball. Houston, we have a problem!

1998. Bally/Williams develops Pinball 2000, touted as a "giant leap forward" in the evolution of pinball technology. The games blend an interactive video monitor with traditional flipper action. In games such as Revenge from Mars and Star Wars Episode 1: The Phantom Menace, the monitor projects virtual images onto the playfield so the ball can interact with video pictures and traditional 3-D targets. Sadly, the name Pinball 2000 may have been a little too optimistic, because in . . .

1999. Williams Electronics Games goes out of business, and Sega's pinball unit is sold to Stern Pinball, in Illinois. For a while there was only one pinball manufacturer left—not just in the U.S. but in the *whole world.* The company turned out just 40 machines a day, including Harley-Davidson and a game based on TV's *South Park.* (Yes, one of the objects of the game is to kill Kenny.) Still, as Cartman might say, that total is pretty lame, compared to the 275 machines that were produced each day during pinball's heyday back in 1992. What happened? CD-ROM games, video arcades, and computer pinball simulations caused the market for real flipper-action tables to dry up. Does this spell disaster for fans of the silver ball? Is it "tilt, game over" for table pinball machines? Not so fast! Because in . . .

2000. A businessman buys up the inventory of the old Williams Company and launches a new business called Illinois Pinball. Its first game, Pool Player, debuts in Las Vegas. Illinois Pinball also acquires the rights to a game called Mystery Castle and six pinballs formerly made by Capcom. Could this mean the revival of real arcade flipper pinball? Find out in the next edition of *The All-New Book of Lists for Kids!*

LANDMARKS IN VIDEO GAME HISTORY

Marcus Webb is the editor of *Replay Magazine,* a publication for people who work in the coin-operated amusement world. Following is his pick of the major events in the evolution of video games over the past 20-plus years.

1972. Nolan Bushnell, the founder of Atari, creates his first smash: Pong. This simple two-player game—like tennis in slow motion—features sliding paddles that intercept a white ball as it glides across the screen. A revolution in entertainment is under way.

1978. Star Fire, by Exidy, is the first video game with a four-color screen. (But it doesn't really have a color screen; it cheats by placing a layer of colored plastic over the black-and-white monitor!)

1980. Bally/Midway introduces Pac-Man. The game is such a smash that the Pac-Man character (a smiley face in profile, his mouth open wide; see "15 Smileys," page 274) soon appears on the cover of *Time* magazine.

1981. Mario (of Brothers fame) makes his first appearance in a wacky game, Donkey Kong. This year, the success of arcade games such as Space Invaders and Galaxian make video a $7.25 billion (that's with a *b*) industry, making more money than the record and movie businesses combined.

1982. Ms. Pac-Man, the first of six spinoffs of the original, appears; it goes on to sell more copies than any other arcade game and is still earning money today. This year also sees the first interactive laser disc games, where players' choices determine which of many cinema-quality animated scenes will play. The most popular one is Dragon's Lair, which in 1994 is reborn as a CD-ROM game.

1983. President Ronald Reagan endorses video games as "teaching tools." Speaking to a group of math and science students at EPCOT Center, he says, "Many young people develop incredible hand, eye, and brain coordination in playing these games. . . . Watch a 12-year-old take evasive action and score multiple hits while playing Space Invaders, and you'll appreciate the skills of tomorrow's pilots." (Reagan reminded his audience, however, that "friends and homework still come first.") No doubt some of the kids weaned on games flew fighter planes during the high-tech Gulf War a decade later.

1984. Data East releases Karate Champ, the first martial arts head-to-head game. A year later, the top three games are all fighting games. The trend continues today, with fighting games blowing away their competitors.

1985. Sega releases Hang On, its first simulator game: a full-size, bright red motorcycle, monitor mounted on the handlebars, with controls in the hand grips and foot pedals.

1986. Gauntlet, by Atari, a Dungeons and Dragons–type fantasy adventure, is the first game to introduce a new perspective. Players look down on the characters from above as they run from room to room in a castle. Also this year, Nintendo launches its first home system just in time for Christmas.

1987. Taito releases the first Double Dragon, which stays on the list of top ten arcade games for an unheard-of two years. The level of violence (a woman gets punched, for example) draws flak from worried adults.

1989. The FBI puts antidrug messages on the "attract screens" of arcade games. Teenage Mutant Ninja Turtles by Konami is one of the year's big hits, as is the first version of Capcom's Street Fighter. This is also the year Nintendo introduces Game Boy.

1990. The first CD-ROM video game appears: "It Came from the Desert," by Cinemaware. The game features live-action, fifteen-frames-per-second digital video footage and computer animation of giant ants. Actors exchange witty dialogue (He: "Ants the size of gas trucks!" She: "I don't even like little ants at picnics!") as they battle the mutants with pistols, flamethrowers, tanks, and fighter planes. Also this year, in Chicago, Virtual World Entertainment creates the first simulator center, "Mech War," in which players sit in "pods" equipped with screens. Each screen shows the field—a post-apocalyptic landscape—from the individual player's point of view. Between four and sixteen players manipulate their huge robots around the field, trying to destroy one another in a high-tech version of Capture the Flag.

1991. The era of true VR—virtual reality—begins. A company called Virtuality creates 'Dactyl Nightmare, in which players wear helmets that respond to their head movements. They "move" around a three-dimensional platform in space, lobbing grenades at their opponent (another player or the computer) while ducking the onslaught of digital pterodactyls.

1992. The first five Virtual Reality Centers—arcades devoted to VR games and simulators—open in St. Louis, New York, and other cities.

1993. The U.S. government demands that the video game industry create a "voluntary" rating system to indicate the amount of sex and violence in a game.

1994. SEGA test-markets the Sega Channel, a cable station that allows subscribers to access and download up to 50 different games directly into their Genesis systems.

1995. Sony begins selling the first version of PlayStation in the U.S. In just two years it becomes the most popular gaming system in the world. Meanwhile, Sega gives up on the Sega CD module.

1996. Nintendo introduces its 64-bit unit, N64, in the U.S., selling nearly 2 million copies in just three months. Also this year, Nintendo sells its one billionth (that's with a *b)* game cartridge. Meanwhile Atari, the pioneer video game maker, goes out of business—just in time to earn a place in Videotopia, the first traveling museum exhibition on the history of video games.

1997. The Tamagochi typhoon strikes! Kids in Japan and the U.S. go wild over the electronic pets that need to be fed and played with . . . or they'll die. F.A.O. Schwarz sells out its complete supply of 30,000 units in three days. Meanwhile, in Seattle, movie magician Steven Spielberg opens the first Gameworks, a huge arcade with all the latest electronic games and gizmos.

1998. Pokémon replaces Tamagochi as the latest fad, and the Nintendo Game Boy version becomes the company's fastest-selling game ever.

1999. A die-hard gamester named Billy Mitchell completes every possible board in the classic game Pac-Man and earns the maximum score: 3,333,360. Also this year, in response to the shootings at Columbine High School in Littleton, Colorado, Sega announces it won't make a light gun for use with its Dreamcast units.

2000. Sony releases PlayStation 2 and causes a buying frenzy. Lucky owners discover they can sell their machines on eBay for as much as $1,000.

2001. Software gorilla Microsoft announces plans to enter the gaming arena with its Xbox and to release more than 50 games, such as Oddworld, Munch's Oddysee, and WWF Raw Is War.

THE 10 BEST-SELLING PC GAMES OF ALL TIME

1. Myst
2. MP Roller Coaster Tycoon
3. The Sims
4. Flight Simulator Version 1
5. Who Wants to Be a Millionaire?
6. Riven: The Sequel to Myst

7. MS Age of Empires II: Age of Kings
8. Monopoly Game
9. Lego Island
10. Diablo

THE 10 BEST-SELLING MAC GAMES OF ALL TIME

(in alphabetical order)

1. Escape Velocity (1996, Ambrosia Software)
2. Fallout (1997, Interplay)
3. Marathon (1995, Bungie Software)
4. Myth: The Fallen Lords (1997, Bungie Software)
5. Quake (1997, Id Software/MacSoft)
6. Spaceship Warlock (1990, Reactor)
7. Spectre (1993, Velocity)
8. TIE Fighter (1997, Lucas Arts)
9. Unreal (1998, Epic/MacSoft)
10. Warcraft II (1996, Blizzard Entertainment)

THE 11 BEST GAME SERIES OF ALL TIME

According to the staff of Gamespy.com.

1. DOOM
2. Ultima
3. Civilization
4. Half-Life
5. The Legend of Zelda
6. Warcraft
7. Quake
8. Super Mario Brothers
9. Diablo
10. Age of Empires (TIE)
11. System Shock (TIE)

7 TIPS FOR KIDS WHO WANT TO BECOME VIDEO GAME DEVELOPERS

Developing a video game takes very hard work and an understanding of games. You must be willing to understand the way all games work and love the process of creating something complicated and exciting from some small ideas.

1. Learn computer programming. Without programming skills, there is no game. Programmers are the ones who take basic ideas and find a way to make them work. They don't create the characters but they do bring them to life.

2. Learn to be an artist. Artists are more important than anyone else in creating an exciting game. They design the characters that the programmers bring to life on the video screen.

3. Learn design. Designers put all the elements of the game package together and create the overall look of the game, including the artwork on the video box. Usually artists are the designers, but sometimes they need the experience of an experienced designer.

4. Learn management skills. The producer or manager of a project is basically the boss. The producer is in charge of raising the money needed to finance a project and oversees every step of a game's creation.

5. Learn to be a team player. Developing any game involves working with many other skilled people; you need to know how to share resources with other people.

6. Develop a strong musical background. Sound effects and background music are important elements of a great video game.

7. Seek out a mentor. A mentor is a person who has worked in the field that you are interested in and is willing to advise you. A mentor can help you understand the business and financial aspects of the video game industry as well as the creative ones.

24 TOYS THAT WERE POPULAR IN THE 1950S AND ARE STILL POPULAR TODAY

1. Backgammon
2. Barbie dolls
3. Bingo
4. Candy Land
5. Careers
6. Checkers
7. Chess
8. Chutes and Ladders
9. Dominoes
10. Erector sets
11. Etch-a-Sketch
12. G.I. Joe
13. Gumby
14. Hula hoops
15. Lincoln Logs
16. Monopoly
17. Parcheesi
18. Play-Doh
19. Pogo sticks
20. Scrabble
21. Silly Putty
22. Spaulding balls
23. Tinkertoys
24. Yo-yos

THE G.I. JOE OATH OF HONOR

G.I. Joe was named after a character in the movie *The Story of G.I. Joe* and was the world's first "action figure," manufactured by Hasbro Toys. Today, the name refers not only to one toy but to a whole line of toys representing every branch of the U.S. armed forces and even some foreign ones. He's been through a lot of wars and became popular all over again when the U.S. went to war after September 11, 2001, but he still believes the same things he did when he started out.

G.I. Joe always:

1. Defends the rights of others and neutralizes evil wherever it exists
2. Maintains good health by eating the right foods, getting plenty of PT (physical training), and staying away from drugs and alcohol

All-New
^

3. Obeys the law and does the right thing
4. Answers the call for help from those who need it

THIS SPUD'S FOR YOU
The Life Story of Mr. Potato Head

1952. Mr. Potato Head is born as a kit with eyes, ears, a mouth, a pipe, and noses. You had to have your own potato!

1953. Mr. Potato Head meets and marries Mrs. Potato Head. They honeymoon in Boise, Idaho, the potato capital of the U.S.

1964. Mr. and Mrs. Potato Head get their plastic bodies, which now come with the kits.

1966. Mr. Potato Head becomes Jumpin' Mr. Potato Head, with a head that moves up and down. All Mrs. Potato Head gets is a vacuum cleaner, a floor polisher, and a bell, to let Mr. Potato Head know when it's time to eat.

1974. At the age of 22, Mr. Potato Head has gained a lot of weight. In fact, he's doubled in size! (Guess that little dinner bell really works!)

1983. Mr. Potato Head now comes with his own storage compartment for all his extra parts. This is the same year he learns to bend his arms.

1985. Four people vote for Mr. Potato Head for mayor of Boise. He loses the election in a landslide!

1987. At the suggestion of those who know that smoking is bad for you, Mr. Potato Head gives up smoking and loses the pipe.

2002. Mr. Potato Head has now sold over 75 million copies of himself and celebrates his 50th birthday by getting his own comic strip, which is written and drawn by Jim Davis (whom you might know from the Garfield comics) and Brett Koth. The strip is all about the adventures of Mr.

and Mrs. Potato Head and their two children, Chip and Julienne.

THE CRAYON HALL OF FAME, PART 1
8 Colors That Crayola Stopped Making in 1990

People were so outraged that these colors were discontinued that two groups were formed: CRAYON (the Committee to Reestablish All Your Old Norms) and the National Campaign to Save Lemon Yellow. Alas, they were not successful, and the colors died.

1. Blue gray
2. Lemon yellow
3. Orange red
4. Raw umber
5. Green blue
6. Maize
7. Orange yellow
8. Violet blue

THE CRAYON HALL OF FAME, PART 2
8 Colors That Replaced the Old Ones

1. Cerulean
2. Fuchsia
3. Royal purple
4. Vivid tangerine
5. Dandelion
6. Jungle green
7. Teal blue
8. Wild strawberry

76 AUTOGRAPHS TO COLLECT

If you're an autograph hound, here are some special autographs to be on the lookout for. These are often sold by professional dealers for high prices, so if you're lucky enough to bump into Steven Spielberg or Arnold Schwarzenegger at the mall, you could be in business. For more information, check out *Autograph Collector* magazine, 510-A South Corona, CA 92879-1420 (909-734-9636).

1. Christina Aguilera
2. Muhammad Ali
3. Jennifer Aniston
4. Any of the Backstreet Boys
5. Drew Barrymore
6. Kim Bassinger
7. Judy Blume
8. Matthew Broderick
9. Coby Bryant
10. George Bush
11. George W. Bush
12. Mariah Carey
13. Dana Carvey
14. Chevy Chase
15. Beverly Cleary
16. Bill Clinton
17. Hillary Clinton
18. Sean Connery
19. Bill Cosby
20. Courtney Cox
21. Cindy Crawford
22. Sheryl Crow
23. Russell Crowe
24. Tom Cruise
25. Billy Crystal
26. Matt Damon
27. Johnny Depp
28. Any of the Dixie Chicks
29. Kirsten Dunst
30. Jenna Elfman
31. Jodi Foster
32. Michael J. Fox
33. Sarah Michelle Gellar
34. Whoopi Goldberg
35. Wayne Gretsky
36. Ken Griffey, Jr.
37. Tom Hanks
38. Melissa Joan Hart
39. Kate Hudson
40. Janet Jackson
41. Michael Jackson
42. Reggie Jackson
43. Pope John Paul II
44. Magic Johnson
45. Michael Jordan
46. Michael Keaton
47. Lisa Kudrow
48. Lucy Lawless
49. Mario Lemieux
50. Jennifer Lopez
51. Mark Magwire
52. Dan Marino
53. Ricky Martin
54. Reba McEntire
55. Eddie Murphy
56. Mike Myers
57. Rosie O'Donnell
58. Tatum O'Neal
59. Shaquille O'Neal
60. Bobby Orr
61. Haley Joe Osmont
62. Gwyneth Paltrow
63. Leann Rimes
64. Julia Roberts
65. Winona Ryder
66. Arnold Schwarzenegger

67. Sammy Sosa
68. Britney Spears
69. Steven Spielberg
70. John Travolta
71. Donald Trump
72. Shania Twain
73. Robin Williams
74. Bruce Willis
75. Oprah Winfrey
76. Tiger Woods

6 TIPS FOR GETTING CELEBRITIES TO RESPOND TO YOUR LETTERS

1. Send a photo of yourself. Celebrities will find it impossible to resist your adorable face.

2. Include a self-addressed stamped envelope. That makes it easier for the celebrity to send something back.

3. Explain early in your letter (maybe in the first sentence) why you are writing. Do you have a question? Are you looking for an autograph? Say so.

4. Don't write a very long letter. These people don't have a lot of time!

5. Make sure your letter is neat and easy to read. If someone has to struggle to read what you write, they'll probably give up and throw it away.

6. Don't send anything that you expect to get back. Chances are, you won't.

22 KINDS OF MARBLES

Marbles have been around since ancient times and have fascinated children, artists, and collectors. You can still buy ordinary marbles at any toy store—or you can pay thousands of dollars for the rarest ones.

1. Aggies
2. Birds' eggs
3. Bumblebees
4. Cat's-eyes
5. Clearies
6. Clouds
7. Comics
8. Corkscrews

9. Cub scouts
10. Flames
11. Gooseberries
12. Indians
13. Lutzes
14. Micas
15. Onionskins

16. Oxbloods
17. Popeyes
18. Purees
19. Ravenswoods
20. Rolled commies
21. Rootbeer floats
22. Whispers

88 THINGS YOU CAN USE TO MAKE A COLLAGE

Here's something to do when there's nothing to do: make a collage! All you need are a stiff piece of paper or board, some colorless glue, and your imagination. Choose from the items listed below or find others. Your collage can even center around a theme. For instance, if you were going to make a collage for someone who works as an accountant, you might use some play money, the stock market section of the newspaper, some pennies, and the person's business card. A get-well collage might consist of some Band-Aids, vitamins, a toy thermometer, and your special message spelled out in pasta alphabet letters. Be creative.

1. Absorbent cotton
2. Acorns
3. Aluminum foil
4. Band-Aids
5. Beads
6. Birthday cake ornaments
7. Birthday cards
8. Bobby pins
9. Bottle caps
10. Bows
11. Business cards
12. Buttons
13. Candy packages

14. Candy wrappers
15. Carpet scraps
16. Cereals and grains
17. Clay
18. Coins
19. Colored mints
20. Comic strips
21. Confetti
22. Cranberries
23. Dried beans
24. Dried leaves
25. Eggshells
26. Fabric scraps

27. Feathers
28. Foil hearts
29. Foil stars
30. Food labels
31. Glitter
32. Graph paper
33. Inexpensive plastic toys
34. Jelly babies
35. Keys
36. Loose-leaf paper hole reinforcements
37. Maps
38. Newsprint
39. Nuts
40. Nuts and bolts
41. Old computer parts
42. Old floppy disks
43. Paper clips
44. Paper doilies
45. Paper plates
46. Pasta
47. Pebbles
48. Pencil shavings
49. Pictures cut out of magazines
50. Pipe cleaners
51. Plastic animal eyes
52. Plastic flowers
53. Play money
54. Popped corn
55. Popsicle sticks
56. Postage stamps
57. Postcards

58. A report card
59. Ribbon
60. Rose petals
61. Rubber bands
62. Rubber-stamped impressions
63. Sand
64. Screws
65. Seeds
66. Sequins
67. Sheet music
68. Shells
69. Snapshots
70. Soda can tops
71. A special date circled on a calendar
72. Sponges
73. Spools of thread
74. Sports emblems
75. Stickers
76. Store receipts
77. String
78. Styrofoam bits
79. Ticket stubs
80. Tinsel
81. Toothpicks
82. Twigs
83. Twist ties
84. Vitamins
85. Wallpaper scraps
86. Wire
87. Wrapping paper
88. Yarn

11 GREAT GIFTS THAT DON'T COST ANYTHING

1. A coupon booklet of special favors. You can draw coupons that look like gift certificates, indicating on each one that this certificate is good for one special chore, such as one hour of babysitting, one breakfast served in bed, one whole week of getting your regular chores done on time, or giving the dog a bath. Staple all the coupons together so that they look like a little book.

2. An autographed picture of someone's favorite movie or TV star.

3. You may not be able to afford to shop in the most expensive store in your neighborhood, but their shopping bags usually don't cost anything. Ask the store owner for one and explain that the bag is a gift. This is an especially great gift if the shopping bag is real fancy. (Get two and call them "matching luggage"!)

4. A personal birthday greeting from the governor of your state. In most states, if you write a letter to the governor in care of your state capitol, within six or eight weeks your friend will receive a birthday greeting, personally signed. This service doesn't cost anything.

5. Tickets to a TV show. These are usually free. Just write to the folks at the show at the address they include in the credits at the end of the program.

6. Dedicate a song to someone over the radio by calling the station and making the request. (Some stations won't do it, but many will.) Make sure that the friend is listening at just the right time. If you have a tape recorder, you can make a permanent recording of that special moment when your friend's name is announced.

7. Cheerios. That might not sound like the world's most exciting gift, but you can make it special by placing a few in a small plastic bag, tying a pretty ribbon to secure the package, and drawing a small attractive label that says "Bagel Seeds." If it's really the thought that counts, you should get extra points for this one.

8. Be a slave for a day. That's right—one whole day (or maybe just an hour) of doing nothing but chores for someone else.

9. The front page of a newspaper printed on the day someone was born. Most large newspapers will send you this if you request it in writing. Many offer the service for free; some may charge a dollar or two.

10. If you can't afford a dozen roses, you can plant flowers instead. What a nice surprise someone will have when those flowers—or vegetables—start to grow. Even some grass seed planted in an interesting container can help bring the outdoors inside. If there is someone in your neighborhood who enjoys gardening, ask them for the seeds.

11. An old sock stuffed with another old sock makes a good gift for a pet.

10 GREAT GIFTS THAT COST UNDER $10

1. A poster of someone's favorite movie or TV star. Or find a camera that can enlarge any snapshot to poster size. Who could resist a life-size portrait of *you!*

2. Personalized pencils. You can order a dozen pencils with any name or message printed on them (like "Happy Birthday") through many large stationery stores and mail-order catalogs. Remember to plan this one in advance, as it usually takes about a month to get the pencils printed.

3. Cold cash, but wrapped and presented with a little imagination. You can put $10 worth of pennies in a fancy box or tape them together to make a very long "necklace." You can also put the pennies in a fancy jar, tie a ribbon around it, and paint the label "Mad Money" on the front. (If your friend takes public transportation to work, you can give $10 worth of subway or bus tokens.)

4. We've all had birthday and anniversary cakes, but consider a "Get Well" cake (nothing too rich) or one that just says "I Love You" or "I'm Sorry," depending on the occasion. If you don't have enough money for a decorated cake, buy a plain one and make your own flag with your personal message to place on the cake.

5. A supply of someone's favorite candy bar.

6. Lottery tickets. Who knows? Your $10 worth of lottery tickets may wind up being worth a lot more! However, most states that conduct lotteries have age requirements for the purchase of tickets, so you'll probably need an adult to help you out.

7. An inexpensive pet—like a goldfish—appropriately named. Name it for the occasion—"Happy Birthday" or "Merry Christmas," for example—or a favorite television or comic strip character. (Very important: Make sure the person really wants to have a pet and that they will take care of it before you make this kind of purchase.)

8. Put on some lipstick, press your lips against a piece of plain paper, and frame your permanent kiss.

9. Write different messages, like "I Love You" and "Happy Birthday" on a piece of paper, insert them in balloons, and then blow up the balloons. Your friend will have a bouquet of good wishes.

10. Call someone using a pushbutton telephone, and when the answering machine picks up, play "Happy Birthday." Be sure to say your name before you hang up.

1 1 4 1 * 9

1 1 4 1 # 0

1 1 # 0 * 7 4

0 * 0 *

14 GAMES YOU CAN PLAY ANYWHERE THAT DON'T REQUIRE PAPER OR PENCILS

These are fun to do while traveling or even if you're just bored waiting for the school bus. See if you can make up your own variations.

1. What Am I Counting? One player who's "It" counts something out loud as they see it (like trucks passing by or billboards) around him, and everyone has to guess what he's counting.

2. What's Next? If you're in a place where cars pass, try to guess the color of the next one that appears.

3. Treasure Hunt. Make a list (memorize it if you don't have paper) of weird things like a lady in a blue jacket or an old green man with a purple dog. The first person who sees each thing gets a point, and the one with the most points wins.

4. Are We There Yet? If you're in a car, try to guess how long it takes before you have traveled five miles. Ask the driver to clock you on the trip odometer.

5. Collect Smiles. Smile at everyone you see and count how many people smile back at you.

6. Who Am I? Think of a person. Everyone else takes turns asking you yes-or-no questions about the person. If they don't guess after 20 questions, you win.

7. Palm Writing. Write a message on someone's palm by outlining each letter, one at a time. They have to guess the message.

8. The Human Dictionary. The first person makes up a sentence. The second person repeats the sentence, only this time using a synonym (a word that means the same things as another word) for one of the words. Keep doing this until you have a really ridiculous sentence. For instance:

"I'm going to the store to buy milk."

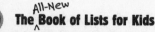

"I'm going to the store to purchase milk."

"I'm going to the store to purchase some of the white stuff that comes out of cows."

"I'm going to the place that sells things to purchase some of the white stuff that comes out of cows."

"I'm going to the place that sells things to purchase some of the white stuff that comes out of certain farm animals who supply us with dairy products."

9. I Know Where You're Coming From. One person says the name of a city, state, or other place, and the next person has to think of another place that starts with the last letter of that place. Keep going around the room until someone runs out of places and thus loses. (You can also play this game using people's names or foods, or toys, or anything else you can think of.)

10. What Am I? One player says things that an inanimate object would say if it could talk, and everyone has to guess what the thing is. For instance, if you said things like "I always get stepped on" and "I lie on the floor a lot," you'd be a rug. (You could also play this pretending that you are a famous person. If you were Christopher Columbus you could say, "It sure was nice sailing around the world" or "I'm a real Italian hero!")

11. Ask Dr. Know-It-All. One person makes up a question like "Why does it rain?" and everyone has to make up what they think might be the real scientific explanation.

12. Tell Me a Story. One person makes up a story, but after one minute, they stop, and the next person has to continue the story.

13. Memorize License Plates. See how many you can remember in a row.

14. .007. Substitute some letters for others in the alphabet —like if you turned all S's into T's, your sister Susan would be your "titter Tutan" and "sassafras" would be "tattafrat." Talk like this until someone figures out your secret code.

35 OF THE YOUNGEST SPORTS STARS EVER

Sports is one area where you'll seldom be told, "Wait until you grow up." Since the end of World War II, there has been a great increase in the number of sports programs available to kids, and the application of science to sports has resulted in great advances in nutrition and sports technique. So it is hardly surprising that many of these athletes earned their special distinctions in recent years.

1. The youngest international competitor in any sport was Joy Foster, who represented Jamaica in the 1958 West Indies Table Tennis Championships at the age of 8.

2. The youngest winner of an individual Olympic event was Marjorie Gestring, from the U.S., who was 13 when she won the springboard diving title in 1946.

3. The youngest jockey was Frank Wooten, an English champion between 1909 and 1912. He rode his first winner at the age of 9.

4. The youngest international gymnastics competitor was Pasakevi Voula Kouna, who was 9 when she entered an international meet in Greece in 1981.

5. The youngest basketball player ever to be signed as a rookie by a major league team was Jorge Lebron, of Puerto Rico. At the age of 14, he was signed by the Philadelphia Phillies in 1974 to play on a farm team.

6. The youngest baseball player to play on a major league team was Joe Nuxhall, who was 15 when he played with the Cincinnati Reds in 1944.

7. The youngest bullfighter was Conchita Cintahn, who became a *rejoeadora* (someone who fights bulls on horseback) at the age of 12.

8. The youngest member of the 111 Mountain Climbing Club was Deborah Wilson, who became a member when she was 11. In order to qualify, she had to climb 111 mountains in the northeastern U.S. In addition, Deborah climbed 111 other mountains, all over 4,000 feet high. She was 3 years old when she first started climbing, and she scaled her first 4,000-foot peak the same year.

9. The youngest boxing champion in any weight class was Wilfredo Benitez, who won the world light welterweight title in 1976 at the age of 17.

10. The only girl to ever compete in a Golden Gloves boxing event was Amber Hunt, who was 12 when she competed in 1977.

11. The youngest champion in the history of the U.S. Open Tennis Championship was Tracy Austin, who won at the age of 16, in 1979.

12. The youngest Wimbledon champion was Martina Hingis, of Switzerland, who won the women's doubles in 1996 (with Helena Sukova of the Czech Republic) at 17.

13. The youngest American to pedal a bicycle across the U.S. was Kirsten Wilhelm, who did it at the age of 9 in 1977. The trip took 66 days.

14. The youngest pair of ice skaters to represent the U.S. in international competition was Tai Babilonia and Randy Gardner, at 12 and 14 respectively, in 1974.

15. The youngest woman to win an international Grand Championship in judo was Margaret Castro in 1977 at the age of 17.

16. The youngest person ever to sign a professional soccer contract was Archie Stark, at the age of 14, in 1911.

17. Boris Becker, at 17, was the youngest tennis player to win at Wimbledon.

18. Nadia Comaneci was only 15 when she won three gold medals in gymnastics at the 1976 Olympics. She was also the first person to record a perfect score of 10 in a gymnastic event.

19. Krisztina Egerszegi at the age of 14 was the youngest person ever to win a gold medal at the Olympics in swimming.

20. Shane Gould retired from swimming at 16, having set five world records in freestyle swimming. He won three gold medals, two silver, and a bronze at the 1972 Olympics.

21. Monica Seles was the youngest tennis player, at 15, ever to win a Grand Slam title in the 20th century.

22. The youngest rodeo star was Anne Lewis, who won a world title in barrel racing in 1968, at the age of 10.

23. Richard Daff, Jr., was the youngest bowler to score a perfect 300 game. He was 11 years old at the time.

24. At age 5, Coby Orr of Littleton, Ohio, was the youngest golfer to shoot a hole-in-one. The hole was 103 yards from where Coby teed off. (Remember, a football field is 100 yards long!)

26. In 1979 Bunny Taylor became the first girl to pitch a no-hitter in Little League Baseball. She was 11 at the time.

27. At the age of 14, golfer Gary Gereson of Milford, Indiana, shot a hole-in-one three days in a row.

28. Twelve-year-old Karen Muir, of South Africa, became the youngest person ever to break a world athletic record. She swam the 100-meter backstroke.

29. Four-year-old Brent Vogle became the youngest American to finish a marathon run (just over 26 miles).

30. In 1975 Metha Brorsen won a world rodeo title. She was 11 when she and her horse won the barrel racing event.

31. The first girl to win the All-American Soap Box Derby was Karren Stead. She was 11 years old.

32. In 1977, 8-year-old Wesley Paul ran the New York City Marathon in three hours, setting a world record for his age group.

33. Thomas Gregory, at 11, was the youngest person ever to swim the English Channel. It took him 12 hours to swim 21 miles.

34. Eight-month-old Frederick Garcia couldn't walk yet, but he did manage to swim well enough to pass the Red Cross water safety beginner's test.

35. Andrea Holmes of Great Britain was the youngest trampoline competitor in an international event when, at 12, she competed in the World Championships in Bozeman, Montana, in 1982.

10 TIPS FOR BUYING ICE SKATES

If you're having difficulty skating, one of the reasons could be that your skates do not fit properly. A skate that is not made well will not give your foot the support it needs. Skates should be of good quality, properly fitted, and comfortable. Here are some guidelines you can follow when buying skates.

1. Your skates should either be the same size as your ordinary shoes or slightly smaller.

2. The boot should be laced loosely and tried on while you are sitting down. When you stand up, there should be enough room for your toes to move slightly. The heel and ball of your foot, however, should not be able to move at all. Make sure that your toes are not uncomfortable.

3. Grip the boot by the back of the heel. Pull up and down. You should hear suction and a snap.

4. Walk on the skate. There should be no motion of the heel.

5. If the skate seems too narrow, you can sometimes adjust the fit by the way you lace up. You can also try on a boot that is a half size larger.

6. The boots should be made of top-grain leather. The counter—the part of the boot your foot rests on—should be waterproof and have a cup that holds your heel in place.

7. The upper portion of the boot should be a soft leather that will allow your ankle to bend backward and forward.

8. The boot should have a full lining. The hooks and eyelets should be securely fastened.

9. Blades should be made of high-tempered steel and be able to hold an edge well.

10. Never try to break in a new pair of skates by walking on them without the blade protectors.

10 SAFETY TIPS FOR ICE SKATERS

These suggestions are recommended by the Ice Skating Institute of America.

1. Never wear skates on any area that is not covered by rubber matting. You can ruin the blades of your skates if you walk on a hard surface.

2. Never skate in the opposite direction of the other skaters.

3. Do not dart across the ice.

4. Do not hang out in the center of the ice or anywhere else where you might interfere with other skaters.

5. Never chain skate.

6. Never skate too fast.

7. Never climb over the boards surrounding the ice.

8. Don't bring food or drinks onto the skating surface.

9. When you have finished skating, leave the ice very carefully so you don't interfere with other skaters.

10. When the session is over and you return your skates, be sure that the laces are tucked into the skates and wipe the blades clean.

TAI BABILONIA TELLS HOW TO FALL DOWN WHILE ICE SKATING WITHOUT HURTING YOURSELF

She should know: She did it a lot while she was practicing to become a world champion figure skater.

1. When you realize you're going to fall, put your arms out behind you so your body doesn't hit the ground first.

2. Don't stiffen your body. Stay loose.

3. Go with the fall—don't fight it.

10 INTERESTING FACTS ABOUT TIGER WOODS'S CHILDHOOD

Tiger Woods is to golf what Michael Jordan is to basketball—a truly gifted superstar. He is the first black golf superstar, and he holds records that may never be equaled or beaten. He has opened the door to golf for thousands of kids by touring the country, giving demonstrations and lessons to young people of all nationalities. Today, over 900,000 kids between the ages of 5 and 11 play golf.

Tiger's dedication to the sport began very early in his life. Here are some facts about Tiger that you may want to know:

1. He was born in 1975 and named Eldrick T. Woods. His father gave him the nickname "Tiger" as a way of honoring a South Vietnamese soldier, Nguyen Phong, who saved his life in the Vietnam War.

2. At the age of 6 months, Tiger saw his father hitting golf balls into a net and began to imitate his swing.

3. At 2 he appeared on TV on *The Mike Douglas Show* and putted against comedian Bob Hope.

4. When he was 3, he shot a 48 over nine holes at the Navy Golf Club in Cypress, California. Many adult players wish they could play as well as that now.

5. At 5 he appeared in *Golf Digest* magazine and on ABC's *That's Incredible*.

6. In 1984, at 8, he won the Optimist International Junior Championship. He went on to win it again when he was 9, 12, 13, 14, and 15.

7. When he was 13, a doctor hypnotized him to help him concentrate and block out distractions on the course.

8. At 15 he became the youngest U.S. Junior Amateur Champion in golf history. He was voted Southern California Amateur Player of the Year for the second consecutive year and was also voted Golf Digest Amateur Player of the Year.

9. The following year he defended his title at the U.S. Junior National Championships and became the first golfer to win this title more than once. He won the same championship the following year.

10. At 18 Tiger won the U.S. Amateur Golf Championship and became the youngest golfer ever to achieve this title, and he was also the first African American to win this tournament.

8 SKATEBOARDING SAFETY TIPS

Although skateboarding is a lot of fun and most injuries, such as scrapes, are minor, skateboarders sometimes do hurt themselves badly. Elbow, head, arm and knee injuries are the most common. Wearing the proper protection and following some basic safety tips may help you prevent a serious injury.

1. Wear proper clothing. Long pants such as blue jeans and long-sleeve shirts are recommended. You should wear rubber-soled athletic shoes. Never wear a shoe with a heel and never skateboard barefoot.

2. Wear protective gear—elbow and knee pads as well as gloves. Helmets are an absolute must!

3. If you are a beginner, start in a flat area that is free of traffic, such as a schoolyard or dead-end street.

4. Learn to fall safely.

5. Never skateboard on a wet or slippery surface.

6. Don't ride your skateboard into an intersection.

7. Don't ride into the street from behind a parked car.

8. Don't show off.

6 WAYS TO MAKE SURE YOUR SKATEBOARD IS SAFE

If you make the mistake of riding on a board that is not safe, you are asking for trouble. Here are some safety measures that you should know.

1. Make sure that your wheels work properly. They should spin freely. Use a bearing spray to remove dust and dirt from your wheels.

2. If your wheels seem too tight, loosen the bearing nut.

3. Before you go riding, place your board on a flat surface and give it a little push. If it doesn't roll in a straight line, something is wrong and the board should not be ridden. Take the board back to the shop and have the problem checked out.

4. Wheel wobble can be extremely dangerous. If your wheels begin to wobble, use your skate key to tighten the truck bolt so that there is pressure between the bolt and the truck plate.

5. To prevent your wheels from wearing down unevenly, you should rotate them every four to six weeks. Rotate from front right to rear left, front left to rear right, rear right to front left, and rear left to front right.

6. If the deck of your board shows any sign of cracking, you should take it back to the shop for repair, especially if the cracks are deep.

9 ROLLERBLADING SAFETY TIPS

Skating in traffic is never recommended. However, if you have to skate in the street to get where you are going, please follow these safety guidelines.

1. Always look up! And always be aware of what is going on around you.

2. Always stay off to the side of the road or on the sidewalk.

3. Never skate against traffic; always go with the flow.

4. Watch for car doors opening and cars pulling out of parking spaces and into the road.

5. Never wear headphones. You need to be able to hear all of the street sounds around you.

6. Never hold on to a moving vehicle to "skitch" a ride.

7. Never zigzag. This will confuse drivers and pedestrians.

8. If you are approaching a parked car, notice the direction of the tires. If they are turned out toward the street, be real cautious. This could mean that the car is about to pull out into the street.

9. Always be courteous to other people using the road.

25 BASIC SOCCER TIPS TO IMPROVE YOUR GAME

Doug Choron, a former high school All-American, has been a soccer coach for the past 25 years. In 2001 he led his team, the Westchester Flames, to a Division 3 PDL (semipro) National Championship. Here are his tips for becoming a better player.

1. Train with dedication and respect the sport.

2. When watching soccer on TV or at a stadium, watch the players without the ball to learn about movement on the field.

3. Always try to play with people better than yourself.

4. Playing 5 on 5 on a small field will sharpen your game.

5. When you play, keep your head and eyes up to see your teammates and the field.

6. Decide what you will do with the ball before it comes to you.

7. When dribbling, touch the ball every step for control.

8. Don't dribble the ball when you can make a constructive pass or cross instead.

9. Play all the different positions.

10. When heading, keep your eyes open, mouth closed, and arms out for balance.

11. When passing, use the inside of your foot.

12. Don't be afraid to shoot and miss the goal.

13. Be the first to show up for practice and the last to leave.

14. A good way to practice by yourself is to kick against a wall.

15. Talk to your teammates on the field. Let them know what is happening in the area they can't see.

16. When throwing in, keep your feet on the ground and release the ball from behind your head.

17. Watch instructional videos.

18. Attend a professional match.

19. Watch the ball at all times and never retreat with your back to the ball.

20. Eat pasta the night before a game.

21. When playing on a hot day, drink a lot of water.

22. Always move toward a pass; never wait for the ball to come to you.

23. Respect the referee's decision.

24. Enjoy the sport all year round and stay in shape.

25. Thank your parents for driving you to all the games and practices so you can enjoy this great sport.

10 THINGS YOU SHOULD KNOW WHEN SELECTING A MARTIAL ARTS SCHOOL

Martial arts schools are not difficult to find, but choosing the right school is important. A good school should not only train you physically but should also teach you courtesy, respect, patience, and how to avoid a fight. These qualities are what martial arts are really all about.

1. Don't choose a school just because it's close to home. Visit a few different ones in your area so you can compare them.

2. Sit in on a class and see if the kids are enjoying themselves. If they aren't getting along, it could be a bad sign. If you aren't allowed to observe a class without paying, don't even think of going there.

3. If there are more than 15 kids for each instructor, you won't get the attention you need. A class of about 10 students is ideal.

4. Instructors should have about 5 years of training. Ask them for details.

5. Talk to kids who train in that school and ask them questions about what it's like.

6. Don't be impressed by a lot of trophies that may be on display. Anyone can go to a hobby shop and buy a trophy.

7. Don't choose a school that tries to pressure you into signing up for a long period.

8. If students are awarded black belts after only 1 or 2 years of training, this is not a serious school. It takes about 5–8 years to earn a black belt.

9. The instructor should talk about nonviolence and respect for others in the class. Ask the other students if he does.

10. Explore the different styles of martial arts that are being taught and choose the one that appeals to you. Martial arts magazines and Web sites can be a good source of information.

4 TIPS FOR THROWING A FRISBEE PROPERLY

Dr. Stancil E. D. Johnson, who has been recognized as one of the world's foremost authorities on the sport, recommends the following guidelines for putting real power into your throwing technique.

1. To throw the Frisbee long distances, take a few short running steps before you throw. The purpose of the run is not to get the Frisbee to fly farther but to put more force into your throwing arm. Try to get your whole body into the throw as you let go. This technique is only used for long-distance throwing.

2. If you're more interested in reaching your target (the other player) accurately, the best way to start is to stand sideways with your throwing arm toward the target and your other hand behind you—or wherever you need it to give your body good balance. Your feet should be spread apart about as wide as your shoulders, and your knees should be bent.

3. A maneuver called "sighting" can help you reach your target with greater accuracy. That is, before you actually throw the Frisbee, swing your arm with the Frisbee in your hand as if you're going to throw it—but don't let go of it. As you do this, try to see if your aim is really as sharp as you want it to be; imagine where the Frisbee would have gone if you had actually let go. Correct your position if you don't think you were right on target. This maneuver will also help you concentrate.

4. When throwing a Frisbee, before you ever let go of it, you need to wrap or curl your wrist around the edge. As you finally do let go, it's important to unwrap—or uncurl—your wrist very smoothly. It's the uncurling, called "wristing," that puts the spin into your throw.

HOW TO CATCH A FRISBEE

Dr. Johnson also tells how to catch a Frisbee properly. Here are some of his pointers.

1. As a Frisbee comes hurling your way, prepare to catch it by standing with your knees bent and your feet about as far apart as your shoulders are wide. Then get up onto the balls of your feet. This position is a good one because you'll be able to move quickly into just the right spot when the Frisbee comes in for its landing.

2. Always look straight ahead when catching so you can see the entire area in front of you. This is important, since you never really know where a Frisbee is going to wind up until it gets there. Looking ahead will keep you prepared for anything.

3. Don't try to catch too soon. Again, Frisbees are unpredictable, and you don't know what one is going to do until it does it. Wait to grab it until just before you can reach it. That way, if it flies to your left but then swings around to your right at the last moment, you won't be reaching to the wrong side.

6 KITING TIPS

1. Most people are under the impression that spring is the best time to fly a kite, but the truth of the matter is that kite-flying is really a four-season proposition. The best days for kite-flying are those when the trees seem to be jiggling against a blue sky dotted with a few clouds to move the breeze along. The best kite-flying weather provides winds traveling 4–18 miles per hour.

2. The best places to fly kites are wide-open spaces, such as beaches, open hillsides, or a stretch of a few acres, like farmland. Empty parking lots and rooftops are also ideal. But be careful.

3. The best kites, whether they cost $100 or $5 or are homemade, are well balanced. They should be weighted evenly from side to side and have a symmetrical shape and frame.

4. The line you use should be strong. It should also be tied to and wound around something, like a stick or even a reel or any kind of winder. Don't just use a ball of string you're likely to get all caught up in knots; fumbling will interfere with the smooth sailing of your kite.

5. The best way to launch a kite is to have a friend act as your assistant (a great job for a little brother or sister who wants to help!). Have your friend hold the kite (while you hold the line) and ask him or her to walk about 100 feet away from you. The wind should be at your back and in the face of your assistant. Your assistant should hold the kite by the center sticks, letting the tail (if there is one) extend to the ground. When the wind seems right, instruct your friend to let go of the kite while you hold the line taut. Now watch it rise!

6. If the wind doesn't seem strong enough to support your kite, there are three things you can do: (1) try a lighter kite; (2) have your assistant launch the kite from a position farther away, such as 200 or even 500 feet from you; (3) go home and accept that some days aren't right for kite-flying.

10 RULES OF KITE SAFETY

1. Don't fly kites in the rain.

2. Pay attention to local rules about kite-flying where you live.

3. Don't fly kites across roads.

4. Don't fly kites near or across power lines. If your kite gets stuck in one of these, do not try to get it down.

5. Never fly kites near live fireworks or sparklers or open bonfires or barbecues.

6. Don't fly kites on crowded beaches.

7. Never use glazed string for your kite or kites that have razor blades in them. (Some do!)

8. Do not fly kites too close to airports or when the visibility is not good.

9. Don't fly kites that have metal in the frame or tail.

10. If you are flying a kite that is more than 5 feet wide, wear gloves.

EVERYTHING YOU NEED TO KNOW ABOUT BICYCLE SAFETY

Bicycles are fun, a great way to get around, and they provide good exercise. But your bicycle is not a toy—it's a vehicle, like a car. For your safety and for the safety of others, be sure you know and practice the following guidelines.

1. Buy the right helmet and ALWAYS WEAR IT! You can grumble about it all you want, but you still have to DO IT! It's already a law in some states and is being considered in many others. Try a helmet on before you buy it to make sure you get a good fit.

2. Buy the right bike. There are three kinds: high-rise bikes, for younger riders (with small wheels and high handlebars); single-speed bikes, with coaster brakes (these are good until you develop strength in your hands); and multispeed lightweight bikes, which are great for high speeds and long distances. Getting the right bike for you will mean that you can manage the ride better and more safely.

3. Size it up. It's important that the bike you choose is the right size for you. In general, a good rule to follow is that when you sit on the seat, you should be able to balance the bicycle with the tips of your toes. You should also be able to reach the pedal in its lowest position with the tips of your toes while sitting in the seat. If you are between 8 and 10 years old, your bicycle should most likely be a 24-inch; if you're 11 or older, try a 26-inch wheeler.

4. Keep your bike in proper working order. That means keeping a constant check to make sure everything is operating the way it should. Before riding, check your brakes, make certain the tires are properly inflated, and test the lights and horn or bell.

5. Give a hand. Hand signals are important. You should know and use these signals just as adults use them when driving cars.

- **Left turn:** Left arm straight out to your side.
- **Right turn:** Left arm raised up in a salute.
- **Slowing or stopping:** Left arm in downward position.

6. Obey all traffic signs and signals.

7. Ride in the same direction as traffic.

8. Pedestrians always have the right-of-way.

9. Never carry passengers on your seat. Bicycles are built for one.

10. Never wear loose or long clothing that can get caught in the wheels as you ride. Don't be long—don't be loose.

11. Beware of parked cars. Be alert when you ride by parked cars in case a door is suddenly opened.

12. Be a smart groupie. When riding with a group of friends, never ride more than two abreast, and make sure to watch the rider in front of you.

13. Handle with care. Always ride with both hands on the handlebars except when signaling.

14. Watch out for slippery surfaces. Damp roads are slippery. Ride slower under these circumstances and brake slowly and earlier than you would normally.

15. Avoid top-overs. You can do this by being especially careful around drain gates, soft road edges, gravel or sand, leaves (especially when wet), potholes, ruts or uneven paving, and any obstacles that might be in your path.

16. Be a night owl. This means keeping your eyes open and acting wisely. Avoid wearing dark clothing (motorists can see bright colors better) or clothing that might cover up your rear light. Also, make sure your reflectors and lights are working, and carry extra batteries just in case.

BOWLING ETIQUETTE

According to the Young American Bowling Alliance, the following rules should be observed whenever you are bowling with or alongside others.

1. Be prepared to take your turn when it comes up.

2. The player to your right always has the right-of-way.

3. If the player on your left picks up the ball from the rack before you do, let her bowl first.

4. Always stay in your approach area. After your ball hits the pins, walk directly back to your approach area.

5. Be on time. Don't make other bowlers wait for you.

6. Don't bother or talk to other players once they have take their position at the approach area.

7. Never go beyond the foul line at any time.

8. Be a good loser and a gracious winner.

YOU'VE COME A LONG WAY, BARBIE!

In 1959 Elliot and Ruth Handler, who founded the Mattel toy company, introduced one of the most successful toys ever—the Barbie doll. By the time Barbie turned 25 in 1984, 200 million Barbie dolls and members of her family had been sold worldwide, and over the years, kids had purchased more than 20 million of her fashions annually. Barbie has lots more competition these days than she did back in 1959, but she's managed to stay among the favorites, mostly due to Mattel's introduction of new developments over the years. For instance, echoing the fashion trends of the '50s, she started out with heavy eyeliner and a long ponytail. Today's Barbie, on the other hand, has long hair and eyeglasses, which she first got in the 1960s. Here are some of the other changes that Mattel initiated to ensure that Barbie kept up with the times.

1961. Barbie was no longer presented as just a glamour doll. She got a job. That year Mattel introduced the stewardess outfit, which led to other occupational clothing kits—a nurse, a doctor, a skin diver, a fashion editor, and even an astronaut in 1965, preceding Sally Ride by nearly 20 years!

1963. Barbie got her first wig.

 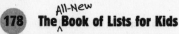

1964. Barbie was able to bend her legs for the first time, made possible by knee joints.

1966. Mattel introduced a special solution that kids could use to color Barbie's hair and clothing.

1967. Barbie learned to bend at the waist.

1971. Barbie got her own mechanical stage, which made the Live Action Barbie dance.

1976. Barbie smiled for the first time, when the Olympic-hopeful Gold Medal Barbie was introduced.

1979. Kissing Barbie came with puckered lips and a button in the back so she could give "real" kisses.

1981. Black Barbie was introduced. She wore an Afro and a bright red African dress. Mattel took this one off the market, since many people complained that the doll didn't represent what black people are really like.

1984. Barbie's "family" had grown to include Ken, Skipper, P.J., Christie, Tracy, Todd, and a host of other friends.

1989. UNICEF Barbie sold in four versions: Oriental, Hispanic, Black, and White.

1990. Ken got his ear pierced: Earring Magic Ken quickly became a collector's item.

1993. Native American Barbie, complete with long black braids and a beaded dress, came and then quickly went. Native Americans accused Mattel of racism, and Mattel responded by removing the doll from stores.

1994. Barbie celebrated her 35th birthday with special Barbie boutiques in toy department stores and with a whole special series of anniversary dolls.

2001. Mattel had to deal with the fact that because of all the new dolls that came out in the 1990s (especially Gina), interest in Barbie declined. So they decided to make some changes, including lowering the price and introducing a whole line of fashion model Barbies. They also decided to only manufacture 35,000 of each of the collectible limited edition Barbies. Before this, they were making 100,000 of each, and because they were so easy to get, people lost interest. But by this year, Barbie was back on her feet, with her own magazines, clubs, chatrooms and books. Barbie lives!

5 TIPS FOR STORING COMIC BOOKS

Most paper has acid in it, and this is what makes paper age: It turns brown and crumples easily. We can't stop the aging process, but we can slow it down. Take care of your comics if you want them to be worth more money later on. Here's how.

1. Place each comic book in its own acid-free plastic bag. (These and the other supplies mentioned here are available from comic book dealers. Check your Yellow Pages.)

2. The comic books, in their bags, should be stored vertically (standing up), not lying on top of one another. They should be stacked in special acid-free boxes.

3. Store the boxes in a cool (40°–50°), dark place with a relative humidity of 50°. Avoid heat, ultraviolet light, and dampness.

4. Keep your collection away from polluted air and dust.

5. Mylar bags should be changed every two or three years.

11 TIPS FOR TRADING CARD COLLECTORS

Collecting trading cards can be a very enjoyable hobby for kids and adults. It's a great way to learn about your favorite sport or hobby and make new friends. It can also be exciting to find out that a card in your collection is worth a lot more than what you paid for it. Here are some tips from the pros.

1. Keep cards away from food and liquids.

2. Don't store cards in places that are very hot or damp.

3. Either store your cards in a notebook with plastic pages or place them in a plastic sleeve or shield and keep them in a storage box. Storage supplies are available at trading card and comic book stores.

4. Never hold cards together with rubber bands. This will damage the cards and reduce their value.

5. Sort cards by manufacturer, year (set), and number, not by team or players.

6. Establish a friendly relationship with your card shop owners. They'll be more willing to help you, and you will learn more about collecting as a result. Never handle cards in the shop without permission.

7. If you buy cards in sets, you will usually spend less money than if you bought the cards one at a time.

8. Have a written list of the cards you're interested in acquiring whenever you are shopping or trading, so you don't wind up getting something you already have.

9. The best cards to collect are cards that have mistakes on them.

10. Always buy, sell, and trade *fair*.

11. Even if you lose interest in collecting, don't throw your cards away. Store them properly. You may become interested in them at a later date—when they'll be even more valuable!

PLAY-DOH HISTORY

Squish it. Squeeze it. Turn it into anything. You've probably been playing with the stuff all your life. But did you know that the Playskool company, which makes Play-Doh, still keeps the top-secret formula under lock and key—or that there was a time when the U.S. government conducted experiments to find out whether Play-Doh could be used for military purposes? (The answer was no!) Here's a history lesson you won't learn in school.

1956. In Cincinnati, scientists experimenting with soap and cleaning solutions discover Play-Doh, a nontoxic modeling compound that's easy to mold. They sell the stuff in one color — off-white — in department stores in 1½-pound cans.

1957. Three new colors are added — red, yellow, and blue. The first TV ads appear, on *Captain Kangaroo* and *Ding Dong School.*

1958. Now you can buy the handy four-pack of Play-Doh — a can for each color.

1959. Play-Doh introduces the first "accessories" to help kids make Play-Doh objects, the Pixie-Pak and the Little Baker's Set. Future accessories include the Play-Doh Forge Press, the Play-Doh Fuzzy Pumper, Shape Makers, the Play-Doh Zoo Set, Funny Frogs, and the Bake 'N Cake Shop, among others. Later, these products will be based on popular TV shows and film characters, such as *Star Wars, The Bionic Woman,* Hanna-Barbera cartoon characters, the Care Bears, Disney's *Duck Tales,* and Beetlejuice.

1960. Play-Doh Boy is born, to be used in advertising.

1963. Mini-cans of the stuff go on sale for the first time.

1964. Play-Doh is introduced in England, France, and Italy.

1972. Play-Doh manufactures its 500 millionth can.

1976. A man in Virginia creates a replica of Monticello with 2,500 bricks made of Play-Doh. His effort is recorded in Play-Doh history as the most ambitious use ever.

1979. Play-Doh is first sold in a 3-pound container.

1980. National Play-Doh Day is celebrated for the first time on September 16.

1983. Four bright colors are added to the original four, so now Play-Doh comes in the Rainbow 8 Pack.

1987. Glow-in-the-dark Play-Doh is sold as part of the Real Ghostbusters Playset.

1991. Play-Doh celebrates its 35th birthday as one of America's most popular toys.

1992. Sparkling Play-Doh, with glitter, is sold for the first time.

2001. It's not just squishy stuff anymore. Now Play-Doh has more than fifteen different sets that come with shape makers and other accessories, including sets that have been authorized by Pokémon, McDonald's, Chuck E Cheese, and Taco Bell. They also add scented Play-Doh and neon colors.

THE 8 HIGHEST SCORING WORDS IN SCRABBLE

All of these are seven-letter words, so you'll get 50 extra points for making them. Do you know what all these words mean? Do you know what *any* of them mean? Can you say "dic-tion-ary"?

1. BEZIQUE	**5.** QUIZZED
2. CAZIQUE	**6.** ZEPHYRS
3. JAZZILY	**7.** ZINCIFY
4. QUARTZY	**8.** ZYTHUMS

THE 10 MOST LANDED-ON SQUARES IN MONOPOLY

The board game Monopoly was designed in 1936. Today it is available in 23 languages, each of which uses the local currency for its play money: In South America you play for *rands* and in Peru you play for *sols*. Monopoly is one of the best-selling games of all time, having sold more than a billion sets. The following are the squares people land on most often when they play the game. Be sure to buy these properties if you have a chance to do so.

1. Illinois Avenue
2. Go
3. B&O Railroad
4. Free Parking
5. Tennessee Avenue
6. New York Avenue
7. Reading Railroad
8. St. James Place
9. Water Works
10. Pennsylvania Railroad

4

Food

19 TABLE MANNERS THAT CAN MAKE YOUR LIFE EASIER

Your first formal meal can be a frightening experience, especially if you're uncomfortable about various rules of etiquette. Here are some things to remember that will help you get through such times.

1. It's OK to eat asparagus with your fingers.

2. When you take a piece of candy from a boxed assortment, you should also take the frilly little cup that the candy comes in. (Also, you should only take one piece at a time.)

3. If you have to remove something from your mouth, like a bone or something you can't swallow, place your napkin up to your mouth and spit it into the napkin as inconspicuously as possible.

4. It's bad manners to sneeze at the table. If you need to do it, excuse yourself and do it someplace else.

5. It's OK to eat parsley and other decorations, but you don't have to.

6. If you hate what's being served, take a small portion anyway and nibble at it if you can. If someone asks why you're not eating the stuff, say it's delicious but that you had a big lunch.

7. If someone asks you to pass the potatoes and you haven't taken any for yourself yet, pass them first and then ask for the bowl so that you can serve yourself.

8. It's never polite to take the last piece of anything.

9. At a formal meal, when someone asks you to pass the salt, it's most polite to pass both the salt and pepper if they're on the table together.

10. When you're eating spaghetti and you're left with all those long strands hanging out of your mouth, it's best to suck them all in rather than bite down, with the ends dropping back onto your plate.

11. When eating fruits with pits, like grapes and cherries, it's OK to remove the pits from your mouth with your fingers.

12. Don't be the first to start eating after the food has been served. Wait until the head of the house has begun. While you're waiting to begin, you can put salt, pepper, and butter on your food.

13. If everyone seems to be doing something that you're not used to doing at the table, follow the house custom and do it anyway. You don't want anyone to feel uncomfortable.

14. If you're uncomfortable with your surroundings and can't think of anything to say, just smile a lot when someone looks at you.

15. If someone puts something on your plate that you'd rather die than eat, just leave it there.

16. It's OK to use a small piece of bread to push tricky foods like peas onto your fork. (Or you can pretend that you are clumsy and don't know about the bread trick in order to avoid eating the peas.)

17. It's always polite and kind to thank your hosts for inviting you.

18. In Japanese restaurants, it's OK to drink the soup out of the little soup bowl. Just try not to make slurping noises when you sip.

19. You can blow loud bubbles into your milkshake if you are younger than 4.

15 FOODS THAT FURTHER FLATULENCE

In other words, they make you fart. Don't eat them before your piano recital. By the way, if you do "let one rip" in the presence of others, the polite thing to do is say "Excuse me" and then go on with what you were doing. If someone else does it, ignore it.

1. apples

2. avocados

3. beans

4. brussels sprouts

5. cabbage

6. corn

7. cucumbers
8. high-fiber cereals
9. lima beans
10. melons
11. peas

12. prune juice
13. radishes
14. raisins
15. turnips

5 PEOPLE WHO HAVE NEVER FARTED

1.
2.
3.
4.
5.

AND YOU THOUGHT BRUSSELS SPROUTS WERE BAD!
23 Delicacies You Might Not Want to Try

While most of us consider hamburgers and French fries a pretty good meal, there are those adventurous souls out there who always seem willing to try something new. The following are gourmet delicacies somewhere in the world, even throughout parts of the U.S. Many of them taste just like chicken—NOT!

1. Iguana flesh
2. Antelope
3. Ground billy goat
4. Locusts
5. Roast bear
6. Ant eggs
7. Butterflies
8. Squirrel

9. Buffalo
10. Caterpillar grubs
11. Goliath beetles
12. Kangaroo
13. Alligator
14. Moose nose
15. Rattlesnake
16. Camel

17. Raccoon pie
18. Moose à la mode
19. Bird's nest soup
20. Dirt (In Nigeria it's seasoned with vinegar and salt.)
21. Grasshoppers
22. Seaweed
23. Thousand-year-old eggs (They're really only about 8 weeks old and are eaten raw. Yum.)

LUNCH COUNTER LINGO

Waiters and waitresses didn't always write your restaurant order down on a pad and pass it back to the kitchen. Starting back in the 1850s, when restaurants were much smaller than they are now, the waiter would simply call your order to the cook. Now, yelling out, "Gimme an order of beef stew," would have been understandable enough, but Americans like to spice up their language, and so a list of code words developed over the years. Beef stew became "Bossy in a bowl" (Bossy is a common name for a cow), a banana split became known as a "houseboat" for its shape, and two poached eggs on toast were referred to as "Adam and Eve on a raft." ("Wreck 'em," called the waitress if those eggs were to be scrambled.) The new lingo—or household Greek, as it was known— must have made the days more interesting for cooks and waiters. Too bad these terms have all but disappeared now.

1. Axle grease: butter
2. Belch water: plain soda water
3. Blast: to heat up
4. A bowl of birdseed: a bowl of cereal
5. Burn the British: a toasted English muffin
6. Burn the pup: a hot dog
7. Campers: people who sit at a table for a long time without ordering anything
8. CB: a cheeseburger
9. CJ: a cream cheese and jelly sandwich

10. A crowd: three of whatever is ordered, as in "a crowd of cowboys," meaning three western omelettes

11. Crumbs: children, because they leave so many

12. Dog biscuits: crackers

13. Eighty: a glass of water

14. Eve with the lid on: apple pie

15. Five: a large glass

16. Fifty-five: a glass of root beer

17. Fifty-one: a cup of hot chocolate

18. Fly cake, or roach cake: a slice of raisin pie

19. Forty-one: lemonade

20. Grass: lettuce ("Keep off the grass" means "without lettuce.")

21. MD—Hold the nail: Dr Pepper, no ice

22. Moo juice: a glass of milk

23. Nervous pudding: Jell-O

24. Paint it red: with ketchup

25. Put out the lights and cry: liver and onions

26. Radio: tunafish salad sandwich on toast

27. Suds: a glass of root beer

28. Warts: olives

8 FOOD FIRSTS

1. In 1912, when the machine that Clarence A. Crane was using to produce a new kind of mint candy malfunctioned and accidentally punched a hole in the center, the first Life Saver was created.

2. George Crum, an Adirondack Indian chief, worked as a chef and was rather proud of his French fries. In 1853, when one of his customers complained that they were too thick, Chief Crum grabbed the nearest potato and, out of spite, carved the thinnest slice he could. He fried it and served it to the customer, who thought it was great. And so potato chips were born.

3. Antoine Feuchtwanger was selling sausages in the U.S. in the 1880s. But they were served so hot that he had to give his customers gloves to wear so they wouldn't be so difficult to hold. This proved highly impractical (and expensive), so Feuchtwanger replaced the gloves with sliced rolls, thus creating the hot dog.

4. In 1902 vendors who were selling ice cream at the St. Louis World's Fair ran out of dishes. Ernest Hamwi, a pastry vendor, saved the day: He came up with a cone-shaped pastry to hold the ice cream. Those were the very first ice cream cones.

5. In 1905 11-year-old Frank Epperson combined soda water with a flavored powder, mixed it up with a wooden stick, and then forgot about it, leaving it outdoors overnight. When he awoke the next morning, he found that he had created the Popsicle!

6. In 1920 Bruce Murrie (whose father was the head of the Hershey Company) and Forrest Mars decided to invent a new kind of chocolate candy for soldiers, so they came up with something that wouldn't get their trigger fingers sticky. They used their own initials to name the new candy; that's how M&M's came to be.

7. In 1931 James Dewar created little log-shaped cakes with cream filling inside. He called them Little Shortcake Fingers, but the name was soon changed to Twinkie Fingers. Today we know them as Twinkies.

8. Pasta is not Italian. It was first made in China over 4,000 years ago.

10 REALLY BIG FOODS
Have It Your Way

1. The biggest frankfurter ever was prepared by the German Butcher's Guild in 1601. It was over a half-mile long.

2. In 1979 students at Smith College made the biggest ice cream sundae ever. It contained 1,800 gallons of ice cream, 150 pounds of fudge, 75 pounds of sprinkles, 90 pounds of walnuts, 12 gallons of cherry halves, and a dozen cans of whipped cream. (Burp!)

3. The world's largest Boston cream pie was baked in honor of Boston's 350th birthday. It weighed an astounding 3,800 pounds.

4. In 1974 the largest Easter egg was made by a group of Australians. It weighed over 600 pounds and measured over 6 feet high.

5. The largest main-course dish was often prepared for Bedouin weddings. Here's how it was made: Cooked eggs were stuffed into fish. The fish were stuffed into cooked chickens. The chickens were stuffed into a roasted sheep, and the sheep was stuffed into a whole camel, and then the whole thing was cooked. Imagine having to do the dishes after that meal.

6. The world's largest chocolate chip cookie weighed 475 pounds and was baked by chef Franz Eichenauer.

7. If you'd been around over 200 years ago, you could have indulged in a slice of the biggest meat pie ever, created by one Sir Henry Gray. His masterpiece was 9 feet in circumference and weighed 200 pounds. Here are the ingredients:

  2 bushels of flour
  6 snipe (a kind of bird)
20 pounds of butter
  2 curlews (a kind of bird)
  4 geese
  2 oxen's tongues
  2 turkeys
  4 partridges (hold the pear trees!)
  2 rabbits
  7 blackbirds
  2 wild ducks
  7 pigeons
  2 woodcock

8. The largest pumpkin ever grown weighed 1,131 pounds, in 1999.

9. The longest sushi roll was made by 600 Japanese chefs in 1997 and was 3,281 feet long.

10. The largest pizza ever made had a diameter of 122 feet and was baked in South Africa in 1990.

7 VEGGIES YOU DON'T HAVE TO HATE ANYMORE

These are really fruits.

1. Cucumbers

2. Eggplant

3. Gherkins

4. Okra

5. Pumpkins

6. Squash

7. Tomatoes

10 TIPS FOR BAKING THE BEST CHOCOLATE CHIP COOKIES EVER

Americans bake over 7 billion chocolate chip cookies each year. You can use these tips with any recipe.

1. Don't use an old cookie sheet. Old, dented cookie sheets will give you badly shaped cookies, plus they absorb heat faster, which leads to the bottom of the cookies getting burned.

2. Use a rubber spatula rather than a plastic one. The rubber kind bends to conform with the curved sides of the bowl, so you can mix all the good stuff into the batter.

3. Use an oven thermometer to measure the heat in your oven. Chocolate chip cookies are very sensitive to high temperatures, and your cookies will benefit from a true oven reading. (The recipe you use will give you the correct temperature.)

4. Transfer your cookies to a cooling rack so they can cool once they're baked. Cookies need evenly circulated air once they're out of the oven, and a cooling rack is your best bet.

5. Use chocolate chips that aren't too sweet. Bittersweet chocolate is best, because the flavor contrasts with the sweetness of the sugar.

6. Cover your cookie sheet with aluminum foil before you use it. That way your cookies won't spread out too much while they bake, and you'll get nice thick ones.

7. If you decide to cut your own chocolate chips from a chocolate bar rather than use the morsels that come in packages, don't cut the pieces too thin or you'll get brittle, hard little chips instead of big, chewy, soft ones.

8. If your recipe calls for vanilla, use real extract of vanilla, not imitation vanilla.

9. You can substitute honey for sugar in your recipe. Use three-quarters as much honey as you would sugar.

10. After you've mixed the batter, leave it in the refrigerator for about 12 hours before you bake it.

36 THINGS YOU CAN ADD TO CHOCOLATE CHIP COOKIES

Once you're happy with a basic chocolate chip cookie recipe, it's time to get creative. Consider adding any of the following (in whatever quantity your palate fancies) to your batter. Use your imagination to come up with even more ideas.

1. Allspice
2. Almond extract
3. Candied ginger
4. Chopped dates
5. Chopped prunes
6. Chopped, candied orange peel
7. Cinnamon
8. Coconut
9. Cream cheese

All-New

10. Crumbled graham crackers
11. Crushed peppermint sticks
12. Crushed Wheaties
13. Granola
14. Grated orange rind
15. Honey
16. Instant coffee
17. Lemon juice
18. Lemon rind
19. M&M's
20. Mashed banana
21. Mashed potato chips
22. Molasses
23. Nutmeg
24. Nuts (any kind)
25. Oatmeal
26. Orange juice
27. Peanut butter
28. Raisins
29. Reese's Pieces
30. Rice Krispies
31. Shredded coconut
32. Sliced Maraschino cherries
33. Sour cream
34. Sunflower seeds
35. Wheat germ
36. White chocolate chips

THE FREQUENCY OF COLORS IN A 14-OUNCE BAG OF M&M'S

1. Orange (46)
2. Blue (53)
3. Green (55)
4. Yellow (81)
5. Red (91)
6. Brown (134)

THE 9 BEST-SELLING CHOCOLATE CANDIES

1. M&M's
2. Hershey candy bars
3. Reese's Peanut Butter Cups
4. Snickers
5. Kit Kat
6. Russell Stover candies
7. Hershey's Kisses
8. Butterfingers
9. Milky Way

THE 9 BEST-SELLING NONCHOCOLATE CANDIES

1. Life Savers
2. Starburst
3. Twizzlers
4. Brach's candies
5. Mentos
6. Skittles
7. Jolly Ranchers
8. Tootsie Pops
9. Werther's candies

14 WEIRD POPCORN FLAVORS

All of these actually exist.

1. Apple
2. Cinnamon
3. Pistachio
4. Banana
5. Fudge
6. Raspberry
7. Butterscotch
8. Honey
9. Vanilla
10. Caramel
11. Peach
12. Watermelon
13. Chocolate
14. Piña Colada

CANDY IS DANDY

It will spoil your appetite, give you an upset stomach, cause pimples to sprout all over your face, and decay your teeth faster than you can say "cavity." Nevertheless, American kids eat an average of 4 pounds of the stuff a week. Here are some of their favorites and the year in which the candies were first sold.

1. Almond Joy (1947)
2. Baby Ruth (1921)
3. Butterfinger (1923)
4. Cracker Jack (1896)
5. Hershey Bar (1894)
6. Hershey's Kisses (1907)
7. M&M's (1920)
8. Milky Way (1923)
9. Mounds (1921)
10. Reese's Pieces (1978)
11. Snickers (1930)
12. 3 Musketeers (1932)
13. Tootsie Roll (1896)

12 INTERESTING FACTS ABOUT CANDY

1. Kids spend more of their own money on candy than anything else.

2. The first people to eat a sweet treat (candy) were cavemen, who ate honey from beehives.

3. The average American eats an average of 26 pounds of candy each year, split almost equally between candy and chocolate.

4. Chocolate is America's favorite flavor. A Gallup survey revealed that 48% of U.S. adults said they preferred chocolate, compared to 15% who preferred berry-flavored candy.

5. Candy is made simply by dissolving sugar in water. The hardness of the candy depends on the amount of heat that is used. If hot temperatures are used, you get hard candy. The cooler the temperature, the softer the candy you can produce.

6. People in Denmark eat more candy per person than people in any other country, and people in Switzerland eat more chocolate than people in any other country.

7. Some 65% of American candy brands have been around for more than 50 years.

8. Chocolate is made from a bean called the cacao bean,

which was worshipped as an idol by the Mayan Indians in Mexico more than 2,000 years ago.

9. The Aztec emperor of Mexico, Montezuma, loved chocolate so much that he drank as much as 50 glasses of chocolate every day.

10. The chewing of gum began 100 years ago when the famous Mexican general Antonio de Santa Anna was exiled to New York after the Mexican revolution. He brought "chicle" (as in Chicklet) with him. Chicle is a gum extracted from sapodilla, a tree that grows in the Yucatán desert.

11. Milk chocolate was invented by Henry Nestlé, a maker of evaporated milk, and Daniel Peter, a chocolate maker. Today, milk chocolate is preferred by 80% of the world's population.

12. It was during World War I that the candy bar became popular. American chocolate manufacturers began sending small blocks of chocolate to soldiers overseas. When these soldiers returned home after the war they wanted to be able to continue eating chocolate bars, and that is how the candy bar manufacturing business started.

THERE'S NO SUCH THING AS A FREE LUNCH
12 Very Expensive Lunchboxes

Old lunchboxes, which some people collect, have sold for very high prices. Here are some examples of really expensive lunchboxes.

1. Gene Autry (1954), $425
2. The Beatles (1966), $400
3. Benny & Cecil (1963), $150
4. Boston Bruins (1973), $525
5. Bullwinkle (1962), $800
6. Bullwinkle (1963), $200

7. Green Hornet (1967), $360
8. Howdy Doody (1954), $450
9. Jetsons dome-shaped box (1963), $1,500
10. Lost in Space (1978–79), $145
11. Mickey Mouse (1935), $1,000
12. Star Trek (1968–69), $250

14 NAMES FOR SUGAR

If you're reading food labels to avoid sugar, you should know that all of the following *are* forms of sugar.

1. Barley malt syrup
2. Brown sugar
3. Corn syrup
4. Dextrose
5. Fructose
6. Honey
7. Lactose
8. Maltose
9. Maple syrup
10. Molasses
11. Raisin syrup
12. Raw sugar
13. Sorghum
14. Turbinado sugar

12 FOODS YOU SHOULD EAT BEFORE A TEST

These foods won't make you smarter than you are, but studies show that they can help you keep alert by fighting the effects of carbohydrates (candy, bread, sugar), which tend to make you more calm or sleepy.

1. Apples
2. Broccoli
3. Fish (especially oysters)
4. Grapes
5. Lean beef
6. Low-fat yogurt
7. Nuts
8. Peaches
9. Peanuts
10. Pears
11. Skim milk
12. Turkey breast

THE 15 TOP ICE CREAM FLAVORS IN THE U.S.

These are according to the International Ice Cream Association.

1. Vanilla
2. Chocolate
3. Butter pecan
4. Strawberry
5. Neapolitan
6. Chocolate chip
7. French vanilla
8. Cookies and cream
9. Vanilla fudge ripple
10. Praline pecan
11. Cherry
12. Chocolate almond
13. Coffee
14. Rocky road
15. Chocolate marshmallow

18 ICE CREAM FLAVORS YOU'VE PROBABLY NEVER HEARD OF

1. American Beauty — containing the petals of real roses!
2. Arab Lunch — the only ice cream we've heard of that includes cheese, in addition to dates and honey
3. Azuki Bean — made from a Japanese sweet bean that is used mostly for dessert toppings
4. Easter Egg — coconut cream, toasted pecans, and caramel
5. Girl Scout Cookie — not made from *real* Girl Scouts!
6. Hard Hat — whiskey and crème de menthe
7. Have a Date, Honey — honey and dates
8. I Yam What I Yam — sweet potatoes
9. Jungle Princess — pineapple, mango, and coconut
10. Nesselrode — containing nine different flavors, including rum, brandy, lemon, and pineapple
11. Pickle — no kidding!
12. Sabra — Based on a chocolate and orange Israeli liqueur

All-New

13. Soursop—a tangy ice cream that gets its flavor from a tropical fruit known as the custard-apple

14. Star Wars—vanilla ice cream with swirls of multicolored marshmallows

15. Strawcot—strawberry and apricot

16. Turtle—tastes better than it sounds, with vanilla ice cream, toasted pecans, and caramel; a whole sundae inside an ice cream cone

17. Veggie—spinach, carrots, tomatoes, and twelve other vegetables (Yechhh.)

18. Wedding Bells—strawberry and champagne

BEN & JERRY'S 10 MOST POPULAR FLAVORS IN THE U.S.

Its top-selling flavors in Japan are Caramel Caramel, Strawberry Garden, and Chunky Monkey.

1. Chocolate Chip Cookie Dough Ice Cream
2. Cherry Garcia Ice Cream
3. Phish Food Ice Cream
4. New York Super Fudge Chunk Ice Cream
5. Chocolate Fudge Brownie Ice Cream
6. Cherry Garcia Low Fat Frozen Yogurt
7. Dilbert's World Totally Nuts Ice Cream
8. Chunky Monkey Ice Cream
9. Chocolate Fudge Brownie Frozen Yogurt
10. Peanut Butter Cup Ice Cream

BEN & JERRY'S FLAVOR GRAVEYARD

Ben & Jerry's no longer sells the following flavors, but the company claims, "These flavors are not dead—some are very much alive, in a limited sort of way, while others float aimlessly in a 'flavor limbo-land.'" That doesn't really help if you have a craving for Rainforest Crunch or Phish Food, neither of which is available. These aren't all the discontinued flavors—just some of our favorites. For more ice cream fun, visit www.benjerry.com.

1. Apple Pie
2. Aztec Harvest Coffee
3. Black Russian
4. Candybar
5. Canteloupe
6. Capecodder
7. Cool Britannia
8. Chubby Hubby
9. Dastardly Mash
10 Egg Nog
11. Holey Cannoli
12. Maniacal
13. Monkey Wrench
14. Mystic Mint
15. Peanutbutter and Jelly
16. Smathies
17. Srape
18. Tiggersblood
19. Wavy Gravy
20. White Russian
21. Wild Maine Blueberry

THE 14 TOP-SELLING HÄAGEN-DAZS FLAVORS

1. Vanilla
2. Chocolate
3. Coffee
4. Butter Pecan
5. Strawberry
6. Dulce De Leche Caramel
7. Vanilla Swiss Almond
8. Rum Raisin
9. Chocolate Chocolate Chip
10. Pineapple Coconut
11. Cherry Vanilla
12. Vanilla Fudge
13. Mango
14. Creme Caramel Pecan

6 PIZZA FACTS

1. Pizza is the most popular of all fast foods.
2. Americans eat 90 acres of pizza every day.
3. The average person eats 60 slices of pizza every year.

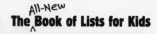

4. The most popular toppings are pepperoni, mushrooms, extra cheese, sausage, green pepper, and onion, in that order.

5. The least favorite topping is anchovies.

6. There is a magazine called *Pizza Today.*

THE 10 MOST POPULAR FAST FOODS

You know that they are not exactly the healthiest foods you could be eating, but they sure taste great. So great that nearly $8 billion a year is spent on junk food. Here is a list of your favorites, starting with the most popular.

1. Pizza
2. Chicken nuggets
3. Hot dogs
4. Cheeseburgers
5. Macaroni and cheese
6. Hamburgers
7. Spaghetti and meatballs
8. Fried chicken
9. Tacos
10. Grilled cheese sandwiches

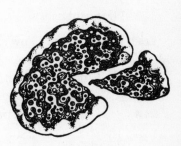

HOW TO EAT HEALTHY AT 5 FAST-FOOD RESTAURANTS

There's bad news here, there's good news, and we even have something in between.

McDonald's

Bad	Quarter Pounder with Cheese	530 calories
Better	Chicken McGrill (no mayo)	340 calories
Best	Grilled Chicken Salad Deluxe (reduced calorie dressing)	230 calories

Burger King

Bad	Double Whopper Cheese Sandwich	920 calories
Better	BK Broiler Chicken Sandwich (no mayo)	390 calories
Best	Chicken Tenders	170 calories

KFC

Bad	Honey Barbeque Wings	607 calories
Better	Honey BBQ Flavored Chicken Sandwich (with sauce)	310 calories
Best	Tender Roast Chicken Sandwich (no sauce)	270 calories

Pizza Hut

Really Bad	Pepperoni Lover's Stuffed Crust Pizza, 2 slices	1,150 calories
Better	Chicken Supreme Thin 'n' Crispy Pizza, 2 slices	400 calories
Best	Ham Thin 'n' Crispy Pizza, 2 slices	340 calories

Wendy's

Bad	Big Bacon Classic	580 calories
Better	Junior Cheeseburger	320 calories
Best	Junior Hamburger	280 calories

BAD NEWS ABOUT MOVIE SNACKS

The next time you go to the movies and order a snack at the candy counter, be real careful. What you get may be a lot more than what you wanted.

1. Buttered Popcorn (medium) = 3 meals consisting of scrambled eggs, bacon and home fries, Spam on rye, and for dinner, a 6-ounce steak, baked potato with cheesecake. (1,538 calories total)

2. Unbuttered Popcorn = 1 double cheeseburger, with (medium) large fries and a chocolate shake. (1,240 calories)

3. Goobers (3.5 ounces) = 3 cheese enchiladas, an order of refried beans and nachos with an onion dip. (810 calories)

4. Milk Duds (5-ounce box) = 1 frozen 12-inch pizza with pepperoni. (360 calories)

5. Peanut M&M's = 4 slices of white bread, each with a pat of butter. (424 calories)

6. Raisinets (3.5-ounce box) = A plate of spaghetti with white clam sauce and 2 brownies for dessert. (570 calories)

7. Junior Mints (5.5-ounce box) = 2 hot dogs on rolls with mustard. (560 calories)

8. Twizzlers (5-ounce pack) = 12 regular rice cakes.

CANDY IS NOT SO DANDY AFTER ALL
The Calorie & Fat Content of
11 Candy Bars

	Calories	Fat Grams
1. Almond Joy (1.76 oz)	250	14
2. Good & Plenty (1.8 oz)	191	0
3. Hershey's Milk Chocolate (1.55 oz)	240	14
4. Junior Mints (1.6 oz)	192	5
5. Kit Kat (1.5 oz)	230	12
6. Life Savers (.9 oz)	88	0
7. Mr. Goodbar (1.65 oz)	240	15
8. M&M's peanut (1.74 oz)	250	13
9. Sugar Daddy (2 oz)	218	1
10. Tootsie Roll (2.25 oz)	252	6
11. York Peppermint Pattie (1.5 oz)	180	4

5 JELL-O FLAVOR FLOPS, FLUKES, AND FAILURES

Those marketing whizzes at General Foods aren't perfect. In past years, they've produced some unusual flavors and discovered—duh—that no one *really* wanted to eat quivering blobs of iridescent goo that tasted like:

1. Apple
2. Celery
3. Cola
4. Mixed vegetable
5. Salad

5

Books, Magazines, the Comics, and Cyberfun

JACQUELINE KENNEDY ONASSIS'S ADVICE TO YOUNG READERS

Jacqueline Kennedy Onassis, who was married to President John F. Kennedy, was one of the most beloved women of our time. As First Lady, she challenged ideas about what her role should be, and she worked throughout her career for many great causes, including children and reading. She even worked for a time as an editor at a publishing company before retiring. Here is her advice to young readers, which was sent to us by the Commission on Literature of the National Teachers of English before she passed away in 1994.

1. "Read for escape, read for adventure, read for romance, but read the great writers." She added that the great writers will always be easier to read and more enjoyable than any others, for it is these writers who can stir your imagination best and open your world to the new experiences that books hold in store. The best of these writers will also help you develop your own language skills.

2. Read the works of Edgar Allan Poe, Jack London, Jules Verne, and Ernest Hemingway.

3. Poetry is important, too. "Rhythm is what should first seize you when you read poetry." Onassis recommends "The Congo," by Vachel Lindsay; "Tarantella," by Alfred Noyes; "The Fog," by Carl Sandburg; and the poetry of Countee Cullen, E. E. Cummings, Emily Dickinson, and Siegfried Sassoon.

4. "If you read, you may want to write," suggests Onassis, pointing out that the great painters learned to paint by copying others. You, too, may want to try to express your feelings by writing about them, and you can learn to do that well by choosing a writer you like and then copying his or her work for practice.

5. Onassis's letter closed with these sentiments: "Once you can express yourself, you can tell the world what you want from it or how you would like to change it. All the changes in the world, for good or evil, were first brought about by words."

WINNERS OF THE NEWBERY MEDAL, 1941–2002

Each year, the Association for Library Services to Children, a division of the American Library Association, awards the Newbery Medal for the most distinguished contribution to American literature for children. Here are the books that have won since 1941, their authors, and the publishers. If you have any questions about the awards or about children's books in general, write to the American Library Association, 50 East Huron Street, Chicago, IL 60611, or visit them at www.ala.org.

1941. *Call It Courage,* by Armstrong Sperry
1942. *The Matchlock Gun,* by Walter Edmonds
1943. *Adam of the Road,* by Elizabeth Gray
1944. *Johnny Tremain,* by Esther Forbes
1945. *Rabbit Hill,* by Robert Lawson
1946. *Strawberry Girl,* by Lois Lenski
1947. *Miss Hickory,* by Carolyn Baily
1948. *The Twenty-One Balloons,* by William Pène du Bois
1949. *King of the Wind,* by Marguerite Henry
1950. *The Door in the Wall,* by Marguerite di Angeli
1951. *Amos Fortune, Free Man,* by Elizabeth Yates
1952. *Ginger Pye,* by Eleanor Estes
1953. *Secret of the Andes,* by Ann Nolan Clark
1954. *. . . And Now Miguel,* by Joseph Krumgold
1955. *The Wheel on the School,* by Meidert DeJong
1956. *Carry On, Mr. Bowditch,* by Jean Lee Latham
1957. *Miracles on Maple Hill,* by Virginia Sorenson

1958. *Rifles for Watie,* by Harold Keith

1959. *The Witch of Blackbird Pond,* by Elizabeth George Speare

1960. *Onion John,* by Joseph Krumgold

1961. *Island of the Blue Dolphins,* by Scott O'Dell

1962. *The Bronze Bow,* by Elizabeth George Speare

1963. *A Wrinkle in Time,* by Madeleine L'Engle

1964. *It's Like This, Cat,* by Emily Neville

1965. *Shadow of a Bull,* by Maia Wojciechowska

1966. *I, Juan de Pareja,* by Elizabeth Borton de Trevino

1967. *Up a Road Slowly,* by Irene Hunt

1968. *From the Mixed-Up Files of Mrs. Basil E. Frankweiler,* by E. L. Konigsburg

1969. *The High King,* by Lloyd Alexander

1970. *Sounder,* by William H. Alexander

1971. *Summer of the Swans,* by Betsy Byars

1972. *Mrs. Frisby and the Rats of NIMH,* by Robert C. O'Brien

1973. *Julie of the Wolves,* by Jean Craighead George

1974. *The Slave Dancer,* by Paula Fox

1975. *M. C. Higgins, the Great,* by Virginia Hamilton

1976. *The Grey King,* by Susan Cooper

1977. *Roll of Thunder, Hear My Cry,* by Mildred D. Taylor

1978. *Bridge to Teribithia,* by Katherine Paterson

1979. *The Westing Game,* by Ellen Raskin

1980. *A Gathering of Days,* by Joan W. Blos

1981. *Jacob Have I Loved,* by Katherine Paterson

1982. *A Visit to William Blake's Inn,* by Nancy Willard

1983. *Dicey's Song,* by Cynthia Voight

1984. *Dear Mr. Henshaw,* by Beverly Cleary

1985. *The Hero and the Crown,* by Robin McKinley

1986. *Sarah, Plain and Tall,* by Patricia MacLachlan

1987. *Whipping Boy,* by Sid Fleischman

1988. *Lincoln,* by Russell Freedman

1989. *Joyful Noise,* by Paul Fleischman
1990. *Number the Stars,* by Lois Lowry
1991. *Maniac Magee,* by Jerry Spinelli
1992. *Shiloh,* by Phyllis Reynolds Naylor
1993. *Missing May,* by Cynthia Rylant
1994. *The Giver,* by Lois Lowry
1995. *Walk Two Moons,* by Sharon Creech
1996. *The Midwife's Apprentice,* by Karen Cushman
1997. *The View from Saturday,* by E. L. Konigsburg
1998. *Out of the Dust,* by Karen Hesse
1999. *Holes,* by Louis Sachar
2000. *Bud, Not Buddy,* by Christopher Paul Curtis
2001. *A Year Down Yonder,* by Richard Peck
2002. *A Single Shard,* by Linda Sue Park

WINNERS OF THE CORETTA SCOTT KING AWARD

Each year the Coretta Scott King Award honors books written or illustrated by African Americans which add to our understanding of African-American culture. The award honors Mrs. King for all the work she has done to continue the job that her husband, Martin Luther King, Jr., started. For more information write to the American Library Association, 50 East Huron Street, Chicago, IL 60611; online, visit www .ala.org/csking.

1978. *Africa Dream,* by Eloise Greenfield
1979. *Escape to Freedom,* by Ossie Davis
1980. *Young Landlords,* by Walter Dean Myers
1981. *Beat the Story-Drum Pum-Pum,* by Ashley Bryan
1982. *Let the Circle Be Unbroken,* by Mildred Taylor
1983. *Sweet Whispers, Brother Rush,* by Virginia Hamilton

1984. *Everett Anderson's Goodbye,* by Lucille Clifton

1985. *Motown and Didi,* by Walter Dean Myers

1986. *People Could Fly: American Black Folktales,* by Virginia Hamilton

1987. *Half a Moon and One Whole Star,* by Crescent Dragonwagon

1988. *Mufaro's Beautiful Daughters,* by John Steptoe

1989. *Fallen Angels,* by Walter Dean Myers

1990. *A Long Hard Journey: The Story of the Pullman Porter,* by Patricia C. and Frederick L. McKissack.

1991. *Road to Memphis,* by Mildred Taylor

1992. *Now Is Your Time!* by Walter Dean Myers

1992. *Tar Beach,* by Faith Ringgold

1994. *Soul Looks Back in Wonder,* by Tom Feelings

1994. *Toning, the Sweep,* by Angela Johnson

1995. *Christmas in Big House, Christmas in the Quarters,* by Patricia and Frederic McKissack

1995. *Creation,* by James W. Johnson

1997. *Minty: A Story of Young Harriet Tubman,* by Alan Schroeder

1997. *Slam,* by Walter Dean Myers

1998. *Forged by Fire,* by Sharon Mills Draper

1999. *Heave,* by Angela Johnson

2000. *Bud, Not Buddy,* by Christopher Paul Curtis

2001. *Miracle's Boys,* by Jacqueline Woodson

WINNERS OF THE PURA BELPRE AWARD

This is a fairly new award honoring books that best portray Latino life. You can find out more by writing to the American Library Association, 50 East Huron Street, Chicago, IL 60611, or visit online at www.ala.org/alsc/Belpre.

1996. *An Island Like You: Stories of the Barrio,* by Judith Ortiz Cofer

1996. *The Bossy Gallito: A Traditional Cuban Folktale,* by Lucia González

1996. *Baseball in April, and Other Stories,* by Gary Soto

1998. *Parrot in the Oven: mi vida,* by Victor Martinez

1998. *Laughing Tomatoes and Other Spring Poems,* by Francisco X. Alarcón

1998. *Spirits of the High Mesa,* by Floyd Martinez

2000. Under the Royal Palms: A Childhood in Cuba, by Alma Flor Ada

2000. *From the Bellybutton of the Moon and Other Summer Poems,* by Francisco X. Alarcón

2000. *Laughing Out Loud, I Fly: Poems in English and Spanish,* by Juan Felipe Herrera

13 WRITERS LIST THEIR FAVORITE BOOKS

1. **Avi**
   The Cat in the Hat, by Dr. Seuss

2. **Natalie Babbitt**
   Make Way for Ducklings, by Robert McCloskey

3. **Betsy Byars**
   The Adventures of Mabel
   Uncle Wiggily Stories
   Desert Sand

4. **Susan Cooper**
   Tom's Midnight Garden, by Philippa Pearce

5. **Bill Cosby**
   The Bible
   The Adventures of Huckleberry Finn, by Mark Twain
   Aesop's *Fables*

6. **Paula Danziger**
   The Catcher in the Rye, by J. D. Salinger
   Pride and Prejudice, by Jane Austen
   A Separate Peace, by John Knowles

7. **Louis L'Amour**
   Treasure Island, by Robert Louis Stevenson
   Kim, by Rudyard Kipling
   The Count of Monte Cristo, by Alexandre Dumas

8. **Lois Lowry**
   The Secret Garden, by Frances Hodgson Burnett

9. **Gregory Maguire**
   The Green Book, by Jill Paton Walsh

10. **J. K. Rowling**
    The Little White Horse, by Elizabeth Goudge
    Manxmouse, by Paul Gallico
    The Narnia series, by C. S. Lewis

11. **Maurice Sendak**
    "The Story of Chicken Little"
    A Child's Garden of Verses, by Robert Louis Stevenson
    Toby Tyler, by James Otis
    Pinocchio in Africa
    The Prince and the Pauper, by Mark Twain

12. **R. L. Stine**
    The Cat in the Hat, by Dr. Seuss
    The Bunnicula books, by James Howe
    Something Wicked This Way Comes, by Ray Bradbury
    Many Moons, by James Thurber
    Earthsea Trilogy, by Ursula K. Le Guin

13. **Jane Yolen**
    The Once and Future King, by T. H. White

11 BOOKS THAT HELP KIDS DEAL WITH REALLY TOUGH ISSUES

The world is changing, and it's sometimes a scary place. We're confused by what we see on the news, and we experience feelings we didn't know we had, like anger and fear. It's often hard to understand why we are having these feelings or what to do about them. Talk to your parents and teachers about this stuff. If no one will listen, talk louder! At the same time, you might also want to check out some books that can help.

Free Spirit is an unusual publishing company. It is one of the only companies that publish books on important personal subjects for young readers; in other words, it takes kids seriously. You won't find all of its books in bookstores, though, so you might want to visit its Web site (www.freespirit.com) to find out more about the hundreds of books they have available. Or write to them at Free Spirit Publishing, 217 Fifth Avenue North, Suite 200, Minneapolis, MN 55401.

1. *Perfectionism: What's Bad About Being Too Good?* by Miriam Adderholdt and Jan Goldberg. Are you trying *too* hard to do everything right? Do you like the idea of being an overachiever? If so, this book will show you how to manage your goals in a more realistic way.

2. *When Nothing Matters Anymore: A Survival Guide for Depressed Teens,* by Bev Cobain. Bev Cobain is the cousin of Kurt Cobain, the famous rock star who committed suicide in 1994. In this book, she describes the causes and symptoms of depression, which is very common among teens, and tells where to go for help.

3. *The Struggle to Be Strong: True Stories by Teens About Overcoming Tough Times,* by Al Desetta. Read about how insight, independence, creativity, and humor helped teens overcome life's biggest obstacles.

4. *When a Friend Dies: A Book for Teens About Grieving and*

Healing, by Marilyn Gootman. The death of a friend is awful for anyone at any age, but it's especially painful for kids. This book answers questions like "How should I act?" and "What should I do if I can't handle this on my own?"

5. *Stick Up for Yourself! Every Kid's Guide to Personal Power and Positive Self-Esteem,* by Gershen Kaufman, Lev Raphael, and Pamela Espeland. This book teaches you about the importance of self-esteem and the dangers of having too much of it.

6. *The First Honest Book About Lies,* by Jonni Kincher. Lying can become a dangerous habit. This book teaches us why it's a bad idea and how to develop a personal value system based on honesty.

7. *What Do You Stand For? A Kid's Guide to Building Character,* by Barbara A. Lewis. As we become a more multicultural society, honesty, kindness, empathy, integrity, and tolerance become more important than ever. This book talks about those traits and suggests activities that point the way toward good character development.

8. *The Power to Prevent Suicide,* by Richard E. Nelson and Judith Galas. Almost half of all kids have thought about suicide at one time or another. Here's an action-oriented guide that tells you what to do if you're having thoughts on the subject and what to do if your friend is thinking about it.

9. *Bullies Are a Pain in the Brain,* by Trevor Romain. Why bullies do what they do and what you can do to become "bullyproof."

10. *Cliques, Phonies, and Other Baloney,* by Trevor Romain. If you've ever felt bad because you were excluded from a group, you know how hurtful cliques can be. This book teaches you how to make friends with the *right* people.

11. *Stress Can Really Get on Your Nerves,* by Trevor Romain and Elizabeth Verdick. If there's a lot going on in your world, you can feel stressed out by it. This book talks about managing stress and about the fact that sometimes your stomachaches and other pains are really symptoms of stress.

12 KIDS WHO WROTE BOOKS THAT GOT PUBLISHED

1. In 1641 Francis Hawkins wrote a book of manners for children called *Youth Behavior*. He was 8 years old at the time.

2. Katharine Hull, 15, and Pamela Whitlock, 16, wrote their novel, *The Far-Distant Oxus,* which was published one year later, in 1937, and was said to be a classic by critics in both Europe and the U.S.

3. Anne Frank's diary describes her family's life in hiding from the Nazis during World War II because they were Jewish. It was published in English in 1952 as *The Diary of a Young Girl.* Her family lived in the attic of a warehouse in Amsterdam, Holland, for two years. They were then discovered by the Nazis and taken to a concentration camp. Anne died there, but her father survived. The diary, which she wrote between the ages of 13 and 15, was later translated into 50 languages.

4. Dorothy Straight was only 4 years old when she wrote *How the World Began.* Her book was published in 1964.

5. S. E. (Susan Eloise) Hinton started writing her first draft of *The Outsiders* at the age of 15. It was about youth gangs and their confrontations and was published in 1967, when she was 17. It has sold more than a million copies and was eventually made into a movie.

6. A West Indian girl named Manghanita Kempadoo wrote *Letters of Thanks* when she was 12 years old. The book is a series of thank-you notes that make fun of the gifts in the carol "The Twelve Days of Christmas."

7. In 1975, actress Ally Sheedy wrote a book at the age of 12 called *She Was Nice to Mice.* It was the story of Esther Esther, an amazing mouse, and became a best-seller. (It must have helped that her mother, Charlotte, was a very successful literary agent.)

8. Jamie DeWitt was 12 years old when he entered his true adventure story "Jamie's Turn" in the 1984 Raintree Publish-a-Book Contest. What was truly amazing about this is that at the time Jamie had a learning disability, which made it difficult for him to write down what he was thinking.

9. Jason Gaes, stricken with Burkitt's lymphoma, a rare form of cancer, decided to write *My Book for Kids with Cansur.* His twin brother, Tim, and 10-year-old brother, Adam, illustrated the book, which was published in 1987. It offers inspiration to people of all ages.

10. Gordon Korman was a seventh-grader when he wrote his first book, *This Can't Be Happening at MacDonald Hall,* in 1980. He continued writing, and by the time he graduated from high school, he had published five more books, including *Go Jump in the Pool* and *Beware the Fish.*

11. Amelia Atwater-Rhodes became the "teen queen of horror fiction" when, at 14, she wrote her first novel, *In the Forests of the Night,* in 2000. She wrote her second book, *Demon in My View,* at 16 and is now often compared to master writers Anne Rice and Stephen King.

12. Sahara Sunday Spain published a book of poetry called *If There Would Be No Light: Poems from My Heart,* in 2001, when she was only 9 years old. Reviewers found it hard to believe that such a young girl could produce such mature poetry. How does she do it? "I don't know where it comes from," she says, "but it feels like I swallow the words down from the sky and they come up again as poems."

40 BOOKS THAT HAVE BEEN BANNED OR CHALLENGED IN PUBLIC SCHOOLS

It's hard to believe that some of the most popular books in the world have been banned or challenged in schools where some people think it's OK to tell you what you can and can't read. Only your parents have the right to guide your reading interests. To make matters worse, the reasons the censors sometimes give for what they do are ridiculous and often more frightening than the stuff they're trying to censor. For instance, Judy Blume's best-selling book *Are You There, God, It's Me, Margaret* was accused of being sexually offensive and amoral. *The Adventures of Sherlock Holmes*, by Sir Arthur Conan Doyle, was banned for having references to the occult. And *The Diary of Anne Frank*, one of the most important accounts we have of what it was like to be Jewish in Holland during World War II, was called "a real downer."

We recommend that you read these books and talk to your parents about your opinions and about censorship.

1. *I Know Why the Caged Bird Sings*, by Maya Angelou
2. *On My Honor*, by Marion Dane Bauer
3. *The Figure in the Shadows*, by John Bellairs
4. *Blubber*, by Judy Blume
5. *Then Again, Maybe I Won't*, by Judy Blume
6. *Curses, Hexes, and Spells*, by Daniel Cohen
7. *My Brother Sam Is Dead*, by James Lincoln Collier and Christopher Collier
8. *The Chocolate War*, by Robert Cormier
9. *Charlie and the Chocolate Factory*, by Roald Dahl
10. *James and the Giant Peach*, by Roald Dahl
11. *Revolting Rhymes*, by Roald Dahl
12. *The Witches*, by Roald Dahl
13. *Annie on My Mind*, by Nancy Garden
14. *My House*, by Nikki Giovanni
15. *Lord of the Flies*, by William Golding
16. *Little Red Riding Hood*, by Jacob and Wilhelm Grimm
17. *A Separate Peace*, by John Knowles
18. *A Wrinkle in Time*, by Madeleine L'Engle
19. *The New Teenage Body Book*, by Kathy McCoy and Charles Wibbelsman
20. *Halloween ABC*, by Eve Merriam

21. *I Have to Go,* by Robert Munsch
22. *Heather Has Two Mommies,* by Leslea Newman
23. *The Great Gilly Hopkins,* by Katherine Paterson
24. *The Learning Tree,* by Gordon Parks
25. *A Day No Pigs Would Die,* by Robert Peck
26. All the Harry Potter books, by J. K. Rowling
27. *How to Eat Fried Worms,* by Thomas Rockwell
28. *The Catcher in the Rye,* by J. D. Salinger
29. *More Scary Stories in the Dark,* by Alvin Schwartz
30. *Scary Stories in the Dark,* by Alvin Schwartz
31. *In the Night Kitchen,* by Maurice Sendak
32. *The Witches of Worm,* by Zilpha Snyder
33. *The Grapes of Wrath,* by John Steinbeck
34. *Of Mice and Men,* by John Steinbeck
35. *The Adventures of Huckleberry Finn,* by Mark Twain
36. *The Adventures of Tom Sawyer,* by Mark Twain
37. *Slaughterhouse-Five,* by Kurt Vonnegut
38. *The Color Purple,* by Alice Walker
39. *Daddy's Roommate,* by Michael Willhoite
40. *The Pigman,* by Paul Zindel

12 BOOKS YOU'LL ENJOY IF YOU'RE INTERESTED IN LATIN CULTURE

1. *Lupita Manana,* by Patricia Beatty (1981). Two young Mexicans must travel to the U.S. to find work.

2. *Where the Deer and the Cantaloupe Play,* by T. Ernesto Bethancourt (1981). A young New York Latino boy tries to find his place in the Wild West.

3. *Sparrow Hawk Red,* by Ben Mikaelsen (1994). A boy flies an airplane over the Mexican border to save his family and lives with the street children there.

4. *Maria Luisa,* by Winifred Madison (1971). Maria Luisa encounters prejudice against Chicanos when she and her younger brother move to San Francisco to live with an aunt.

5. *Yagua Days,* by Cruz Martel (1976). Adam Bure visits his parents' homeland, Puerto Rico, for the first time.

6. *Felita,* by Nicholasa Mohr (1979). A Puerto Rican family moves from a friendly neighborhood to one where Spanish is not spoken.

7. *Juan's Eighteen-Wheeler Summer,* by Marian T. Place and Charles G. Preston (1982). A Mexican-American boy spends a summer working with a truck driver so he can buy a bicycle.

8. *The Circuit: Stories from the Life of a Migrant Child,* by Francisco Jiménez (1997). The struggles and triumphs of the author's Mexican family as they worked as field laborers in 1940s California.

9. *Parrot in the Oven: Mi Vida,* by Victor Martinez (1996). Manny relates his coming-of-age experiences as a member of a poor Mexican-American family in which his alcoholic father only adds to everyone's struggle.

10. *Encounter,* by Jane Yolen (1996). A Taino Indian boy on the island of San Salvador tells of the landing of Columbus and his men in 1492.

11. *An Island Like You: Stories of the Barrio,* by Judith Ortiz Cofer (1996). Twelve stories describe young people caught between their Puerto Rican heritage and their American surroundings.

12. *Breaking Through,* by Francisco Jiménez (2001). Francisco and his family are caught by immigration officers and forced to leave their California home but soon find their way back.

15 BOOKS YOU'LL ENJOY IF YOU'RE INTERESTED IN JEWISH CULTURE

1. *Dmitry: A Young Soviet Immigrant,* by Joanne E. Bernstein (1981). A Russian-Jewish family leaves the Soviet Union for a life in the U.S.

2. *Stories My Grandfather Should Have Told Me,* by Deborah Brodie (1977). Twelve stories from a variety of authors that explore many aspects of 20th-century Jewish life.

3. *King of the Seventh Grade,* by Barbara Cohen (1982). Vic Abrams's secure world becomes unstuck when his mother reveals she is not Jewish and, therefore, there will be no bar mitzvah.

4. *Anne Frank: The Diary of a Young Girl* (1947). On her thirteenth birthday, just a few weeks before her family goes into hiding to avoid the Nazis, a young girl is given a blank diary. This is what she wrote before she was killed in 1945.

5. *The Hidden Children,* by Howard Greenfeld (1993). Greenfeld has spoken to Holocaust survivors now living in the U.S. and explains what it was like to be a Jewish child at that time.

6. *Letters from Rifka,* by Karen Hess (1992). A young Jewish girl chronicles her family's flight from Russia to America in 1919.

7. *The Murderer,* by Felice Holman (1978). A young Jewish boy growing up in the days of the Great Depression is bullied by local boys and accused of murdering Christ.

8. *The Turning Point,* by Naomi J. Karp (1976). Hannah and her brother Zach encounter anti-Semitism when their family moves from the Bronx to the suburbs.

9. *Gershon's Monster,* by Eric A. Kimmel (2000). A beautiful retelling of the traditional Hasidic legend for the Jewish New Year in which people gather at the seashore or by a river to turn their pockets inside out, allowing bread crumbs to fall into the water—a symbolic casting off of sins.

10. *Masada: The Last Fortress,* by Gloria D. Miklowitz (1999). As the Roman army marches across the Judean desert toward the fortress of Masada, Simon, a 17-year-old, and his Jewish community prepare to fight.

11. *The Chosen,* by Chaim Potok (1995). An unlikely friendship forms between two boys: Reuven, who is a secular Jew, and Danny, the son of a strict Hasidic rabbi.

12. *Thanks to My Mother,* by Schoschanna Rabinovici (1998). A young Jewish girl and her mother struggle to survive in Nazi-occupied Lithuania.

13. *The Upstairs Room,* by Johanna Reiss (1987). In Holland, before the outbreak of World War II, Ani and her family flee from the Nazis.

14. *Speed of Light,* by Sybil Rosen (2001). An 11-year-old Jewish girl struggles with the anti-Semitism and racism in her small southern community in the 1950s.

15. *All of a Kind Family,* by Sydney Taylor (1980). Five sisters grow up on the Lower East Side shortly after the turn of the century.

20 REALLY GOOD BOOKS THAT DEAL WITH AFRICAN-AMERICAN ISSUES

1. *Through My Eyes,* by Ruby Bridges (1999). Ruby Bridges recounts the story of her involvement as a 6-year-old in the integration of her New Orleans school in 1960.

2. *Bud, Not Buddy,* by Christopher Paul Curtis (1999). Set in 1936, the book is about Bud, a foster child who goes in search of his father and meets, along the way, characters such as Doug the Thug, Doo-Doo-Bug, and Steady Eddie. Especially enjoyable if you're into music.

3. *The Ear, the Eye and the Arm,* by Nancy Farmer (1995). General Matsika's three children are kidnapped and put to work in a plastic mine while three mutant detectives use their special powers to search for them.

4. *The Slave Dancer,* by Paula Fox (1996). This historical tale is about a young boy who is kidnapped and placed on a slave ship. It's a powerful book about the horrors of slavery.

5. *Return to South Town,* by Lorenz Graham (1976). In this fourth volume of a celebrated series, David Williams, now a doctor, returns to the southern town from which his black family fled years ago.

6. *Bluish,* by Virginia Hamilton (1999). Ten-year-old Dreenie is a girl nicknamed Bluish, not because she is half black and half Jewish, but because her leukemia has made her pale.

7. *Many Thousand Gone: African-Americans from Slavery to Freedom,* by Virginia Hamilton (1999). African-American slaves journey to freedom via the Underground Railroad.

8. *Circle of Fire,* by William H. Hooks (1982). Three friends — a white boy and two black boys — try to thwart an attack on some Irish Gypsies by the Klan.

9. *Heaven,* by Angela Johnson (2000). Fourteen-year-old Marley's seemingly perfect life in the small town of Heaven is disrupted when she discovers that her father and mother are not her birth parents.

10. *Go Well, Stay Well,* by Toeckey Jones (1980). A white girl in South Africa meets a black girl her own age, and a friendship begins in spite of social pressures.

11. *Bizou,* by Norma Klein (1983). Bizou, a French child with a black American mother, learns about her family roots.

12. *Dave at Night,* by Gail Carson Levine (1999). Dave, just orphaned, is treated cruelly at the Hebrew Home for Boys, so he sneaks out at night and is welcomed into the music- and culture-filled world of the Harlem Renaissance.

13. *It Ain't All for Nothin',* by Walter Dean Myers (1979). A 12-year-old boy is cast adrift in Harlem.

14. *145th Street: Short Stories,* by Walter Dean Myers (2000). Ten tales about the residents of a single Harlem block.

15. *The Cay,* by Theodore Taylor (1991). This well-loved book is about a boy and his racist family, who are shipwrecked and saved by an old black man.

16. *Roll of Thunder, Hear My Cry,* by Mildred D. Taylor (1997). Cassie Logan learns the importance of family and sticking together when she first encounters racism at the age of 9.

17. *The Well: David's Story,* by Mildred D. Taylor (1995). In Mississippi in the early 1900s, a time of racial tensions, 10-

year-old David Logan's family generously shares their well water with both white and black neighbors.

18. *Leon's Story,* by Leon Walter Tillage (2000). The son of a North Carolina sharecropper recalls the hard times faced by his family in the first half of the 20th century.

19. *The Integration of Mary-Larkin Thornhill,* by Ann Waldron (1975). Because her parents insist, a white northern girl must attend a black junior high school.

20. *Ludell,* by Brenda Wilkinson (1975). A tender story of a girl's year in the fifth grade in a southern segregated school during the mid-1950s.

11 BOOKS ABOUT NATIVE AMERICAN CULTURE

1. *Mak,* by Belle Coates (1981). A young boy is torn between Indian and white cultures.

2. *Indian School: Teaching the White Man's Way,* by Michael L. Cooper (1999). This moving photo essay tells the brutal history of the Indian boarding schools, which removed children from their homes to teach them to live like white people.

3. *Morning Girl,* by Michael Dorris (1990). A magical tale, it illustrates the transformation of a place before it is discovered by white men.

4. *The Whipman Is Watching,* by T. A. Dyer (1979). Children living on an American Indian reservation try to retain their identity in an all-white school.

5. *The Birchbark House,* by Louise Erdrich (1999). A 7-year-old Ojibwa girl lives through the joys of summer and the perils of winter on an island in Lake Superior in 1847.

6. *People of the Dream,* by James D. Forman (1972). This novel concerns the flight of Chief Joseph and his Nez Perce people and the gross injustice inflicted on them.

7. *Stone Fox,* by John Reynolds Gardiner (1980). Little

Willy competes against the Indian Stone Face in the National Dogsled Races.

8. *Julie of the Wolves,* by Jean Craighead George (1974). This Eskimo tale is about Miyax—or Julie, as the white people call her—who is trapped in the wilderness of a freezing Arctic winter with a pack of wolves.

9. *The Scared One,* by Dennis Haseley (1983). The story of an Indian boy living in fear.

10. *Island of the Blue Dolphins,* by Scott O'Dell (1987). This fast adventure is about a young girl who is trapped alone in the wilderness and must train the dog who killed her brother in order to survive.

11. *Weave Little Stars into My Sleep: Native American Lullabies,* by Neil Philip (editor), Edward S. Curtis (photographer) (2001). These beautiful lullabies combine Native American themes with universal concerns of parenthood.

9 BOOKS YOU'LL ENJOY IF YOU'RE INTERESTED IN ASIAN CULTURE

1. *In The Year of the Boar and Jackie Robinson,* by Bette Bao Lord (1984). A Chinese girl leaves China to join her father in New York in 1947.

2. *Chinese Cinderella,* by Adeline Yen Mah (1999). Wu Mei describes her sad and lonely childhood with an abusive family in China during the 1940s and 1950s.

3. *A Step from Heaven,* by An Na (2001). Young Ju's parents don't want her to become too American, and in turn, Ju is ashamed of their Old World ways. The stories here blend together into a beautiful novel that takes Ju through her teenage years until she's ready to leave for college.

4. *Talent Night,* by Jean Davies Okimoto (2000). Rodney, an aspiring Japanese-American rap musician, learns about his heritage and the importance of being oneself.

5. *A Jar of Dreams,* by Yoshiko Uchida (1981). A young girl grows up in a closely knit Japanese-American family in California during the 1930s, a time of great prejudice.

6. *Journey Home,* by Yoshiko Uchida (1975). A Japanese-American family is released from a World War II internment camp.

7. *I Rode a Horse of Milk White Jade,* by Diana Lee Wilson (1998). Oyuna tells her granddaughter the story of how her love for her horse enabled her to win a race and bring good luck to her family in Mongolia in 1339.

8. *Dragon's Gate,* by Laurence Yep (1995). In 1867, when he accidentally kills a Manchu, a 15-year-old Chinese boy is sent to America to join his father, uncle, and other Chinese workers building a tunnel for the transcontinental railroad.

9. *Sea Glass,* by Laurence Yep (1979). An awkward Chinese-American boy moves to a new junior high school and has trouble adjusting.

13 SEQUELS TO <u>THE WIZARD OF OZ</u>

Even if you've seen the movie *The Wizard of Oz* a hundred times, *read the book!* Written by L. Frank Baum in 1900, it remains a classic. But did you know that afterward, Baum wrote 13 other books depicting the adventures of his famous characters? You can connect with other Ozmaniacs by joining the International Wizard of Oz Club, 1407 A St., Suite D, Antioch, CA 94509. Or visit its very cool Web site: ozclub.org.

1. *The Land of Oz* (1904). Tip, an Oz boy, makes a Pumpkinhead Man, and an old witch brings him to life. They run away to the Emerald City and are "conquered," along with King Scarecrow, by General Jinjur's girl army. Their escape, aided by the Saw Horse, the Woggle-Bug, and the wonderful Flying Gump, makes a lively tale that ends with a real surprise!

2. *Ozma of Oz* (1907). A storm at sea strands Dorothy on the shores of Ev, where she finds Tik-Tok the Machine Man and Billina the Talking Hen. She also meets her old friends the Scarecrow and Tin Man—and Ozma, the lovely Queen of Oz. But they are soon imprisoned by the tricky Nome King and have a strange adventure in his weird underground castle.

3. *Dorothy and the Wizard in Oz* (1908). An earthquake plunges Dorothy and her cousin Zed into a magical land in the depths of the earth, where they meet again the jolly Wizard of Oz. After amazing experiences with the Live Vegetables, the Invisible Family, the Gargoyles, and the Dragonettes, they are rescued—in the nick of time—by Ozma.

4. *The Road to Oz* (1909). This book tells how to reach the Wonderland of Oz over an enchanted road that leads Dorothy into all kinds of adventures. On the way she meets the funny Shaggy Man, Button-Bright (who is not so bright), and Polychrome, the Rainbow's Daughter. At the end of the road is the Emerald City—and Ozma's wonderful birthday party.

5. *The Emerald City of Oz* (1910). Dorothy is finally invited to live in Oz permanently. But while she is on an Ozian sight-seeing tour with her Aunt Em and Uncle Henry, the vengeful Nome King is plotting to tunnel under the surrounding desert and capture the Land of Oz! How the Emerald City is miraculously saved makes an amazing—and delightful—ending.

6. *The Patchwork Girl of Oz* (1913). Ojo, a little Munchkin boy, sees a Crooked Magician make a rag doll servant out of a patchwork quilt and bring her to life! Ojo's Unk Nunkie, the Magician's wife, the zany Patchwork Girl, and the haughty Glass Cat set out to find the magic antidote, making this one of the best of the Oz stories.

7. *Tik-Tok of Oz* (1914). Queen Ann of Oogaboo goes forth to conquer the world. Betsy Bobbin and Hank the Mule are shipwrecked on the island of Talking Flowers. The Shaggy

Man sets out to seek his long-lost brother. How they all fall into the clutches of the Nome King — and are rescued by Tik-Tok, the intrepid Mechanical Man — is related in this strange and funny tale.

8. *The Scarecrow of Oz* (1915). Tiny Trot and Cap'n Bill are exploring caves off the California coast when a whirlpool engulfs their boat! They finally reach far-off Jinxland, where King Krewl has made a witch freeze the heart of a lovely princess. Things go from bad to worse before our old friend the Scarecrow arrives on the scene and saves the day.

9. *Rinkitink in Oz* (1916). Prince Inga of Pingaree is the hero of this perilous quest in the islands of the Nonestic Ocean. Jolly King Rinkitink and his surly goat, Bilbil, provide the comic relief. They sail off to rescue Inga's parents from the pirates of Regos. How they find, lose, and find again the Three Magic Pearls that are their only hope of success adds up to a thrilling adventure.

10. *The Lost Princess of Oz* (1917). Ozma is stolen! So are all the magical treasures of Oz, including the Cookie Cook's diamond dishpan. Dorothy and the Wizard head a search party and hunt for the thief until they discover the enchanted Wickerwork Castle and its eerie secret. Who the scoundrel was, where Ozma has been, and where her friends find her will surprise you!

11. *The Tin Woodman of Oz* (1918). The Tin Woodman, with the Scarecrow and Woot the Wanderer, sets out to find his long-forgotten sweetheart. A wicked Giantess transforms them into a Tin Owl, a Straw-stuffed Bear, and a Green Monkey! How they manage to regain their real forms, and what the Tin Woodman really finds, make a bizarre and mirth-filled tale.

12. *The Magic of Oz* (1919). A mischief-bent boy with a magical secret meets the spiteful old Nome King, and they decide to invade Oz. Trot and Cap'n Bill, lured by a wonderful Magic Flower, are trapped on a deadly island. Dorothy and the Wizard go off to search for a magic birthday present for Ozma. Their paths all cross, and the result is "Mixed Magic," indeed!

13. *Glinda of Oz* (1920). Ozma and Dorothy travel to a distant part of Oz to make peace between the warring Flatheads and Skeezers' glass-domed island city when it mysteriously submerges! Finally Glinda, the Good Sorceress of Oz, and the Wizard pool their magic to bring about a thrilling underwater rescue.

12 THINGS YOU CAN DO TO FIGHT CENSORSHIP

1. Find out which books have been banned from your school and read them. Think about why they were censored. You may be surprised to know that some of your best buddies —including Judy Blume and Bart Simpson—have had to deal with censors who felt their work wasn't suitable for young people.

2. Talk to your friends about starting a group to fight censorship. Talk about how censorship works and how your school and library are affected.

3. Write letters to newspapers, radio stations, publishers, and members of the local media, explaining your opinions on the subject.

4. Contact a group called People for the American Way to learn more about censorship (2000 M St., NW, Suite 400, Washington, DC 20036; www.pfaw.org).

5. Write to the American Booksellers Association for a complete list of books that have been banned and ask how you can support the annual event called Banned Books Week (828 S. Broadway, Tarrytown, NY 10591; www.bookweb.org).

6. Talk to your parents about censorship and urge them to get involved working against the censorship movement in your community.

7. Get your friends and other members of your community to sign petitions against censorship and make sure they are delivered into the hands of public officials who can help. Force them to guarantee their support. If they don't, make sure everyone who signs the petition knows it.

8. Write to your favorite performers and ask what they're doing to help preserve freedom of expression. (When the freedom of one artist is threatened, *all* artists are threatened.)

9. Create art with anticensorship themes.

10. Create your own T-shirt and get the message on your chest. Here are some ideas for slogans:

"Book Burning Burns Me Up"

"Freedom Is Not a Dirty Word"

"I Support the First Amendment"

11. Support your public library in its efforts against censorship. If it isn't doing anything, find out how you can get something started.

12. Read the list of "Banned Books" on pages 219–20 of this book.

10 LEGENDARY PLACES ANYONE CAN VISIT

1. Camelot, the magical capital of Logres, which was King Arthur's kingdom, is a great place to visit if you like enchanted castles. Merlin the Magician built a palace there and decorated it with mystical symbols. To get there, read *The Legend of King Arthur.*

2. Speranza. Plenty of wildlife but no wild beasts, so you're safe. If you like exotic birds and turtles, you'll find this place as awesome as Robinson Crusoe did when he was shipwrecked here in 1659. Directions: Read *The Life and Surprising Adventures of Robinson Crusoe,* by Daniel Defoe, and make a left at the lemon trees.

3. Lilliput. If you're over 6 inches in height, you'll feel out of place on this tiny island south of Indonesia. Gulliver sure did when he landed here by mistake. Read about his adventures in *Gulliver's Travels,* by Jonathan Swift.

4. Middle-earth, where elves, dwarfs, and men speak to wizards, and hobbits go on the most amazing journeys. J.R.R. Tolkien wrote of Middle-earth in *The Hobbit, The Lord of the Rings,* and other books.

5. Narnia. Created by a Lion named Aslan, Narnia is filled with centaurs, fauns, dryads, and a witch. Getting there is complicated: You can only enter through a wardrobe (a closet), by magic rings, or by the power of Aslan. It helps if you have a copy of *The Chronicles of Narnia,* by C. S. Lewis.

6. Never Land. Mermaids, pirates, fairies, red Indians, and adventure. They're here, where Peter Pan takes Wendy Darling to be the mother of the Lost Boys. Read *Peter Pan,* by J. M. Barrie.

7. Oz. Munchkinland is only one region of Oz. Winkie Country, where everyone wears yellow, is another. In Quadling Country they wear red, in Gilliken it's purple, and we all know what color they wear in the capital, Emerald City. *The Wonderful Wizard of Oz,* by L. Frank Baum, is *way* different from the movie!

8. Sleepy Hollow. If you keep your eyes open when you come to Sleepy Hollow, you'll notice that everyone here is just a little bit "dreamy," as if they're in a trance. But try not to lose your head, like poor Ichabod Crane. *The Legend of Sleepy Hollow,* by Washington Irving, makes a great Halloween "vacation."

9. Wonderland. Go to Oxford, England, follow the Thames River, and enter the rabbit hole. Take the long tunnel straight down and you can't miss it. Don't eat or drink anything when you get there, though; strange things can happen. Of course, you can take the easy route by reading *Alice's Adventures in Wonderland,* by Lewis Carroll.

10. Redwall. If you like wildlife, this is the place for you.

It's a medieval wonderland inhabited by peace-loving mice, moles, shrews, squirrels, and their friends. But it's a crowded place: Redwall gets "visitors" each year from kids from 126 different countries. There are almost 15 different "guidebooks" to Redwall, with great titles such as *Redwall, Mossflower, Matimeo, Salamandastron,* and *Marlfox.* These wonderful stories are written by Brian Jacques.

10 BOOKS TO READ WHILE YOU'RE WAITING FOR THE NEXT HARRY POTTER BOOK TO BE PUBLISHED

1. *The Dark Is Rising,* by Susan Cooper. On his eleventh birthday, Will Stanton discovers that he possesses ancient and mysterious powers.

2. *Time Stops for No Mouse: A Hermux Tantamoq Adventure,* by Michael Hoeye. Hermux's life is forever changed after he goes in search of famed adventuress Linka Perflinger, who has mysteriously disappeared. Hermux's encounters involve spies, thieves, killers, betrayal, and the Fountain of Youth.

3. *The Phantom Tollbooth,* by Norton Juster. A wonderful story about a boy named Milo who is always bored. One day he comes home to find a tollbooth and a car in his room. He gets in the car and, after going through the booth, enters another land.

4. *The Gammage Cup,* by Carol Kendall. This epic tale tells about the race of people called the Minnipins, tiny folk who become big heroes.

5. *Owl in Love,* by Patrice Kindl. Owl's wild, wise, and witty ways make this tale truly enjoyable. She is an owl by day and a werewolf by night. Falling in love, making friends, and trying to figure out who and what she is brings Owl nearly to the end of her wits.

6. *The Chronicles of Narnia,* by C. S. Lewis. Four children travel repeatedly to a world in which they are far more than just children and everything is much more than it seems. Issues of good and evil, faith and hope, make these books especially interesting to kids.

7. *A Wrinkle in Time,* by Madeleine L'Engle. The story of 13-year-old Meg Murry, a misfit, who discovers her own abilities. Meg, her 5-year-old brother Charles, and their friend Calvin O'Keefe are led on a fantastic journey.

8. *The Giver,* by Lois Lowry. An old man known as the Giver enables 12-year-old Jonas to discover the truth about his world, in which there is no poverty, no crime, no sickness, and where every family is happy. But in order to have this perfect society, people have to sacrifice their individuality and human qualities.

9. *The Ghosts of Austwick Manor,* by Reby Edmond MacDonald. Hillary and Heather MacDonald are excited when their brother, Don, inherits a dollhouse made to look like the family's old home in England. They find four sets of dolls with a note that says not to touch any of them. What do you think they do?

10. *The Hobbit,* by J.R.R. Tolkien. Hobbits are furry humanlike creatures who love nothing better than a leisurely life, free of adventure. But Bilbo and Frodo and their elfish friends get swept up into a mighty conflict with the dragon Smaug, the dark lord Sauron, the monstrous Gollum, the Cracks of Doom, and the awful power of the Magical Ring.

7 THINGS YOU PROBABLY DIDN'T KNOW ABOUT J. K. ROWLING

Joanne Kathleen Rowling has become one of the most cherished and popular children's authors of all time. Here are some facts about her that you might find interesting.

1. She began her writing career by making up fantasy stories to tell her little sister Di.

2. She wrote her first story at the age of 6.

3. She had childhood friends named Ian and Vicki Potter.

4. When she answered a math problem incorrectly at a new school she was attending, her teacher sat her in the dumb row. After she proved her writing abilities, she was placed with the bright kids.

5. Her favorite holiday is—you guessed it—Halloween.

6. She once autographed a thousand books in just 2 hours.

7. Her favorite TV shows are *Frasier* and *The Simpsons*.

25 CHARACTERS THAT APPEAR IN THE HARRY POTTER SERIES AND 5 THAT WE MADE UP
(Can You Spot the Phonies?)

1. Edwina Biggle—Professor Sinistra's niece and assistant. She wears a black cloak that has golden stars embroidered all over it.

2. Geoffrey Black—The not-so-serious brother of Sirius Black.

3. Sirius Black—Azkaban's most notorious prisoner. He was accused of murdering 13 people with a single curse. He is Harry's godfather.

4. Cho Chang—Seeker for the Ravenclaw's Quidditch team. Harry has a crush on her.

5. Crookshanks—Hermione's mysterious cat in *The Prisoner of Azkaban*.

6. Dobby—A house-elf that appears in *The Chamber of Secrets*. He warns Harry not to return to Hogwarts.

7. Dopey—The Ravenclaw's elfin mascot.

8. Professor Albus Dumbledore—The headmaster of

Hogwarts. He is a wise wizard with powerful magic skills. A true friend of Harry.

9. Vernon Dursley—Harry's mean uncle.

10. Fang—Hagrid's very large black pet boarhound.

11. Fat Lady—Her talking portrait hangs at the entrance of Gryffindor Tower.

12. Fluffy—The vicious three-headed dog that guards the hiding place of the Sorcerer's Stone.

13. Cornelius Fudge—Minister of Magic, head of the Ministry of Magic.

14. Hermione Granger—She is a bright overachiever and one of Harry's closest and loyal friends. She is a half Muggle.

15. Hagrid—The giant-size groundskeeper at Hogwarts. He is also Harry's protector and loves just about any type of creature.

16. Hedwig—Harry's pet owl and postal service.

17. Neville Longbottom—A bumbling student who is always losing things and forgetting passwords.

18. Professor Remus J. Lupin—Teacher of Defense Against the Dark Arts in Harry's third year at Hogwarts and a loyal friend to Harry's dad.

19. Draco Malfoy—Nasty, snobbish know-it-all who constantly bullies Harry. Malfoy's father is rumored to have been an ally of You-Know-Who.

20. Quinella Strange Malfoy—Lucius Malfoy's wife.

21. Aunt Marge—Vernon Dursley's cruel sister who is fond of making Harry's life miserable. She appears in *The Prisoner of Azkaban*. Harry puts a spell on her and makes her blow up like a balloon.

22. Finneus McFood—Always the first person to arrive for dinner and the last to leave.

23. Professor Minerva McGonagall—Deputy headmistress of Hogwarts and head of Gryffindor. Another Harry supporter.

24. Moaning Myrtle—A ghost that haunts one of the toilets in the girls' bathroom.

25. Madam Pomfrey—The school nurse at Hogwarts.

26. Tom Riddle—A past student at Hogwarts who received a school award for special services. He has a secret identity and his diary is discovered in book two.

27. Scabbers—Ron Weasley's old and tired pet rat (or is he?), who was passed down from his older brothers.

28. Professor Severus Snape—He is a hook-nosed, nasty teacher of Potions. Seems to have it in for Harry. Snape was an enemy of Harry's father at Hogwarts.

29. Voldemort—Also known as You-Know-Who. He is an evil and much-feared wizard who killed Harry's parents and is responsible for giving Harry his lightning bolt scar.

30. Ron Weasley—One of Harry's best pals at Hogwarts. Ron comes from a loving and friendly family of many siblings, all with red hair.

The Imposters are numbers 2, 3, 9, 20, 28.

4 HIGHLY COLLECTIBLE HARRY POTTER BOOKS

If you have already started a Harry Potter collection, you know that there are a wide range of items available. From trading cards to electronic games, to clothing, to photo frames, albums, storage boxes, and framed mirrors, you can go nuts deciding where to begin. The following is a list of what we consider to be the most interesting and unfortunately the most expensive collectibles of all—the books themselves. If you do decide to become a collector, be on the lookout for Harry Potter books published in these languages: Afrikaans, Bahasa Indonesian, Bulgarian, Chinese, Croatian, Czechoslovakian, Danish, Dutch, Estonian, Finnish, French, German, Greek, Hebrew, Hungarian, Icelandic, Italian, Japanese, Korean, Norwegian, Polish, Portuguese, Romanian, Slovenian, Spanish, Swedish, Thai, and Turkish!

1. The first editions of the first four books released in Great Britain are very valuable. A set of all four is worth $40,000.

2. The first printings of *Harry Potter and the Philosopher's Stone* (the original title of *Harry Potter and the Sorcerer's Stone*) are extremely rare; only 200 were printed. This first edition is worth $23,000.

3. The British Deluxe Editions feature cloth covers with J. K. Rowling's signature stamped in gold, gilt-edged pages, and a sewn-in bookmark. Each edition is worth approximately $2,500–$3,000.

4. The editions published by Scholastic Publishing in the U.S. are a little different from the British ones. The American books have different covers and an Americanized vocabulary. A first printing of the American edition of *Harry Potter and the Sorcerer's Stone* is valued at $5,700.

10 TIPS FOR YOUNG WRITERS

Lots of kids have learned that writing is one of the most rewarding hobbies you can have. It's a great way to explore ideas, practice communicating, and save your thoughts for later reference. It's also a lot of fun. Here are some ideas that might help you along the way.

1. Write about things you really know about instead of spending a lot of time trying to come up with exotic subjects and situations. If you write from your own experience—and from the heart—your story will be a lot more believable.

2. If you think your own life is boring and not worth writing about, remember that different people have different experiences, and your life may very well be what other readers can only dream about. Also pay attention to what goes on around you, even the "boring details." These could help make your story more realistic.

3. If you're having trouble deciding how to begin (lots of

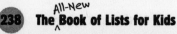

writers have the same problem), just start writing from the point where you feel comfortable. You can always go back and add a beginning when you're done.

4. Try to outline your story before you start writing it. Then make sure your story has a beginning, a middle, and an end. The outline technique is also useful for writers who are overwhelmed with all they want to say. Once you have the outline done, you can just write the story one part at a time.

5. After you've finished your first version of the story, which is commonly called a first draft, review what you've done. Ask yourself if you've used exactly the right words to get your point across. Use a thesaurus to find other words that mean almost the same thing. Also, use a dictionary to check your spelling before you write a final version of the story. Keep in mind that many writers go through numerous versions before they are satisfied with what they've written. Paula Danziger once said that she went through four different endings for *The Cat Ate My Gymsuit* before she finally found one that seemed right.

6. Even if you're not ready to write a story, you can still work on your writing skills by keeping a diary of everything you see and hear and practicing putting those observations into words. You can use these observations later if you need ideas for details.

7. Don't worry about getting your stories published. Most kids' stories never get into print, but you shouldn't let this discourage you. Your writing will serve as great practice for the stories or books you may write when you get older, and in the meantime, you can enjoy the experience and dream about the future.

8. Don't be shy about sharing your stories with friends and family. This is sometimes hard, especially if you're afraid that others won't like what you've written. Right now, it's important that *you* like what you've written. But be open-minded, too. It's often hard to take criticism about something that's so personal, but others may have good ideas that will help you improve your craft in the future. So listen to what they say and then be as objective as you can in deciding if what they're saying makes sense.

9. Enjoy yourself! No matter how serious you are about what you are doing, it will come out a lot better if you can relax a little and take pleasure from the experience. Writing is hard work, but the roads you travel in the course of doing it and the doors it opens can serve as some of the most gratifying experiences in your life.

10. Learn to write by reading a lot—everything you can find. Reading the works of others will give you ideas and teach you all about the variety of styles that are possible. Thomas Rockwell, who wrote *How to Eat Fried Worms,* believes in this method. As he put it, "The best way to learn to write is to write a lot and read a lot."

25 SPECIAL-INTEREST MAGAZINES YOU MIGHT WANT TO SUBSCRIBE TO

These magazines also publish articles by and for kids. Be sure to also check out the list called "30 Magazines . . . That Publish Stuff by Kids," page 246.

1. *Biography Today*
Omnigraphics
Penobscot Bldg.
Detroit, MI 48226
Profiles of newsmakers in fields such as entertainment, politics, sports, and literature.

2. *Boys' Life*
Boy Scouts of America
1325 W. Walnut Hill La.

P.O. Box 15079
Irving, TX 75015
All about scouting for boys.

3. *Business Kids*
1300 1st St., NW, Suite 1080 E.
Washington, DC 20005
Profiles teens who own their own businesses.

4. *Cobblestone*
7 School St.
Peterborough, NH 03458
Each issue concerns a particular theme related to American history.

5. *Disney Adventures*
Walt Disney Publications
500 S. Buena Vista
Burbank, CA 91521
For kids ages 7–14. Articles on music, movies, trends, games, travel, and adventure.

6. *Faces*
7 School St.
Peterborough, NH 03458
Articles about the customs and cultures of different races around the world.

7. *Falcon Magazine*
P.O. Box 15936
N. Hollywood, CA 91615
Articles, games, and lots of interesting stuff for kids who care about nature and conservation.

8. *Home Education*
P.O. Box 1083
Tonasket, WA 98855
Nonfiction articles and interviews about kids who are educated at home.

9. *i*
Cousteau Society Membership Center
870 Greenbriar Circle, Suite 402
Chesapeake, VA 23320
Exploration of oceans, rivers, waterways, and marine life.

10. *Kidsports*
P.O. Box 8488
Coral Springs, FL 33075
Posters, games, fiction, and facts about sports.

11. *Little Leaguer*
Little League Baseball
P.O. Box 3485
Williamsport, PA 17701
Baseball-related articles.

12. *National Geographic World*
1145 17th and M St., NW
Washington, DC 20036
Artwork, photos, and poems about the natural world.

13. *National Wildlife*
National Wildlife Federation
8925 Leesburg Pike
Vienna, VA 22184
Photos and articles about wildlife, conservation, and ecology.

14. *Nintendo Power*
Nintendo of America
4820-150th Ave., NE
Redmond, VA 98052
Game review, tips, and stories.

15. *Odyssey*
7 School St.
Peterborough, NH 03458

Scientific articles related to a particular theme.

16. *Owl*
255 Great Arrow Ave.
Buffalo, NY 14207
Articles and photos on animals, science, and nature.

17. *Plays*
120 Boylston St.
Boston, MA 02116
Original one-act plays and programs for kids interested in theater.

18. *Ranger Rick*
National Wildlife Federation
8925 Leesburg Pike
Vienna, VA 22184
Science, conservation, and study via articles, photos, and stories.

19. *Sports Illustrated for Kids*
P.O. Box 830609
Birmingham, AL 35283
Articles, games, comics, and *loads* of inside information about your favorite sports stars.

20. *Superscience Blue*
Scholastic
2931 E. McCarty St.
Jefferson City, MO 65102
Science and technology news and experiments.

21. *3-2-1 Contact*
P.O. Box 53051
Boulder, CO 80322
Science, technology, nature study, and current events.

22. *U*S* Kids*
Children's Better Health Institute
P.O. Box 7036

Red Oak, IA 51591
True stories about nature, pets, and family life.

23. *YM*
Young Miss
Gruner & Jahr
685 Third Ave., 30th Floor
New York, NY 10017
Fashion- and beauty-related articles

24. *Zillions*
P.O. Box 54861
Boulder, CO 80322
Probably the most interesting magazine we've come across, with lots of articles on how to get the most for your money.

25. *Zoobooks*
Wildlife Education
3590 Kettner Blvd.
San Diego, CA 92101
Each issue covers a particular animal or group of animals.

12 TIPS FOR SUBMITTING YOUR WORK TO MAGAZINES FOR PUBLICATION

If you're an aspiring writer, you've probably daydreamed about seeing your name in print. Maybe you will someday. But until that happens keep trying, and keep trying new things. What you do before you become successful is just as important as what you do after. Here are some ways to present yourself professionally to publishers. If they take you seriously, maybe they'll give you their opinions, which is *very* helpful. See the list that follows of "29 Magazines (and One Publishing Company!) That Publish Stuff by Kids."

1. Do not send money to anyone in return for publishing work.

2. Be sure that the work you submit is original, which means that you wrote it by yourself and that none of it was copied.

3. Only submit your best work. Keep working on your piece until you're sure it says exactly what you want it to.

4. Make sure you send your work to the right place. No matter how good your story is, you'll get turned down if a magazine never publishes that kind of story. For this reason, write to magazines and contests for their exact guidelines before you send in anything. Send a self-addressed stamped envelope with your request.

5. Some submissions require that a parent or guardian fill out a certain form. Follow this and other rules very carefully.

6. Write or type your entry on one side of 8½ by 11 sheets of paper. If you write by hand, use lined paper. If you type, double-space the lines. Be neat, but remember that even the most professional-looking essay won't get published if it's not a good essay. (Generally, if you're under 13, you're not expected to type.)

7. On the first page of your work, include your name, address, phone number, and the date.

8. Do not tell an editor your life story unless you are asked to do so.

9. Always make a copy of anything you send before you send it. *Most magazines and contests do not return the copy you send them.*

10. Most magazines don't pay kids for submissions. Send your work in anyway. Young writers need all the experience they can get, and it *is* fun to see your name in print.

11. Learn that failing is the thing that comes before success —and *keep trying!*

12. Be patient. It may take *months* before you get a response.

29 MAGAZINES (AND ONE PUBLISHING COMPANY!) THAT PUBLISH STUFF BY KIDS

You'll learn *tons* about getting your stories and poems published by consulting a reference book called *The Market Guide for Young Writers,* by Kathy Henderson.

Magazines aim themselves at different kinds of readers, so you may want to find out more about their specific interests before you send in your stories or poems. For instance, your short story about your boat trip to Alaska may be great, but *Calliope* won't publish it no matter how good it is if it's not looking for adventure stories. On the other hand, *Field and Stream Jr.* would probably be very interested in your story. It's a good idea to read an issue of a magazine before you send in your material.

Check out the list on pages 244–45 of this book for general instructions for submitting material to magazines.

Good luck!

1. *American Girl Magazine*
8400 Fairway Pl.
Middletown, WI 53562
A glossy magazine with a section for kids' poems, tips, and suggestions. No short stories.

2. *Boodle: By Kids, for Kids*
P.O. Box 1049
Portland, IN 47371
Aimed at kids aged 6–12, it publishes lots of stories, poems, and illustrations. It stays away from sad subjects.

3. *Calliope*
7 School St.
Peterborough, NH 03458
Each issue has a specific theme—like adventure, family,

travel—so you have to write first and find out what subjects it's looking for. It publishes stories, poetry, games, and puzzles (no word finds) and occasionally has contests.

4. *Child Life*
1100 Waterway Blvd.
P.O. Box 567
Indianapolis, IN 46202
Poetry, stories, and jokes for kids 9–11. The magazine is mostly about health and nutrition, but your submissions don't have to be about these subjects.

5. *Creative Kids*
P.O. Box 8813
Waco, TX 76714
One of the best we've come across. Publishes stories, poetry, plays, and photography by kids for kids, anywhere from ages 5 to 18. Get this magazine to find out what really talented kids are up to.

6. *Creative with Words*
P.O. Box 223226
Carmel, CA 93922
Another excellent magazine with plenty of space for submissions from young people. Sometimes, when they can't publish your work, the editors will take the time to offer opinions. (This is rare. Most times you just get the same rejection letter that everyone else gets, which basically says "thanks but no thanks.")

7. *Dogwood Tales Magazine*
P.O. Box 172068
Memphis, TN 38187
It only publishes fiction—anywhere from 250 to 3,000 words—on southern themes. No poetry or nonfiction.

8. *Field and Stream Jr.*
2 Park Ave.

New York, NY 10016
This magazine is all about hunting, fishing, and nature. It publishes stories, letters, and puzzles (no poetry). Very picky about the stories it publishes.

9. *Highlights for Children*
803 Church St.
Honesdale, PA 18431
This magazine, for kids 2–12, publishes short stories, factual articles, jokes, plays, and art (color and black-and-white) by kids.

10. *How on Earth!*
P.O. Box 339
Oxford, PA 19363
"Teens supporting compassionate ecological living." Publishes anything concerning ecology, ethics, animal, and global issues, by and for people 12–20. This is a nonprofit magazine completely run by volunteers.

11. *Ink Blot*
901 Day Rd.
Saginaw, MI 48609
A monthly newsletter especially designed for the voices of new, young writers. Submit nonfiction essays, short stories, poetry, or black-and-white art.

12. *It's Your Choice*
P.O. Box 7135
Richmond, VA 23221
An informal monthly newsletter that gets kids interested in the subject of ethics, especially crime, capital punishment, racism, and personal responsibility. No poetry.

13. *Kid's Byline*
P.O. Box 1838
Frederick, MD 21702

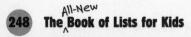

For grades 4–12, this magazine encourages kids to send in letters to the editors, but it also publishes stories. It's more interested in the experience you're writing about than the quality of your writing.

14. *Kids N' Sibs*
191 Whittier Rd.
Rochester, NY 14624
A newsletter that allows kids to share the views and experiences of disabled kids and their siblings. The publication is free.

15. *Kids' World*
1300 Kicker Rd.
Tuscaloosa, AL 35404
Poems, short stories, and art from kids up to the age of 17. They are sticklers about grammar and punctuation, so ask a parent to check your piece before you send it in.

16. *Listen, Celebrating Positive Choices*
P.O. Box 51
Cadillac, MI 49601
This magazine about good habits and positive physical and mental ideas also accepts short essays and poems for its "Listening" column.

17. Majestic Books
P.O. Box 19097M
Johnston, RI 02919
This company publishes collections of stories by kids up to the age of 18. You don't get paid, but you get a copy of the book. They encourage originality.

18. *Merlyn's Pen*
P.O. Box 1058
East Greenwich, RI 02818
This national magazine of student writing is for kids in grades 6–12, and it publishes everything—stories, plays, poems, essays, even puzzles. There's one magazine

for grades 6–9 called the *Middle School Edition,* and another for grades 9–12 called the *Senior Edition.* Be sure to specify which edition you are writing for.

19. *Muse*
Cricket Magazine Group
332 S. Michigan Ave.
Chicago, IL 60604
A science and discovery magazine for kids, with articles on art, zoology, and everything in between. This is a kids' version of the magazine called *Smithsonian.* Great color photos and original humor throughout.

20. *New Moon*
P.O. Box 3620
Duluth, MN 55803
"The magazine for girls and their dreams" was created by girls and is written for girls aged 8–14. Publishes a huge variety of things, from stories, biographies, and daydreams to book, movie, and electronics reviews. A publication that promotes the idea that all of us, *all over the globe,* are connected. Totally recommended.

21. *Poets at Work*
P.O. Box 113
Butler, PA 16001
A monthly magazine for poets of all ages that encourages free expression, especially among young poets.

22. *Skipping Stones*
P.O. Box 3939
Eugene, OR 97403
Publishes writing and art by kids 7–18. In addition to stories, poems, and art, it also publishes jokes, recipes, magic tricks, science experiments, toys, games, and movie and book reviews.

23. *Skylark*
Purdue University Calumet

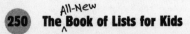

2200 169th St.
Hammond, IN 46323
Mostly written by adults, each issue has 15–20 pages of prose, poetry, and art by writers and artists from 8 to 18. Interested in publishing well-stated opinions on many subjects.

24. *Spring Tides*
Savannah Country Lower School
824 Stillwood Dr.
Savannah, GA 31419
Publishes stories and poems, with or without illustrations, in black-and-white or color. By kids 5–12.

25. *Stone Soup*
P.O. Box 83
Santa Cruz, CA 95063
One of the most famous of the magazines for kids, probably because it's so often used in schools. Includes stories, poems, personal experiences, book reviews, and art by children up to 13.

26. *Thumbprints*
928 Gibbs
Caro, MI 48723
This monthly newsletter publishes poetry, short fiction, articles, essays, and opinions, but wants them to relate to the subject of writing and expressing yourself. You don't have to type your submission if you're under 12.

27. *Time Magazine For Kids*
Cricket Magazine Group
332 S. Michigan Ave.
Chicago, IL 60604
A kids' version of the news magazine featuring news, humor, help with studying, games, and more.

28. *U*S*Kids*
1100 Waterway Blvd.

P.O. Box 567

Indianapolis, IN 46202

Even though the magazine is mostly about health,
safety, and exercise, it accepts material on any subject.
Drawings and poetry are considered for its "Best for the
End" column.

29. *Writers' International Forum, Junior Edition*
P.O. Box 516

Tracyton, WA 98393

Publishes short stories about the lives of young people.
If they publish your story, you get $5 and a copy of the
magazine.

14 SUPERHEROES AND THEIR SUPERPOWERS

1. Batman. He is superpowerful and supersmart. Gets
around in his Batmobile with his sidekick, Robin. Batman
lives in his laboratory, the Batcave. He also owns a Batplane
and lassos criminals with his Batarang.

2. Captain America. Steve Rogers is an American patriot
who wants to fight against the Nazis at the time of World War
II. He is tested by the American government and is given a
new serum and Vita-rays. The test is succesful: Steve gains immense strength, and he is given a powerful shield.

3. Captain Marvel. The following powers were given to
him by a 3,000-year-old wizard: Solomon's wisdom, Hercules' strength, Atlas' stamina, Zeus' power, Achilles' courage,
and Mercury's speed.

4. Flash. He became the fastest man on earth when he was
hit by a bolt of lightning.

5. The Green Lantern. He gains his enormous powers
when given a ring by the guardians of the planet OA. The ring

gives him the power to do anything he imagines, as long as his will is strong enough.

6. Hercules. Because his father was Zeus, king of the gods, and his mother was human, Hercules became half mortal and half god and possesses superhuman strength.

7. The Incredible Hulk. When Bruce Banner gets upset, he turns into the Hulk, who has green skin, weighs 1,000 pounds, and is 7 feet tall. His strength, which he acquired when he was caught in a nuclear explosion, is incredible.

8. Iron Man. Tony Stark is a genius scientist who developed an armor with immense power. Tony was part of a circle of scientists who believed in a golden age for humans, which included Bruce Banner and V. Van Doom.

9. Popeye. Just give him a can of spinach, and Popeye turns into a human dynamo who can beat up anyone or anything.

10. Sabraman. A popular superhero in Israel, Sabraman can shoot radioactive rays from his eyes, cross oceans in a split second, and surround himself with a magic field that prevents anyone from attacking him.

11. Siopawman. If you've never been to the Philippines, you've probably never heard of Siopawman, since that's where he's popular. Bullets and blows can't hurt him, and he's kind of ugly, with a big nose, a fat body, and a bald head. He wears an *S* on his chest, like Superman. His enemies are all criminals, like Jelloman, who quivers with fear at the very thought of Siopawman.

12. Spiderman. When he was bitten by a radioactive spider, Peter Parker turned into a superhero with the power to climb walls and act like a human spider. His web-shooters spin rope lines, and he can grow new arms.

13. Superman. He can fly faster than a speeding bullet, leap tall buildings in a single bound, and travel to the very edges of the universe. He has superhearing and X-ray vision, not to mention his superstrength, with which he can lift a whole railroad train. His breath can blow supercold. Superman's only problem is that he can be hurt by kryptonite, especially the green variety.

14. Wonder Woman. Wonder Woman was born with her incredible strength, which allowed her to tear a tree out by the roots when she was 3 years old and to run as fast as a deer by the time she turned 5. She has a radio in her headband, her belt keeps her honest, and her invisible robot plane can travel at 3,000 miles per hour.

10 COMIC BOOK HEROES AND THEIR SECRET IDENTITIES

(Can you connect them?
See the answers below.)

1. Batman	**a.** Dick Grayson
2. Green Hornet	**b.** Bruce Banner
3. Green Lantern	**c.** Tony Stark
4. The Incredible Hulk	**d.** Bruce Wayne
5. Iron Man	**e.** Peter Parker
6. The Lone Ranger	**f.** Dan Reid
7. Robin	**g.** Alan Scott
8. The Shadow	**h.** Clark Kent
9. Spider Man	**i.** Lamont Cranston
10. Superman	**j.** Britt Reid

Answers: 1d, 2j, 3g, 4b, 5c, 6f, 7a, 8i, 9e, 10h.

THE JUSTICE SOCIETY OF AMERICA

Back in the 1940s, when America was at war, comic book characters, too, were busy keeping the world safe, fighting for "truth, justice and the American way." To this end, the Justice Society of America was formed. Here were its members.

Atom	Red Tornado
Batman	Sandman
Black Canary	Spectre
Green Lantern	Starman
Dr. Fate	Superman
Flash	Johnny Thunder
Hawkman	Mr. Terrific
Hourman	Wildcat
Dr. Midnight	Wonder Woman

POPEYE'S VITAL STATISTICS

Height: 5 feet 6 inches

Weight: 158 pounds

Hair: red

Biceps: 7 inches

Forearm: 20 inches

Chest, expanded: 60 inches

Thigh: 7 inches

Calf: 20 inches

Spinach capacity: 36 tons

OLIVE OYL'S VITAL STATISTICS

Height: 5 feet 10 7/8 inches

Weight: 96 pounds 3 ounces

Arms: long

Nose: pickle

Neck: swan

Shoe size: 14AAAAAA

NETIQUETTE
14 Rules for Online Courtesy

Computer forums and chat lines are great ways for you to share information and ideas, meet new people — and have a lot fun to boot. With the information superhighway becoming more and more a part of our lives, a new kind of community is forming. Thousands of kids are already hooked into (and hooked on!) computer networks like CompuServe, America Online, and Prodigy. In the years ahead, chances are you'll be plugged directly into that vast computer network called the Internet. Whether you realize it or not, right now you are a citizen of a global village—and you'll want to be a good neighbor.

Swapping messages in forums and chatting live online are no different from sending letters or talking with a group of people at a party. There are right ways and wrong ways to go about it. No one likes someone who interrupts, who hogs the conversation or changes the subject, or who isn't tolerant of other people's opinions or mistakes. So you don't come off looking like a total feeb, here are some expert tips to make yourself welcome on computer forums.

1. Listen before you leap. Plunging into a forum discussion is like trying to jump in while your buddies are turning the jump rope. If your timing and rhythm are off, you'll get all tangled up—and no one will have any fun. Take some time just to read a lot of messages on the message board before sending any of your own. Before joining in a live forum discussion, just listen in for a while. You'll learn a lot by watching how the "pros" handle themselves.

2. Get your FAQs straight. FAQs are "frequently asked questions." Everyone who's new to the online world has lots of questions. Chances are, you're not the first person to wonder how to download a file or send a message to a pen pal. Before taking up other people's time with a question that's been asked a squillion times already, check to see if the forum's library has an FAQ file that contains answers to the basic questions everyone has. Access it and read it carefully. Then, if you still don't understand something or if you need other information, feel free to post a message to other members.

3. Don't send test messages. There's no need to waste time (and money) sending messages like "Hello! Just testing to see if this works." Better to go ahead and say what you want to say. When you get a response, you'll know the system is functioning—and you won't take up valuable cyberspace in the process. (Sometimes people on forums waste so much time saying "Hi!" and "Hello" to each other that they never say anything important. There are even some forums that have a rule: "No hi!")

4. Stay "on topic." If everybody in the forum is discussing pets, it's impolite to say, "Hey, did anybody see that new *Power Rangers* episode yesterday?" And post your questions to the appropriate forum. A forum on in-line skating is no place to start discussing the way-cool fatalities in the latest war-'n-gore game.

5. Think twice; post once. Once you've sent a message, you can't take it back. Before you hit the "send" button—and experience that twinge of regret an ohnosecond later (see "The Top 18 Techno-Jargon Terms," page 259), read over what you've written. If there's a chance it might be misunderstood, that it might hurt someone's feelings, or that it might make you look like a total dweeb, erase it. After all, that's what the "DEL" key is for.

6. Watch your tone of voice. If you call your best buddy a dweeb, he'll know from your smile or that playful punch in the arm that you're just giving him a hard time. Online, though, you don't have that luxury. Words on a computer screen don't always carry the teasing or joking tone of the voice we intended. If your joke might be misinterpreted, you can soften it a little by using an expression like <grin> or one of the "smileys," like the ones listed on page 274). Be careful, though—some grouchy people really hate those things. :>(

7. DON'T USE ALL CAPITAL LETTERS WHEN YOU WRITE! It looks like you're shouting, and that's what people will think you're doing IF YOU WRITE LIKE THIS.

8. Watch your temper. There's a great temptation to be real snotty when we're talking to people whose faces we can't see and whose names we don't know. If someone makes a goof or says something clueless, it's all too easy to say "What an idiot!" (or worse). In computer talk, this is known as "flaming." All too often, forum discussions wind up as insult wars. This is an utter waste of time for everyone. If you *must* respond with a strong comment, do everyone a favor: At least give a little warning by writing "Flame" or "Flame on!" before launching your tirade. Or ask your fellow net-neighbor to continue the discussion privately, via e-mail (or Instant Messages), instead of mucking up the public forum. And you'd better be sure of your facts, or you risk getting flamed yourself. Better yet: Just chill out. Thumper's mother was right: If you can't say something nice, clam up.

9. Don't correct people's grammar or spelling. Nobody's perfekt. Some forum users are better typists than others. Other people are in a hurry to post their comment and will send messages without bothering to clean them up. Remember, too, that online services let you talk with people from all kinds of places and backgrounds. Some people may not even be from your country and may not be as adept at using English as you. Be tolerant of other people's errors, and hope that others will be tolerant of yours!

10. Do correct your own grammar or spelling! Try to clean up your own act as much as possible. Nobody likes struggling to read sloppy writing, whether it's on a piece of paper or a computer screen. Do the proofreading. You'll be more likely to receive responses to your postings if you look like a careful and conscientious writer and not some slob.

11. Don't believe everything you read. Some people use the forum to create new identities for themselves. They pretend to be smarter, richer, better looking, older, or younger than they really are. Just because they sign their message "Shaq" or "Chelsea Clinton" doesn't mean that's who's on the other end of the wire. Computer forums are open to everyone —and unfortunately that sometimes means a few creeps and losers will be hanging out.

12. Don't be a spoiler. If you're talking about a great movie you saw or a book you read, don't ruin it for others by giving away the surprises. If you just *gotta* say something to make your point, give fair warning: Print the word SPOILER! before your comment.

13. Don't assume your e-mail will be kept private. You may think your remarks to another person are no one else's business. But once you've posted a message, you have no control over what might happen to it. If you're using a school's system or your parents' computer service account, your notes might wind up in some unexpected places — like the principal's office or your mom's boss's desk. You may even find your flames included in a Top Online Insults list in the next edition of this book!

14. Share what you know. After a few weeks online, you'll be a pro. If you see messages from people who are struggling to catch up, help them out. Maybe you've discovered some great new way to make your computer dance and do tricks. Tell others! Remember, the info highway is a two-way street. Download the program onto your hard drive, and you're up and running. Having all those programs sitting there waiting for you on the disc is a big (and expensive) temptation. If you sample something you think you'd like, don't just pick up the phone. Show the program to your mom or dad. Talk about what the program does and how you'd use it. Best of all, find out if any of your friends — at school or online — use and like the program. Go to the software store and ask for a complete demonstration — and see if there's another program that does the same thing but costs less.

THE TOP 18 TECHNO-JARGON TERMS

1. A little short on RAM: Lacking the brains ("wetware") to complete the task at hand.

2. Alpha geek: The person with the most technological skills.

3. Banana problem: Something that less technically

minded people (that is, big dumb gorillas) can't handle. The more bananas, the bigger the problem. Example: "Installing this game is a two-banana problem."

4. Blog: Short for Weblog; a Web page featuring short, frequent updates.

5. Boat anchor: An obsolete computer. (Also, "doorstop.")

6. Cobweb: A Web page that hasn't been updated in ages.

7. Dancing baloney: Animated doodads added to a Web page to cover up bad design.

8. Dot snot: A young dot-com millionaire.

9. Double geeking: Using two computers at the same time.

10. Frob: A thing. Useful when you have two "unspecified objects" on hand. "Stick that frob on the thing over there."

11. Hactivism: Anything from online activism (e-mail campaigns, online petitions) to the actual malicious hacking of Web sites, "denial of service" attacks on Web servers, "mail bombs," and other acts of online sabotage.

12. Muggle: In Harry Potter's world, the muggles are the nonwizards. In its real world usage, a muggle is an unimaginative person. In the hacker world, it means anyone who's not a hacker.

13. Screen-saver mode: When you're so bored that your brain shuts down and your face goes into neutral.

14. Spamoflage: Methods used by e-mail spammers to hide the true nature of their messages.

15. Tetwrist: A form of repetitive stress injury caused by extended sessions playing computer games.

16. User Eye-D: To meet someone face-to-face for the first time after having only an online relationship.

17. Vulcan nerve pinch: The key combination that resets or reboots a computer or program (such as Ctrl-Alt-Delete, which is also known as the "three-fingered salute").

18. Wombat: "Waste of Money, Brains, and Time." Applies to a person, product, or project.

10 WAYS TO USE ONLINE SERVICES TO GET HELP WITH YOUR HOMEWORK

If you thought it was tough studying history now, check out this factoid: Some future-minded folks predict that by the year 2010, the amount of information in the world will *double every 70 days!* This means that on the last day of your school year there will be 4 TIMES as many facts to keep straight as there were on the first day! Some day soon, "knowbots" will be available to track down information for us. For now, though, if you wanna keep up—better get wired!

1. Join forums, chat lines, and bulletin boards. Ask other kids in your grade for help.

2. Post messages asking for responses from experts in the field. Many professionals are glad to share what they know, especially to help promote the cause of education.

3. Scour electronic encyclopedias—plenty of good, basic information.

4. Search databases—magazines, newspapers—for up-to-the-minute facts. Sometimes these searches can be costly, especially if you download a whole lot of articles. But for doing research on current topics, they're hard to beat.

5. Explore other facets of the reference sections. Depending on your service, you can get book and movie reviews, information about health and medicine, an astounding array of government facts and statistics—just about anything you can imagine. And a lot of it is available at no extra charge!

6. One picture is worth a thousand bytes (give or take a million). Clip art, screen-capturing programs, or online image libraries might have just the pix you need to make your point visually.

7. Check out shareware forums for programs that can jazz up your work: Phat fonts, powerful presentation programs, even sound bites—chances are someone out there has created just the tool you need.

8. Plug in to your public library. In some communities, you can tap directly into your library's computer to find out what's available. Knowing whether the library carries a certain book or periodical, and if it's there on the shelf, can save you time, trips, and trouble.

9. Beg, plead, and cajole your parents to turn your home computer into a direct Internet node. (Fat chance!)

10. Fool around! Sometimes playing with the computer can lead you into unexpectedly rich areas—databases, discussion groups, resources—that you might not have found otherwise. Follow your hunches and see where they lead.

7 GREAT SEARCH ENGINES FOR KIDS

A search engine is a service on the World Wide Web that allows you to browse links to any specific interests you might have. All the search engines listed here are aimed at kids. To use them, you just go to their Web sites and then search for whatever you want. You'll get a much more interesting selection of choices than if you just looked for the information on AOL or Microsoft Network.

1. AOL Search for Kids Only. **www.aol.com/netfind/kids**

2. Ask Jeeves for Kids. A great educational search engine. Ask a question and find the answer. **www.ajkids.com**

3. Berit's Best Sites for Children. Links to 1,000 great kids' sites. **www.beritsbest.com**

4. KidsClick! Great site with links to Web sites covering a wide range of interests. **www.kidsclick.org**

5. LycosZone. Colorful and user-friendly.
www.lycoszone.lycos.co

6. Net-mom's Internet Safe House. Safe and secure, this search engine has lots of great links. **www.netmom.com**

7. Yahooligans. A database of about 20,000 sites that are kid-safe. You can search or select from a directory for the topic you want. www.yahooligans.com

9 GREAT WEB SITES FOR KIDS WHO ARE INTERESTED IN READING AND WRITING

If you want to sharpen your reading skills or become a better writer, you'll find something useful at each of these sites.

1. Biography Maker. Learn how to research a person and write a biography.
www.bham.wednet.edu/bio/biomaker.htm

2. Children's Writing Resource Center. It's an extensive site that helps kids learn to write and also posts writing done by kids. www.write4kids.com/index.html

3. Fake Out! The Definition Guessing Game. Choose one of the listed words and guess its definition.
www.eduplace.com/dictionary/

4. KidNews. A writing service for students and teachers around the world. www.kidnews.com/

5. National Scholastic Press Association. Helps students become better reporters, writers, and editors.
www.studentpress.org/nspa/

6. Storyteller. Kids can contribute stories about themselves or read the many stories written by children from around the world. www.edbydesign.com/storyteller/index.html

7. Word of the Day. *Webster's* dictionary presents a new word every day. www.m-w.com/cgi-bin/mwwod.pl

8. Writing Room for Kids. Learn how to write poetry, stories, essays, letters, and jokes. kidslangarts.about.com/kids/kidslangarts/cs/writingroom/index.htm

9. The Young Writers Club. Encourages children of all ages to enjoy writing as a creative pastime.

> www.cs.bilkent.edu.tr/~david/derya/ywc.html

11 GREAT WEB SITES IF YOU LOVE MUSIC

Whether you want to learn more about the history of music or you are interested in learning a particular instrument, you'll probably enjoy these sites.

1. Beatles Lyric Archive. All the lyrics arranged alphabetically by song title.

> www.geocities.com/SunsetStrip/Limo /3518/

2. Children's Music Web. Links to 5 great music sites.

> www.childrensmusic.org

3. The Classical MIDI files. Listen to classical music right on the Web. **www.prs.net/midi.html**

4. Garden State Pops Youth Orchestra. Learn how to read music and listen to musical instruments. **www.gspyo.com/**

5. Harmonica Lessons. The most complete, in-depth technique instruction anywhere and instruction on how to jam to the blues. **www.harmonicalessons.com/**

6. Music Notes. **www.library.thinkquest.org/15413**

7. Musical Instrument Encyclopedia. This multimedia Instrument Encyclopedia is a student project constructed for entertainment and educational purposes.

> www.Lehigh.edu/zoellner/encyclopedia.html

8. Piano on the Net. A complete set of piano lessons on the Web. Put your keyboard next to your keyboard and off you go! **www.artdsm.com/music.html**

9. PlayMusic! **www.playmusic.org**

10. Rock & Roll Hall of Fame and Museum. Listen to audio clips of inductees to the Rock & Roll Hall of Fame and learn about rock and roll history. **www.rockhall.com/**

11. TV Theme Songs and More. Popular TV and movie theme songs. **themes.editthispage.com/**

7 GREAT WEB SITES FOR KIDS INTERESTED IN FILM AND TV

If you want to learn more about your favorite movies and TV shows, check out these sites and find out all there is to know.

1. About TV for kids. Learn about your favorite shows. Updated daily. **www.kidstv.about.com/mbody.html**

2. Disney. Complete site for everything Disney, including games, music, and activities, all connected to the Disney channel. **www.disney.com**

3. Imax. This site is both fun and educational.
  www.imax.com

4. The Force.net. A daily dose of *Star Wars*.
  www.theforce.net

5. Mr. Showbiz. Recent movie releases, interviews with stars, and daily headlines about movies.
  www.mrshowbiz.go.com

6. Nickelodeon. A great site. Colorful and loads of fun. Covers all of Nickelodeon's shows and characters. **www.nick.com**

7. Warner Brothers Kids Page. Shows, games, contests, and free stuff. **www.kidswb.com**

13 GREAT WEB SITES FOR KIDS WHO LIKE TO PLAY ONLINE GAMES

Some of the games you'll find on these sites are easy, while some are very difficult, but they will all keep you entertained for hours.

1. Big Nate. Nate's the star of Big Nate.

www.unitedmedia.com/comics/bignate/

2. Bonus.com. Great games. **www.bonus.com**

3. Checkers. Will the black or the red pieces win this time? **darkfish.com/checkers/Checkers.html**

4. Chess Is Fun. Want to learn how to play chess? **www.princeton.edu/~jedwards/cif/intro.html**

5. Chinook. Computer-generated Checkers. This is a very tough game. **http://web.cs.ualberta.ca/~chinook/**

6. Comic Zone. Your very own newspaper comics section! Includes "Dilbert," "Peanuts," "Rose Is Rose," and a lot more. **www.unitedmedia.com/comics/**

7. DangerMouse. An adventure game with the greatest secret agent in the world. **www.dangermouse.org/index2.html**

8. Enigma. This is a puzzle site based on a toy that was popular many years ago. Great challenges! **www.stephen.com/enigma/enigma.html**

9. Headbone.com. Win prizes at this site. **www.headbone.com/games**

10. Javagameplay.co. Arcade games. **www.javagameplay.com**

11. Kids Domain. Educational games. **www.kidsdomain.com**

12. Kidscom Games. You'll need signed parental approval to register. This is a great site. **www.kidscom.com**

13. The Riddler. Arcade games. **www.riddler.com**

8 GREAT WEB SITES FOR GIRLS

Go to these sites to learn about the accomplishments of women in all walks of life, to communicate with other girls, and for advice on just about anything.

1. Distinguished Women. Biographies of writers, educators, scientists, heads of state, politicians, civil rights crusaders, artists, entertainers, and others. **www.DistinguishedWomen.com**

2. 4,000 Years of Women in Science. This site lists more than 125 names from our scientific and technical past and links you to more extensive sites about each of these people.
www.astr.ua.edu/4000WS/

3. Girl Power! A national public education campaign sponsored by the U.S. Department of Health and Human Services and one of the hottest sites for girls.
www.health.org/gpower/index.htm

4. Girl Tech and GirlTech Game Cafe. Web pages just for girls. An opportunity for girls to read about and communicate with one another; you can also create stories or work on science and math games.
www.girltech.com/Game_Cafe/GC_menu_frame.html

5. Girls Incorporated. Girls Incorporated is a national youth organization dedicated to helping every girl become strong, smart, and bold. www.girlsinc.org/

6. Go Girl! An online magazine for girls on sports and fitness. www.gogirlmag.com/

7. National Women's Hall of Fame. Short biographies of 125 remarkable women.
www.sbaonline.sba.gov/womeninbusiness/fame.html

8. Women of NASA. The Women of NASA resource was developed to encourage more young women to pursue careers in math, science, and technology.
quest.arc.nasa.gov/women/intro.html

10 GREAT WEB SITES TO VISIT IF YOU NEED HELP WITH HOMEWORK

1. B. J. Pinchbeck's Homework Helper
tristate.pgh.net/~pinch13

2. Kid's Web www.npac.syr.edu/textbook/kidsweb/

3. Encarta Encyclopedia encarta.msn.com

4. ePlay Homework Help www.eplay.com/homework

5. Factmonster www.factmonster.com
6. Homework Central www.homeworkcentral.com
7. KidsInternet.dk.com. www.kidsinternet.dk.com
8. School Age www.charleston.net/kids/
9. StudyWeb www.studyweb.com
10. ZoomSchool www.enchantedlearning.com/school

6 COOL CHAT ROOMS

If you love to communicate with other kids and are interested in making new friends around the world, you will love these chat rooms. They are safe for kids, which means that someone monitors them very closely, and only kid-appropriate subjects are allowed. Even so, when you communicate with strangers online, be careful. Read the lists of 5 FBI Tips for Internet Safety, on page 30, and Netiquette, page 255.

1. Beadbone Zone. Talk about anything, find great jokes, and get advice from Velma. www.headbonezone.com
2. Cyber Safe Kids Club. International chats that allow children to communicate safely with other kids from around the world. www.cybersafekids.com
3. Key Pals Club. A place for young people, teachers, and students to locate and correspond with other students around the world. www.mightymedia.com/keypals
4. Kid City Live Kids Chat. Lots of different topics you can choose from here. www.child.net/kcchat.htm
5. Kidscom Graffitti Wall. Excellent chat rooms here on just about everything. Nicely designed and easy to use.
www.kidscom.com
6. Zeeks. Kids can chat with their friends in adult-monitored rooms. www.zeeks.com/

12 GREAT WEB SITES FOR KIDS INTERESTED IN SCIENCE AND TECHNOLOGY

If you are curious and want to learn about the world around you, if you want to know how things work or need to research a project for school, these sites will be helpful.

1. Ask Dr. Math. From the Math Forum at Swarthmore College. Find math information or ask a specific question.
forum.swarthmore.edu/dr.math/dr-math.html

2. Bill Nye, the Science Guy. The online lab for this popular TV show. **nyelabs.kcts.org**

3. Cells Alive! All the facts on cells, including pictures.
www.cellsalive.com

4. The Constellations and Their Stars. Everything you need to know about the Milky Way.
www.astro.wisc.edu/~dolan/constellations/

5. Cool Science for Curious Kids. Answers to some interesting questions. **www.hhmi.org/coolscience**

6. Desert Life. Information about and pictures of the plants, animals, and people of America's deserts.
www.desertusa.com/life.html

7. Discovery Online. The Discovery Channel's Web site.
www.discovery.com

8. The Exploratorium **www.exploratorium.edu**

9. How Stuff Works. For the curious student who wants to know everything. **www.howstuffworks.com**

10. Kids @ Nationalgeographic. Interesting facts from around the world. Great photos. **www.nationalgeographic.com/kids**

11. Periodic Table of the Elements. Atomic number, symbol weight, and history. **pearl1.lanl.gov/periodic/**

12. Whelmers. Demonstrated experiments for all ages— designed to "whelm" (as in "overwhelm") students!
www.mcrel.org/whelmers/

22 GREAT WEB SITES
FOR SPORTS FANS

1. The Ancient Olympic Games. In this exhibit, you can compare ancient and modern Olympic sports.

www.perseus.tufts.edu/Olympics/

2. Athletes in Gold. Athletes in Gold hopes to inspire future champions. **home.earthlink.net/~athngold/**

3. Bigleaguers. The only place on the Internet where you can find personal Web sites for every player in the Major League Baseball Players Association.

www.bigleaguers.com/showpage.asp?thepage=home

4. Black Baseball's Negro League. Learn about the origins of the Negro Baseball League: what it was, why it was founded, and why it no longer exists.

www.blackbaseball.com/

5. International Tennis Federation. Player biographies and tournament info. Excellent section of rules of tennis.

www.itftennis.com/

6. Judo Information Site. World's biggest virtual Judo club, with the most complete information about the sport and art of Judo on the Internet. **www.JudoInfo.com**

7. Little League Baseball. Useful information on Little League, and you can gain access to the Little League Museum.

www.littleleague.org

8. The Locker Room: Sports for Kids. Facts and tips on almost all popular sports.

members.aol.com/msdaizy/sports/locker.html

9. Major League Baseball. The official site of Major League Baseball has an enormous amount of information.

www.majorleaguebaseball.com/

10. Major League Soccer. The official site of Major League Soccer. **www.mlsnet.com/index.html**

11. National Baseball Hall of Fame. History of the game of baseball. **baseballhalloffame.org/index.htm**

The ^All-New^ Book of Lists for Kids

12. National Basketball Association (NBA). This official site of the NBA contains information on games and players.
www.nba.com/

13. National Football League (NFL). Official site of the NFL provides the latest news and statistics. www.nfl.com

14. National Hockey League (NHL). Official site of the NHL has statistics and information on players and games.
www.nhl.com

15. Sports Illustrated for Kids. Get the latest issue online.
www.sikids.com

16. Tennis Worldwide. Provides sound tennis information, including information on Junior Tennis. www.tennisw.com/

17. USA Gymnastics Online. This site lists every top-level directory on USA Gymnastics Online, plus selected documents within each area.
www.usa-gymnastics.org/index-text.html

18. USATF Site. This is a rich site of the U.S. Track & Field Organization. Filled with information and statistics, it includes sections on juniors and the Olympics.
www.usatf.org/index.htm

19. U.S. Soccer Web Pages. Soccer fans gathered information from various sources in order to provide some general information for their fellow fans across the U.S.
www.Sams-Army.com

20. U.S. Fencing Association. Enormous amount of information on a sport that is not as well known as some of the highly popular professional sports. www.USFencing.org

21. WebSwim. Information on a range of swimming sports, including diving, synchronized swimming, lifeguard training, and water polo. www.webswim.com/index.htm

22. Women's National Basketball Association (WNBA). Find out about the Women's NBA. www.wnba.com

10 GREAT WEB SITES FOR KIDS INTERESTED IN THE ARTS

Improve your artistic abilities, learn more about your favorite artists, or visit some of the world's finest museums by using the sites listed here.

1. A. Pintura, Art Detective. Outstanding, clever, and stimulating site. **www.eduweb.com/pintura/**

2. The Art Institute of Chicago. Includes activities for kids. **www.artic.edu/aic/kids/index.html**

3. The @rt Room. Provides a learning environment for exploring the world of art. **www.arts.ufl.edu/art/rt_room/index.html**

4. The Fine Arts Museums of San Francisco. Fantastic site. Combines multiple museum holdings in an over-75,000-item database. **www.thinker.org/index.shtml**

5. Inside Art. An adventure inside art history. **www.eduweb.com/insideart/index.html**

6. Metropolitan Museum of Art, New York. From one of the largest and finest art museums in the world. The page for young people includes family guides, museum hunts, and art games. **www.metmuseum.org/explore/index.asp; www.metmuseum.org/htmlfile/education/kid.html**

7. National Gallery of Art, Washington, D.C. Full-screen views of whole paintings. Includes information on artists. **www.nga.gov/**

8. National Gallery of Canada, Ottawa. Contains the largest collection of Canadian art in the world. Requires plug-ins. **national.gallery.ca/**

9. National Museum of the American Indian, Washington, D.C. Part of the Smithsonian. Arts of Native Americans. **www.si.edu/nmai/**

10. Origami. Instructions in the traditional Japanese art of paperfolding. **www.origami.vancouver.bc.ca/**

22 ONLINE ACRONYMS

An acronym is an abbreviation made up of the first letters of other words. Two common acronyms that actually graduated into honest-to-Pete real words are *laser* (Light Amplification by Simulated Emission of Radiation) and *scuba* (Self-Contained Underwater Breathing Apparatus).

Acronyms (pronounceable and otherwise) are popular in the computer world because they save precious time, space, and bytes.

1. BRB — Be right back
2. BTW — By the way ...
3. FAQs — Frequently asked questions
4. FWIW — For what it's worth
5. FUBAR — [Fouled] up beyond all recognition
6. FYI — For your information
7. GDR — Grinning, ducking, and running (after making a smart remark)
8. IAE — In any event
9. IMCO — In my considered opinion
10. IMHO — In my humble opinion
11. IMO — In my opinion
12. IOW — In other words
13. NRN — No response necessary (to prevent lots of "thanks for the message!" messages)
14. OIC — Oh, I see!
15. OTOH — On the other hand
16. PITA — Pain in the ASCII
17. ROF — Rolling on floor, laughing
18. RSN — Real soon now
19. RTFM — Read the [flippin'] manual!
20. SNAFU — Situation normal, all [fouled] up
21. TAL — Thanks a lot
22. TIA — Thanks in advance

BONUS: 9 ACRONYMS THAT DON'T EXIST BUT SHOULD

1. HDYWTDT   How do you work this dratted thing?
2. ICTIAM   I can't take it anymore.
3. IGU   I give up.
4. MPADMC   My parents are driving me crazy.
5. NGA   No geeks allowed.
6. POD   Party on, dude.
7. SHMUK   Shows how much you know.
8. TIC   This is cool.
9. TWYT   That's what you think.

14 SMILEYS

Smileys are also known as emoticons and are used by computer hacks to bring a little humor to the world of high technology. When you're communicating online, use these symbols (or make up your own) to help get your messages across.

1. :-)   Basic smile
2. ;-)   A wink and a smile
3. :-(A frown
4. (-:   User is lefthanded
5. 8-)   User is wearing sunglasses
6. :-[User is a vampire
7. :'-(User is crying
8. :-#   User wears braces
9. O :-)   User is an angel
10. :-D   User is laughing
11. :-X   User's lips are sealed
12. =):-)=   User is Abe Lincoln
13. d:-)   User likes baseball
14. @@@@@@:)   User is Marge Simpson!

6

TV, Movies, and Music

56 TV NETWORK ADDRESSES

"Fifty-seven channels and nothing's on," sang Bruce Springsteen in 1992. If you feel that way, too, write to the TV networks and let them know. You can also use these addresses to find out more about your favorite show or TV personality.

1. A&E Network
   235 E. 45th St.
   New York, NY 10017

2. ABC
   New York, NY 10017
   77 W. 66th St.
   New York, NY 10023

3. American Movie
   Classics
   150 Crossways Park W.
   Woodbury, NY 11797

4. Black Entertainment
   Television
   1900 W Pl., NE
   Washington, DC 20018

5. Bravo
   150 Crossways Park W.
   Woodbury, NY 11797

6. C-SPAN
   400 N. Capitol St., NW,
   Suite 600
   Washington, DC 20001

7. Cable News Network
   One CNN Center
   P.O. Box 105366
   Atlanta, GA 30348

8. Cartoon Network
   One CNN Center
   P.O. Box 105366
   Atlanta, GA 30348

9. CBS
   51 W. 52nd St.
   New York, NY 10019

10. Cinemax
    1100 Ave. of the
    Americas
    New York, NY 10036

11. CNBC
    2200 Fletcher Ave.
    Fort Lee, NJ 07024

12. CNN Headline News
    One CNN Center
    P.O. Box 105366
    Atlanta, GA 30348

13. Comedy Central
    1775 Broadway
    New York, NY 10019

14. Court TV
    600 Third Ave., 2nd
    Floor
    New York, NY 10016

15. The Discovery Channel
7700 Wisconsin Ave.
Bethesda, MD 20814

16. The Disney Channel
3800 W. Alameda Ave.
Burbank, CA 91505

17. E! Entertainment
Television
5670 Wilshire Blvd.
Los Angeles, CA 90036

18. Encore
5445 DTC Pkwy.,
Suite 600
Englewood, CO 80111

19. ESPN
ESPN Plaza
935 Middle St.
Bristol, CT 06010

20. The Family Channel
2877 Guardian La.
P.O. Box 2050
Virginia Beach, VA
23450

21. FLIX
1633 Broadway
New York, NY 10019

22. Fox Broadcasting
Company
P.O. Box 900
Beverly Hills, CA
90213

23. Fox News Channel
1211 Ave. of the
Americas
New York, NY 10036

24. fX and fXM: Movies
from Fox
P.O. Box 900
Beverly Hills, CA
90213

25. Galavision
9405 NW 41st St.
Miami, FL 33178

26. The Golf Channel
7580 Commerce
Center Dr.
Orlando, FL 32819

27. HBO
1100 Ave. of the
Americas
New York, NY 10036

28. The History Channel
235 E. 45th St.
New York, NY 10017

29. Home & Garden
Television
9701 Madison Ave.
Knoxville, TN 37932

30. Home Shopping
Network
1529 U.S. Rte. 19 S.
Clearwater, FL 33546

31. The Learning Channel
7700 Wisconsin Ave.
Bethesda, MD 20814

32. Lifetime
309 W. 49th St.
New York, NY 10019

33. The Movie Channel
1633 Broadway
New York, NY 10019

34. MSNBC
2200 Fletcher Ave.
Fort Lee, NJ 07024

35. MTV
1515 Broadway
New York, NY 10036

36. The Nashville Network
2806 Opryland Dr.
Nashville, TN 37214

37. NBC
30 Rockefeller Plaza
New York, NY 10112

38. Nickelodeon
1515 Broadway
New York, NY 10036

39. PBS
3120 Braddock Pl.
Alexandria, VA 22314

40. QVC
1365 Enterprise Dr.
West Chester, PA
19380

41. Sci-Fi Channel
1230 Ave. of the
Americas
New York, NY 10020

42. Showtime
1633 Broadway
New York, NY 10019

43. STARZ
5445 DTC Pkwy.,
Suite 600
Englewood, CO 80111

44. TBS SuperStation
One CNN Center
P.O. Box 105366
Atlanta, GA 30348

45. Telemundo
2290 W. Eighth Ave.
Hialeah, FL 33010

46. The Travel Channel
2690 Cumberland
Pkwy., Suite 500
Atlanta, GA 30339

47. Turner Classic Movies
One CNN Center
P.O. Box 105366
Atlanta, GA 30348

48. Turner Network
Television
One CNN Center
P.O. Box 105366
Atlanta, GA 30348

49. TV Food Network
1177 Ave. of the
Americas
New York, NY 10036

50. United Paramount
Network (UPN)
(UPC)
5555 Melrose Ave.
Marathon 1200
Los Angeles, CA 90038

51. Univision
9405 NW 41st St.
Miami, FL 33178

52. USA Network
1230 Ave. of the
Americas
New York, NY 10020

53. VH1
1515 Broadway
New York, NY 10036

54. WB Television
Network
4000 Warner Blvd.
Building 34R
Burbank, CA 91522

55. The Weather Channel
2600 Cumberland
Pkwy.
Atlanta, GA 30339

56. WGN
2501 W. Bradley Pl.
Chicago, IL 60618

14 STAR WARS CHARACTERS YOU CAN WRITE TO FOR AUTOGRAPHS

1. R2-D2
Kenny Baker
c/o Star Wars Fan Club
P.O. Box 111000
Aurora, CO 80042

2. C-3PO
Anthony Daniels
c/o Star Wars Fan Club
P.O. Box 111000
Aurora, CO 80042

3. Princess Leia Organa
Carrie Fisher
1700 Coldwater Canyon
Beverly Hills, CA 90210

4. Han Solo
Harrison Ford
P.O. Box 49344
Los Angeles, CA 90049

5. Darth Vader
David Prowse
12 Marshalsea Rd.
London SE1 1HL, England
Dave Prowse, who played Darth Vader, is trying to raise
money for Dave Prowse's Force Against Arthritis and
asks that you send in a contribution of $15 for a signed
photograph of himself or $10 for an autograph on
something you send him.

6. The Voice of Darth Vader
James Earl Jones
P.O. Box 610
Pawling, NY 12564

7. Chewbacca
Peter Mayhew
c/o Star Wars Fan Club
P.O. Box 111000
Aurora, CO 80042

8. Uncle Owen Lars
Phil Brown
10907 Magnolia Blvd., Suite 284
N. Hollywood, CA 91601
Brown charges $15 for signed color photos, $10 for
signed black-and-whites, and $10 for his signature on
your item.

9. Red Leader
Drewe Henley
c/o Star Wars Fan Club
P.O. Box 111000
Aurora, CO 80042

10. Wedge Antilles–Red Two
Denis Lawson
c/o Star Wars Fan Club
P.O. Box 111000
Aurora, CO 80042

11. Biggs Darklighter–Red Three
Garrick Hagon
c/o Conway–Van Gelder–Robinson
18/21 Jermyn St., #300
London SW1Y 6HP, England

12. Jek Porkins–Red Six
William Hootkins
c/o Star Wars Fan Club
P.O. Box 111000
Aurora, CO 80042

13. Dutch–Gold Leader
Angus MacInnes
c/o Star Wars Fan Club
P.O. Box 111000
Aurora, CO 80042

14. Lt. Pol Treidum ("TK421")
Peter Sumner
c/o Morrissey Management Corporate Voices
77 Glebe Point Rd.
Glebe, NSW 2037, Australia

12 TV CHARACTERS YOU CAN WRITE TO

1. Barney
   c/o Lyrics Studio
   2435 N. Central Expy.
   Richardson, TX 75680

2. Bozo the Clown
   c/o WGN Television
   2501 W. Bradley Pl.
   Chicago, IL 60618

3. Buffy the Vampire
   Slayer
   c/o Studio Fan Mail
   1122 S. Robertson
   Blvd., #15
   Los Angeles, CA 90035

4. Felicity
   c/o Studio Fan Mail
   1122 S. Robertson
   Blvd.
   Los Angeles, CA 90035

5. Little Bear
   c/o Nick, Jr.
   Nickelodeon Viewer
   Services
   1515 Broadway
   New York, NY 10036

6. Malcolm in the Middle
   c/o Fox Television
   P.O. Box 900
   Beverly Hills, CA 90213

7. Moesha
   United Paramount
   Network (UPN)
   5555 Melrose Ave.
   Marathon 1200
   Los Angeles, CA 90038

8. The Muppets
   P.O. Box 20726
   New York, NY 10023

9. Nikki
   c/o Nikki
   The WB Network
   4000 Warner Blvd.
   Burbank, CA 91522

10. Scooby Doo
    WB
    4000 Warner Blvd.
    Burbank, CA 91522
    e-mail: scooby@car-
    toonnetwork.com

11. Bart Simpson
    c/o Twentieth Century
    TV
    Matt Groening's Office
    Box 900
    Beverly Hills, CA 90213

12. Titus
    P.O. Box 900
    Attn: Titus
    Beverly Hills, CA 90213

5 OF THE MOST POPULAR VOICEOVER ARTISTS AND THEIR ROLES

1. **Kelsey Grammer (the star of TV's *Frazier*).** Vladimir in *Anastasia*, Snowball in *Animal Farm*, Dr. Frankenollie in *Runaway Brain*, Sideshow Bob on *The Simpsons*, and Stinky Pete the Prospector in *Toy Story 2*.

2. **James Earl Jones.** Darth Vader in *The Empire Strikes Back*, the Narrator in *Judge Dredd*, Mufasa in *The Lion King*, Mufasa in *The Lion King II: Simba's Pride*, Emperor of the Night in *Pinocchio*, and the Emperor of the Night and the Narrator on *The Simpsons*.

3. **Eddie Murphy.** Mushu in *Mulan*, Superintendent Thurgoode Orenthal in *The PJs*, and the donkey in *Shrek*.

4. **Robin Williams.** The narrator in *A.I. Artificial Intelligence*, the Genie in *Aladdin*, Batty Koda in *Ferngully: The Last Rainforest*.

5. **Bruce Willis.** Muddy Grimes in *Beavis and Butt-head Do America*, Bruno the Kid in *Bruno the Kid*, and Mikey in *Look Who's Talking* and *Look Who's Talking Too*.

8 TIPS FOR KIDS WHO WANT TO BECOME VOICEOVER ARTISTS

1. **Be an interesting person.** To create an entertaining character, you have to have an imagination and be curious about life and the world around you.

2. **Read out loud.** Spend at least one hour a day reading out loud. It doesn't matter what you read. It could be a novel, a play, or even a newspaper. While you are doing this, try to play the roles you are reading. Get into it.

3. **Train your voice.** Singing lessons are a great way to start. They will strengthen your voice and help you develop an ear for different sounds.

4. Watch cartoons and listen to commercials. Try to imitate what you hear.

5. Record yourself. If you record yourself while you are practicing, you'll be able to hear what you really sound like to yourself and other people.

6. Put your body into it. If you are practicing a role, you'll put a lot more intensity into it if you are acting the role and not just speaking it. Imagine that you are that character and how the character might act.

7. Learn from life. Pay attention to what is going on in the world. Pay close attention to people you may meet who have interesting characteristics or quirks, and especially interesting voices.

8. Be good to yourself. Keep yourself fit. Don't smoke. You'll need a lot of energy for voiceover work. Have respect for and try to learn from others.

6 "DOUBLE DARE" SLOPPY SUPER SUPPLIES

If you've ever watched the Nickelodeon TV show *Double Dare,* you know that it can get *real* messy. How messy is it? Here's a list of the stuff they use in an average season of stunts.

1. 16,800 gallons of gak
2. 3,000 cans of whipped cream
3. 67,200 eggs
4. 1,600 gallons of pudding
5. 3,520 pies
6. 20,736 paper towels to clean it all up

THE 48 TOP-GROSSING KIDS' MOVIES OF ALL TIME

Here are the movies that made the most money at box offices around the world. Remember when you look at these numbers that when *Bambi* was released in 1942, it only cost about 10 cents to get into the movies. Had it been released today, when ticket prices are up over $5 almost everywhere, it would have made a lot more money.

1. *Star Wars: Episode I—The Phantom Menace* (1999), $922,300,000

2. *Jurassic Park* (1993), $919,700,000

3. *Harry Potter and the Sorcerer's Stone* (2001), $827,900,000

4. *Star Wars* (1977), $797,900,000

5. *The Lion King* (1994), $767,700,000

6. *E.T. the Extra-Terrestrial* (1982), $704,800,000

7. *The Lost World: Jurassic Park* (1997), $614,300,000

8. *Men in Black* (1997), $587,200,000

9. *The Lord of the Rings: The Fellowship of the Ring* (2001), $587,100,000

10. *Star Wars: Episode VI—Return of the Jedi* (1983), $572,700,000

11. *Star Wars: Episode V—The Empire Strikes Back* (1980), $533,800,000

12. *Home Alone* (1990), $533,700,000

13. *Aladdin* (1992), $501,900,000

14. *Indiana Jones and the Last Crusade* (1989), $494,700,000

15. *Toy Story 2* (1999), $485,700,000

16. *Shrek* (2001), $468,700,000

17. *Tarzan* (1999), $435,200,000

18. *Mrs. Doubtfire* (1993), $423,100,000

19. *The Mummy Returns* (2001), $415,100,000

20. *The Mummy* (1999), $413,300,000

21. *Batman* (1989), $413,100,000

22. *Robin Hood: Prince of Thieves* (1991), $390,400,000
23. *Raiders of the Lost Ark* (1981), $383,800,000
24. *Jurassic Park III* (2001), $364,200,000
25. *The Flintstones* (1994), $358,500,000
26. *Toy Story* (1995), $358,100,000
27. *A Bug's Life* (1998), $357,900,000
28. *Beauty and the Beast* (1991), $351,800,000
29. *Back to the Future* (1985), $350,600,000
30. *Who Framed Roger Rabbit?* (1988), $349,100,000
31. *Dinosaur* (2000), $347,800,000
32. *Pocahontas* (1995), $347,100,000
33. *How the Grinch Stole Christmas* (2000), $340,400,000
34. *Batman Forever* (1995), $335,000,000
35. *Indiana Jones and the Temple of Doom* (1984), $333,000,000
36. *Back to the Future Part II* (1989), $332,000,000
37. *The Hunchback of Notre Dame* (1996), $325,500,000
38. *The Mask* (1994), $320,900,000
39. *101 Dalmatians* (1996), $304,200,000
40. *Mulan* (1998), $303,500,000
41. *Hook* (1991), $300,800,000
42. *Stuart Little* (1999), $297,600,000
43. *X-Men* (2000), $294,100,000
44. *Ghostbusters* (1984), $291,600,000
45. *Doctor Dolittle* (1998), $290,100,000
46. *Batman Returns* (1992), $282,800,000
47. *Caspar* (1995), $282,200,000
48. *Home Alone 2: Lost in New York* (1992), $279,600,000

100 OF THE FIRST DISNEY CHARACTERS

Between 1920 and 1950, Walt Disney revolutionized animated film by creating techniques and effects that the world had barely dreamed of. These accomplishments alone would

 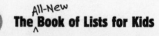

have ensured him a place in film history, but Disney went on to create some of the best-loved characters we've ever known. Mickey Mouse, for instance, was an immediate success when he was first presented to the world in 1928 in a film called *Steamboat Willie,* but Mickey was just one of the many who went on to become stars of the stage, screen, books, songs, toys, underwear — you name it.

The following list includes the first 100 Disney characters, the years in which they were introduced, and the movies in which they first appeared. These are not necessarily the most popular; some were selected for the interesting historical facts they represent. For instance, Donald Duck did not start out as a star but as a character in a film called *The Little Wise Hen.* Others are on the list for their charming names. And did you know that Disney created characters based on such real personalities as Albert Einstein and Adolf Hitler?

1. Abner   1936   *Country Cousin*
2. Agnes   1942   "Mickey Mouse" comic strip
3. Apollo   1940   *Fantasia*
4. Aunt Ena   1942   *Bambi*
5. Aunt Jemimi   1935   *Broken Toys*
6. Baby Weems   1941   *The Reluctant Dragon*
7. Bambi   1942   *Bambi*
8. Bambi's Mother   1942   *Bambi*
9. Bashful   1937   *Snow White and the Seven Dwarfs*
10. Ben Ali Gator   1940   *Fantasia*
11. Ben Buzzard   1943   *Flying Jalopy*
12. Big Bad Wolf   1933   *Three Little Pigs*
13. Blynken   1938   *Wynken, Blynken and Nod*
14. Br'er Bear   1946   *Song of the South*
15. Br'er Fox   1946   *Song of the South*
16. Br'er Rabbit   1946   *Song of the South*
17. Captain Churchmouse   1932   "Bucky Bug" comic strip

18.	Captain Doberman	1933	"Mickey Mouse" comic strip
19.	Captain Katt	1936	*Three Blind Mouseketeers*
20.	Casey	1946	*Make Mine Music*
21.	Casey, Jr.	1941	*The Reluctant Dragon*
22.	Chicken Little	1943	*Chicken Little*
23.	Chip	1943	*Private Pluto*
24.	Christopher Columbus	1949	*So Dear to My Heart*
25.	Clarabelle Cow	1929	*The Plow Boy*
26.	Clementine	1941	*The Reluctant Dragon*
27.	Cock Robin	1935	*Who Killed Cock Robin?*
28.	Daisy Duck	1937	*Donald Duck*
29.	Dale	1943	*Private Pluto*
30.	Dewey	1938	*Donald's Nephews*
31.	Doc	1937	*Snow White and the Seven Dwarfs*
32.	Donald Duck	1934	*The Little Wise Hen*
33.	Dopey	1937	*Snow White and the Seven Dwarfs*
34.	Ducky Lucky	1943	*Chicken Little*
35.	Dumbo	1941	*Dumbo*
36.	Eega Beeva	1948	"Mickey Mouse" comic strip
37.	Einstein	1941	*The Reluctant Dragon*
38.	Eli Squinch	1934	"Mickey Mouse" comic strip
39.	Ezra Beetle	1947	*Bootle Beetle*
40.	Ferdinand the Bull	1938	*Ferdinand the Bull*
41.	Figaro	1940	*Pinocchio*
42.	Gepetto	1940	*Pinocchio*
43.	Goosie Gander	1933	*Old King Cole*
44.	Grumpy	1937	*Snow White and the Seven Dwarfs*
45.	Henny Penny	1943	*Chicken Little*
46.	Hitler	1943	*Education for Death*
47.	Hortense	1937	*Donald's Ostrich*

All-New
The ^ Book of Lists for Kids

48.	Huey	1938	*Donald's Nephews*
49.	Humpty Dumpty	1931	*Mother Goose Melodies*
50.	Ichabod Crane	1949	*The Adventures of Ichabod Crane*
51.	Jack Horner	1931	*Mother Goose Melodies*
52.	Jack Spratt	1933	*Old King Cole*
53.	Jenny Wren	1935	*Who Killed Cock Robin?*
54.	Jiminy Cricket	1940	*Pinocchio*
55.	Johnny Appleseed	1948	*Melody Time*
56.	King Neptune	1932	*King Neptune*
57.	Little Hiawatha	1937	*Little Hiawatha*
58.	Little Minnehaha	1940	"Little Hiawatha" comic strip
59.	Little Toot	1948	*Melody Time*
60.	Mademoiselle Upanova	1940	*Fantasia*
61.	Mammy Two Shoes	1935	*Three Orphan Kittens*
62.	Mary, Mary, Quite Contrary	1933	*Old King Cole*
63.	Max Hare	1935	*Tortoise and the Hare*
64.	Mickey Mouse	1928	*Steamboat Willie*
65.	Minnie Mouse	1928	*Steamboat Willie*
66.	Monstro	1940	*Pinocchio*
67.	Montmorency Rodent	1941	"Mickey Mouse" comic strip
68.	Mortimer Mouse	1936	*Mickey's Rival*
69.	Mother Goose	1931	*Mother Goose Melodies*
70.	Mother Hubbard	1933	*Old King Cole*
71.	Mr. Bluebird	1946	*Song of the South*
72.	Noah	1933	*Father Noah's Ark*
73.	Nod	1938	*Wynken, Blynken and Nod*
74.	Pecos Bill	1948	*Melody Time*
75.	Pegleg Pete	1928	*Steamboat Willie*
76.	Phantom Blot	1939	"Mickey Mouse" comic strip
77.	Pied Piper	1933	*Old King Cole*
78.	Pinocchio	1940	*Pinocchio*

79.	Pluto	1930	*The Chain Gang*
80.	Reason	1943	*Reason and Emotion*
81.	Red Riding Hood	1934	*The Big Bad Wolf*
82.	Santa Claus	1932	*Santa's Workshop*
83.	Satan	1946	*Make Mine Music*
84.	Simple Simon	1931	*Mother Goose Melodies*
85.	Sleepy	1937	*Snow White and the Seven Dwarfs*
86.	Sluefoot Sue	1948	*Melody Time*
87.	Sneezy	1937	*Snow White and the Seven Dwarfs*
88.	Snow White	1937	*Snow White and the Seven Dwarfs*
89.	Stromboll	1940	*Pinocchio*
90.	Sylvester Shyster	1930	"Mickey Mouse" comic strip
91.	Tar Baby	1946	*Song of the South*
92.	Tetti Tatti	1946	*Make Mine Music*
93.	Three Blind Mouseketeers	1936	*Three Blind Mouseketeers*
94.	Thumper	1942	*Bambi*
95.	Thursday	1940	"Mickey Mouse" comic strip
96.	Turkey Lurkey	1943	*Chicken Little*
97.	Ugly Duckling	1931	*The Ugly Duckling*
98.	Widomaker	1948	*Melody Time*
99.	Wynken	1938	*Wynken, Blynken and Nod*
100.	Yensid	1940	*Fantasia*

THE MOVIE MONSTER HALL OF FAME

You probably wouldn't want to have one for a pet, and let's face it: You'd go crawling out of your skin in a minute if one slithered up to your bed on Halloween night. Still, we love to hate movie monsters. Here are some of the most vile creatures from the early days of the silver scream—uh, screen.

1. The Blob. In 1958 a meteor crashes to the earth. Amid the smoke and rubble, the Blob is born. Made of jelly, though not the kind you'd want on your peanut butter sandwich, it starts out weighing just a few ounces and grows until it's about the size of a house and weighs a few tons. The Blob devours everything in sight, including an entire diner and most of the other characters in the movie. But the hero, Steve McQueen, figures out the Blob's weakness: cold. Using carbon dioxide from fire extinguishers, he and his buddy freeze the thing and ship it off to Antarctica, where it remains until later that year, when Paramount brings out *The Return of the Blob.*

2. Dracula. No monster hall of fame would be complete without Dracula, who got his first starring movie role in a film called (what else?) *Dracula.* Related to the bat, he is a Transylvanian vampire. Once he bites his victims, that's it: They, too, become sadistic vampires, living off the blood of others, always searching out their next meal. Extremely handsome and invulnerable to bullets and knives, Dracula is finally done in by a wooden stake driven through his heart (see "8 Ways to Kill or Repel Dracula," page 298), but not for long. He returns in a long list of films that are being made right up to the present.

3. The Fly. We first meet him in the movie called *The Fly,* and you have to feel sorry for this creature. He gets his start when a scientist, Andre Delambre, screws up an experiment and winds up trading heads with a poor little innocent fly. Delambre's huge fly head makes him and everyone around him crazy until his wife finally squooshes him. We see him again in three more films: *Return of the Fly, Curse of the Fly,* and *The Fly II.*

4. Frankenstein. You have to give him credit—he started the ball rolling in 1931 as one of the first hideous movie monsters ever. He starred in a long list of films and even got his son, daughter, and bride into the act. Tall, superstrong, and completely horrifying, Frankenstein was known to break people in half and destroy anyone who tried to prevent him from performing his ghastly deeds. You'd be cranky too if you were made up of parts of dead bodies that had been brought to life by electricity. At the end of the classic film *Frankenstein,* the monster is finally trapped in a windmill and burned to death.

5. Ghidrah. Talk about rude house guests. In *Ghidrah: The 3-Headed Monster,* a Japanese film, we meet one of the strongest monsters in movie history. Visiting here from another planet, this fire-breathing, dragonlike monstrosity manages to destroy Tokyo, mess up half of Japan, and even nearly finish off three other movie-monster favorites—Godzilla, Mothra, and Rodan. But as things turn out, three heads are not better than one, and Ghidrah is finally flung back into outer space by his earth-born monster enemies. Keep an eye out for Ghidrah—he was never actually killed.

6. Godzilla. Before Godzilla learned the error of his ways and fought to save mankind in movies such as *Childrah—The 3-Headed Monster, Godzilla's Revenge, Godzilla vs. the Smog Monster,* and others, he was as bad as the rest in his own film called *Godzilla.* Known as the King of the Monsters, he was created by radiation from atomic testing (a popular monster-movie theme), stood about 200 feet tall, and weighed hundreds of tons. Godzilla managed to destroy ships, entire villages, and thousands of screaming Japanese before his creator, the peace-loving Dr. Serizawa, figured out that his superweapon, which will cut off all of Godzilla's oxygen, is the answer. Godzilla and the good doctor are both reduced to a pile of bones at the end of the film, with Tokyo left in ruins.

7. King Kong. What's 50 feet tall, has a chest that measures 60 feet all around, a 6-foot-wide mouth, and ears that are a foot long? A man-eating ape with a voracious appetite for humans as well as trains known as King Kong. The difference between Kong and most other movie monsters is that he had a heart. In the 1933 movie *King Kong,* he falls in love with lovely Ann Darrow. As if being shot by Cupid's arrow isn't bad enough, King Kong is finally felled by planes armed with machine guns that buzz all around him like flies on a hot summer's day. One of the most popular monsters of all time, King Kong actually had people rioting in the streets when his first film was released. Back for a number of encores, he also appeared in *King Kong Escapes, King Kong vs. Godzilla, King Kong vs. Frankenstein,* and in a 1977 remake of the original film.

8. Mighty Joe Young. In the film *Mighty Joe Young* we meet the kindest monster of all time. Discovered in an African jungle by a bunch of movie producers, our 12-foot-tall ape is brought to the U.S., where someone has the bright idea to make him a nightclub star. But Joe can't seem to adjust to performing in front of an audience, and he breaks out of his cage in an uncontrollable rage during which he terrorizes all in his path. Unfortunately, the authorities decide that anything that big has to be dangerous, and Joe is pursued by policemen ordered to shoot him dead. But there's a happy ending. Joe manages to prove his good intentions by saving a little girl from the top floor of a burning orphanage. He is finally forgiven his past destruction and returned to the African jungle, where he lives happily ever after.

9. Mothra. Picture a moth with wings the size of ocean liners and you've got a fair idea of one of the most popular film monsters of all time. In *Mothra,* the first of many Japanese films in which he starred, our old friend starts out as a giant caterpillar with silver eyes and goes on to become a virtually indestructible 200-ton moth whose wings can create tornadoes. Even a specially built atomic heat cannon does not faze him, but this turns out to be for the good of all, as we learn that all Mothra wants out of life is to protect his homeland and live in peace. After he saves some little girls (destroying much of Tokyo in the process), he flies back home.

10. The Mummy. Here's a present you definitely don't want to unwrap. When he's discovered in an ancient tomb by a group of archaeologists, the Mummy is actually dead. The trouble is, he doesn't know it, and he spends most of the movie chasing down and gruesomely killing his discoverers. The Mummy probably would have gotten all of them, except that in the end he falls in love with the wife of one remaining archaeologist and, in a moment of weakness, is shot by him. Nevertheless, he manages to return in a number of subsequent films. If you ever come across the Mummy on some dark night, you won't have any trouble recognizing him. He'll be wrapped in gauze from head to toe, have one eye closed and one open, and will be dragging one foot behind him. He's not terribly fast, but if he corners you, watch out! Chances are, he'll strangle you with one incredibly strong fist. (Joking.)

11. Nosferatu. "He bites, he sucks, he drains, he destroys." He's also one of the first vampires ever, having made his first appearance in the film *Nosferatu* in 1922 in the starring role. In the 1979 film *Nosferatu the Vampyre,* the "chiller of the night" manages to take over an entire ship and its sailors, whose blood he uses to quench his evil thirst. Although Nosferatu seems indestructible with his superstrong snapping fangs and irresistible hypnotic powers, he is, after all, vulnerable to daylight. When he is detained into the morning by Lucy, with whom he is in love, the sun's rays strike him like flames, and he dissolves into a mess of smelly, awful flesh.

12. Phantom of the Opera. Eric, as he was called before a fire seriously destroyed his face in the film *Phantom of the Opera,* was a music lover whose whole life centered around the Paris Opera House. Unfortunately, circumstances lead him to become a mean hermit living in a bizarre underground world, where he plays music, eats gourmet meals, and finds time to fall in love with one of the young opera stars,

Christine. For most of the film, he is hidden behind a mask, but when the kidnapped Christine finally rips it off his face, we encounter the real Eric: "Extraordinarily thin, his dress coat hung on a skeleton frame," with "eyes so deep one could hardly see the fixed pupils." Like many of his friends in the movies, the Phantom has a heart, and he spends many days teaching Christine to sing like an opera star. He is killed trying to save her from death in an accident that takes place in the midst of a performance.

13. Rodan. Sesame Street's big bird must have learned a lot from the original "Big Bird," Rodan, who thrilled movie audiences in the 1957 film in which he had the starring role. With a wingspan of over 500 feet and weighing over 150 tons (the egg from which he hatched was a whopping 100,000 cubic feet large), Rodan is the product of H-bomb tests that crack open the earth and hatch eggs that have been lying around for millions of years. For a bird, Rodan looks a lot like a lizard, with a long neck like a turkey and a steel-hard beak, which he uses to eat planes and ships. Bullets, missiles, and artillery can't kill him, and Rodan has a monstrously good time blasting apart cities all over the world. After Peking and Singapore are gone, Rodan meets his match in the form of a volcano, whose hot lava eventually burns him to death. Gone but not forgotten.

7 MORE MOVIE MONSTERS AND HOW THEY WERE FINALLY KILLED

1. The Deadly Mantis: It was gassed with cyanide bombs.

2. Them!: Got burned to death by flamethrowers.

3. The Mole People: Were killed in an earthquake.

4. The Tarantula: Got burned to death by an aerial napalm bomb.

5. The Beast from 20,000 Fathoms: Got shot in the throat with a radioactive isotope.

6. The Creeping Unknown: Was electrocuted by high-powered wires.

7. The Saucermen: In *Invasion of the Saucermen,* these guys were dissolved by high-intensity auto headlight beams.

4 FILMS WITH MONSTER VEGETABLES

1. *Attack of the Killer Tomatoes** (1978). Much tomato juice is shed.

2. *Attack of the Mushroom People* (1963). A real fungus.

3. *Invasion of the Star Creatures* (1965). An army of carrots terrorizes Earthlings.

4. *Please Don't Eat My Mother* (1973). A giant vegetable has its revenge.

* Okay, so the tomato is really a fruit.

16 WAYS IN WHICH MOVIES CHEAT

Ever wonder why, when the bad guy in a movie throws a knife, it always hits the target blade first? Have you noticed that only in films do caves have flat floors, heroes go for 72 hours without sleep, or that when a character turns on the radio, it's always just in time to hear whatever special announcement he's waiting to hear? Even the most realistic films cheat. Here are some other ways in which movies try to make you believe that the reel world is real.

1. If a villain takes an elevator, the hero can always beat him by taking the stairs, even if they're on the twentieth floor of the building.

2. Thunder and lightning always happen at the same time.

3. When the hero and villain are about to kill each other, they always have a conversation about it first.

4. All families have big breakfasts together each morning.

All-New
^

Mom makes scrambled eggs, pancakes, and French toast, even if she works.

5. Villains have no trouble renting helicopters with pilots who don't mind getting shot at.

6. Shooting people eight times will not necessarily kill them.

7. The hero doesn't feel any pain when he is shot at or beat up. But when his girlfriend tries to treat the wound, he winces.

8. The phone can ring about ten times before anyone picks it up.

9. Most laptop computers can penetrate even the most powerful programs and can even help blow up the world.

10. It can take weeks to travel into outer space, but it only takes about an hour to get back home.

11. Kids always know more than adults.

12. Even kids whose parents are off in Europe for a month have no problem taking care of themselves.

13. All foreigners speak English.

14. When someone lights a match in a dark place, the whole place lights up.

15. Minority characters such as Native Americans and Asians always know more stuff than Caucasians do.

16. When people talk on the telephone, they never say hello or good-bye.

8 MISTAKES IN <u>WILLY WONKA</u> AND THE CHOCOLATE FACTORY

1. When Willy Wonka plays the musical lock, Mrs. Teevee identifies the tune as one by Rachmaninoff. But it's really from the overture to *The Marriage of Figaro,* by Mozart.

2. In the TV room, Mike Teevee says, "Lights, camera, action," and you see the Oompa Loompa holding the camera put on a set of goggles. But a few seconds later he's putting them on *again.*

3. When Willy Wonka is first in the main candy room, he "picks" a mushroom and sings, "If you want to view Paradise," as he pokes a hole in the mushroom with his cane. But the mushroom already has about six or seven holes in it.

4. When Charlie is in the Fizzy Lifting Drink room going up in the air, you can see the harness he's attached to and the way it bunches up his pants.

5. When the passengers get onto the Wonkamobile, you can see a fancy design on the back wheel cover. But when they get out of the Wonkamobile, the design is gone, probably due to a lighting mistake.

6. Lots of times in the movie, people's hair gets messed up, but a few seconds later, it looks combed again.

7. When Charlie goes into Bill's candy store to buy a Wonkabar, Bill takes a clear glass jar off a shelf and opens it to see what's inside. Why would he have to open a see-through jar to see what's inside?

8. At the end of the movie, Grandpa George (Ernest Ziegler), Grandma Georgina (Dora Altman), and Grandma Josephine (Franziska Liebing) are not listed.

8 WAYS TO KILL OR REPEL DRACULA

If things start going "bump" in the middle of the night and you think you've trapped him at last, use one of the following easy methods to rid the world once and for all of this terrible monster!

1. Exposure to sunlight will kill him.

2. Failure to return to his coffin before morning will kill him.

3. He hates garlic and won't go near the stuff.

4. Holy water will destroy him.

5. Flashing a crucifix will burn him.

6. A shot with a silver bullet will be fatal.

7. A wooden stake hammered through his heart will nail him for good.

8. Turning off the TV usually works.

18 BAT-THINGS

1. Batarang
2. Batawake
3. Batboat
4. Batcave
5. Batcopter
6. Batcostumes
7. Batcuffs
8. Batcycle
9. Bathook
10. Batmobile
11. Batmobile Mobile Crime Computer
12. Batostat Antifire Activator
13. Batphone
14. Batpoles
15. Batrope
16. Batshield
17. Batsignal
18. Batsleep

12 DINOSAUR MOVIES THAT PREDATE JURASSIC PARK

1. *Baby . . . Secret of the Lost Legend* (1985). The baby dinosaur featured in this movie is adorable.

2. *Caveman* (1981). Starring Ringo Starr, of the Beatles, this is a comedy with some very funny effects and silly-looking dinosaurs.

3. *Dinosaurs* (1960). Cavemen face danger. The effects are so silly you'll laugh, even though it's not supposed to be a comedy.

4. *Gertie the Dinosaur* (1914). The first animated movie ever made.

5. *Godzilla, King of the Monsters* (1956). This Japanese movie features a fire-breathing lizard that threatens mankind. There were nine sequels to this movie, including *Godzilla vs. the Smog Monster*.

6. *Journey to the Center of the Earth* (1959). Based on the famous novel by Jules Verne, this film features scenes with prehistoric monsters discovered miles below the earth's surface. A classic adventure movie — don't miss this one.

7. *The Land Before Time* (1988). An animated movie about an orphaned dinosaur trying to find a new home and family.

8. *The Land That Time Forgot* (1975). Sailors on a submarine during World War I discover an unknown region of South America. Bad effects also make this one funny.

9. *The Lost World* (1925). A silent movie based on an adventure tale by Arthur Conan Doyle, the guy who invented Sherlock Holmes. Great special effects for its time.

10. *One Million B.C.* (1940). The special effects in this film were considered so great that they were used in many other movies, too.

11. *Teenage Caveman* (1958). A teenager searches for adventure and finds dinosaurs instead.

12. *When Dinosaurs Ruled the Earth* (1970). Good acting, great effects, and beautiful scenery make this one worth watching.

25 BLACK-AND-WHITE MOVIES (AND 1 IN COLOR) YOU SHOULD WATCH

Yes, they are old. And yes, they are in black-and-white. But they are all great, and each has something special to offer. So if you come across one of these movies while you're channel surfing or see one in your local video rental store, don't be so quick to pass it up. You'll find, as you watch these, that some of your favorite modern movies aren't as original as you thought they were.

1. *Abbott and Costello Meet Frankenstein* (1948). Dracula as played by Bela Lugosi wants to put Lou's brain into the monster's head. Abbott and Costello were around way before the Three Stooges, Beavis and Butt-head, or Pete and Pete ever hit the airwaves. They were funny half a decade ago and are still funny (but dead) today. Do you think we'll say the same thing about Beavis and Butt-head 50 years from now?

2. *The Adventures of Robin Hood* (1951). A great swashbuckler with an all-star cast. If you liked *The Princess Bride, The Three Musketeers,* or any similar movie, you'll be shocked to see that a lot of the best stuff that goes on in those movies (great duel scenes, for instance), were developed long ago.

3. *The Adventures of Tom Sawyer* (1928). Some hilarious scenes in this production of the Mark Twain's classic book. If you haven't read the book, see the movie. The book is much better, but you'll get an idea of what the story is about, and once you read this, you'll want to read more books by Mark Twain, like *The Adventures of Huckleberry Finn* (Tom Sawyer's mischievous best friend) and *The Prince and the Pauper.*

4. *Androcles and the Lion* (1952). A satire of ancient Rome. During the final days of the Roman Empire, a gentle Christian tailor named Androcles helps an ailing lion by removing a thorn from its paw. When Caesar, the Roman emperor, sentences a group of Christians to death by this beast, the lion refuses to harm the man who was so kind to him. Alan Young, who plays Androcles, later went on to become the star of the popular TV show *Mr. Ed.*

5. *Babes in Toyland* (1934). Laurel and Hardy star in this wonderful fantasy featuring storybook characters like Mother Goose and Mary and her lambs. Laurel and Hardy were a great comic duo, as silly as they come, and this is one of their best. The bogeymen scenes are great.

6. *The Bellboy* (1960). Possibly Jerry Lewis's funniest movie. He both wrote and directed this film, which basically has no plot. What the movie has, though, are some truly hilarious scenes in which Jerry plays a bumbling bellboy who can't seem to do anything right. By the way, Jerry was the original Nutty Professor. Check it out, it's better than the Eddie Murphy version.

7. *Call of the Wild* (1935). Based on Jack London's tale. Set in the Yukon, this adventure is about an abused husky named Buck. The movie was remade in 1972, 1976, and again in 1997 as *Jack London's Call of the Wild,* in which the story is told from the viewpoint of the husky. If you liked the movie *White Fang* you'll love *Call of the Wild.*

8. *Captains Courageous* (1937). An adaptation of Rudyard Kipling's novel. A spoiled 12-year-old boy, the only child of a millionaire business tycoon, leans too far over the rail of a luxury ocean liner, after consuming six ice cream sodas, and falls into the ocean, unbeknownst to anyone. He is rescued by a crusty but likable and kindly Portuguese fisherman named Manuel, who takes him under his wing.

9. *The Court Jester* (1956). This movie is actually in color, but because it's so wonderful, we just had to get it on our list. Starring Danny Kaye, this is one of the funniest movies ever made. Kaye plays a phony jester who gets involved in romance, court intrigue, and a deadly duel with Basil Rathbone. There are some scenes in this movie that are so funny, they will have you clutching your sides. The scenes in which they try to remember the lines "The pellet with the poison's in the vessel with the pestle; the flagon with the dragon has the brew that is true" are hilarious. This movie is a must.

10. *Curly Top* (1935). Shirley Temple, the cutest, most talented kid who ever starred in a movie (no kidding!) sings her famous "Animal Crackers in My Soup" in this one. It's a typical Shirley Temple setup: She's an orphan, and a rich guy adopts her, and then she helps him find a wife. But the songs are wonderful ("When I Grow Up," "Curly Top"), there are some really nice costumes, and Shirley was only 8 when she made the film. Adorable!

11. *David Copperfield* (1935). Freddie Bartholomew is the young David in this film based on the Charles Dickens classic novel. Dickens created an abused child who, like himself, struggles to become a writer. The film takes us through David's school days and next presents us with David as a young man and as an adult. With an all-star cast featuring comic legend W. C. Fields as Mr. Micawber, it's a great film from beginning to end.

12. *The Day the Earth Stood Still* (1951). A great science fiction movie even by today's standards. A humanlike alien lands on Earth protected by a robot. He offers mankind the cures to all of our major diseases, but in return, mankind must stop producing nuclear weapons. To make his point, he freezes all earthly machines, except for planes in flight and hospital equipment, for one hour. No special effects, but the robot is fascinating. Remember: Klaatu barada nikto!

13. *Great Expectations* (1946). Charles Dickens's story of an orphan brought to London society by a mysterious benefactor. From the nightmarish opening sequence on the windswept graveyard to the shadowy, musty mansion of the widow Havisham, there's a great, eerie feel to this one.

14. *Gunga Din* (1939). Based loosely on the poem "The Charge of the Light Brigade," by Rudyard Kipling, this movie takes place in British India during the Thuggee uprising. Three British soldiers, with the aid of an Indian waterboy, Gunga Din, fight the rebel forces in this comic adventure. This movie cost so much money to make that it nearly bankrupted RKO Studios.

15. *A Hard Day's Night* (1964). Great music and visual madness. This is the best Beatles movie of all, and it was wacky enough to affect not only our TV taste (The Monkees got most of their tricks from this movie) but the whole idea of weird rock videos. A must for Beatles fans and absolutely required viewing (there'll be a test on Friday!) if you don't know who the Beatles are.

16. *The Jackie Robinson Story* (1950). Jackie Robinson portrays himself as the first black man to play major league baseball. He encounters lots of racism while working his way up as a great ballplayer, and he paves the way for other black athletes to enter the major leagues. A great movie with lots of baseball history.

17. *Jailhouse Rock* (1957). One of Elvis Presley's better films. He portrays a convict who learns to play the guitar in prison and becomes a rock and roll star after being released. The dance sequence to the song "Jailhouse Rock" is one of the most memorable dance scenes in film. This movie explains why Elvis is called the King of Rock & Roll.

18. *King Kong* (1933). Everyone needs to see this classic film, not only because King Kong has become a folk hero of sorts but also because the effects here—some of the earliest uses of "live" animation—are hilarious. Kong's fur looks like a wet rug, and his size seems to change depending on the building he's trying to destroy. But the movie, especially the final scene, with Kong at the top of the Empire State Building, is a classic.

19. *The Mark of Zorro* (1940). Tyrone Power as the masked avenger of the poor. This movie has some great swordplay. Actor Basil Rathbone, who also appears in *The Adventures of Robin Hood* and was in real life a great swordsman, taught Tyrone Power how to fence for the film. This is the best of the Zorro movies.

20. *Mighty Joe Young* (1947). Joe was another one of those early film monsters with a heart of gold. Like King Kong, he falls in love with a beautiful girl, and when he gets upset, only her voice, singing "Beautiful Dreamer," will calm him down. There's a great scene in which Joe risks his own life to save some children from a burning building.

21. *Miracle on 34th Street* (1947). Kris Kringle goes to court to prove that he is Santa. Margaret O'Brien plays the little girl who is too grown up to believe in him but who eventually comes to face reality: There is a Santa. This movie has been remade a few times, but none is better than the original. If you've ever been to the Macy's Thanksgiving Day Parade, you *must* see this movie.

22. *The Thief of Baghdad* (1940). An amazing fantasy adventure. It has native boy Sabu up against an evil magician. There is a scene in which Sabu finds a sealed oil lamp on a beach. He rubs the lamp to dry it off, and an enormous genie appears and grants Sabu three wishes in exchange for his own freedom. What happens next is probably the funniest segment of the movie. Great scenes with a flying mechanical horse that needs to be wound up in order to fly.

23. *Treasure Island* (1934). Based on Robert Louis Stevenson's classic, *Treasure Island* is the tale of the young Jim Hawkins and his search for the buried treasure of the notorious pirate Captain Flint. In his journey, he meets gallant swashbucklers, bloodthirsty buccaneers, and the legendary scoundrel Captain Long John Silver.

24. *Oliver Twist* (1948). After spending his first nine years in a horrible "workhouse," Oliver Twist's troubles get far worse when, painfully hungry at mealtime, he asks for more. As a punishment for calling attention to his empty belly, Oliver is apprenticed to an undertaker. He is treated so cruelly that he escapes and becomes involved with a bunch of young thieves led by the evil Fagin. A great Dickens classic.

25. *Stagecoach* (1939). Considered one of the greatest American films ever made, its great action scenes made actor John Wayne a huge Hollywood star. This movie elevated westerns from cheaply made, low-budget, Saturday matinee "B" films to a serious art form. If you like this movie, you'll like *Dodge City, The Oklahoma Kid,* and *Destry Rides Again.*

HOW TO USE YOUR <u>WHOLE</u> BRAIN WHEN YOU WATCH TV

Actually, you don't *need* your whole brain to understand most of what's on TV. On the other hand, if you find yourself watching something that *deserves* your whole brain:

1. Look up words that you haven't heard before in a dictionary.

2. Ask questions about the opinions you hear.

3. Think about why the characters do what they do. Analyze their personalities.

4. Think about how the story is developing. What will happen next?

5. Talk to friends about what you saw and share your opinions.

NICK AT NITE'S 20 BEST ADULT TV SHOWS FOR KIDS

1. *I Love Lucy*
2. *The Simpsons*
3. *The Wonder Years*
4. *Buffy the Vampire Slayer*
5. *7th Heaven*
6. *Roswell*
7. *Freaks and Geeks*
8. *Angel*
9. *Happy Days*
10. *Kids Say the Darndest Things*
11. *The Dick Van Dyke Show*
12. *Laverne & Shirley*
13. *That '70s Show*
14. *Taxi*
15. *WKRP in Cincinnati*
16. *The Family Guy*
17. *All in the Family*
18. *The Famous Jett Jackson*
19. *The Brady Bunch*
20. *Malcolm in the Middle*

THE GREAT SATURDAY MORNING HALL OF FAME

Ask any TV addicts who grew up in the '50s or '60s, and they'll tell you that the most important day of the week was Saturday. Saturday morning, to be specific. Unlike today, when Saturday morning television is dominated by cartoon shows, programs back then included adventures, dramas, great westerns, science fiction voyages into the unknown, puppet shows, rock 'n' roll showcases, quiz shows, and a great deal more. Here are some of the best. (While many of these were originally aired on weekdays and in the evening, they all wound up on the Saturday morning lineup.) Ask your parents and grandparents if they remember any of them!

1. *The Adventures of Black Beauty.* The famous horse starred in a half-hour live-action adventure.

2. *The Adventures of Kit Carson.* A great old-time western starring Kit and his sidekick, El Toro.

3. *The Adventures of Rin Tin Tin.* A German shepherd starred in this series, set in Fort Apache (not the one in the Bronx) in the 1880s.

4. *The Adventures of Robin Hood.* The English hero fights evil in Sherwood Forest by robbing from the rich and giving to the poor.

5. *The Adventures of Superman.* The Man of Steel made his first TV appearance in 1953; the show is still syndicated today.

6. *American Bandstand.* A TV dance party, with Dick Clark hosting, featured the hottest pop stars of the day. Artists such as the Doors, Linda Ronstadt, Simon and Garfunkel, the Supremes, the Temptations, and Stevie Wonder all made their TV debuts on this show.

7. *Andy's Gang.* Andy Devine was the emcee of one of the most bizarre kids' shows ever. The "cast" included Froggy the Gremlin (who insulted everyone) and the very weird Midnight the Cat.

8. *Annie Oakley.* The first western heroine had every girl on the block dreaming of horses and six-shooters.

9. *Batman.* The Dynamic Duo in dangerous doings.

10. *Beany and Cecil.* A 15-minute puppet show featuring the voices of some famous performers of the day, including Spike Jones and Jerry Lewis.

11. *The Big Top.* A live circus showcase with Ed McMahon as one of the clowns.

12. *Bozo the Clown.* A variety show with games, cartoons, and contests hosted by a clown who looked something like the original Ronald McDonald.

13. *Buck Rogers in the 25th Century.* A live-action science fiction adventure about a World War I flier who wakes up after a 400-year nap.

14. *Captain Midnight.* An aviator hero battles enemy agents and gangsters.

15. *Captain Video and His Video Rangers.* One of the first sci-fi TV shows, first broadcast in 1949.

16. *Circus Boy.* The life and times of Corky, an orphaned boy who gets to join the circus and ride around on his own elephant.

17. *Commando Cody: Sky Marshal of the Universe.* More live action sci-fi fun. Only 13 episodes were produced, but the show still managed to become one of the most popular of its kind.

18. *Crusader Rabbit.* One of the earliest cartoon shows, first shown in 1949, featured the irrepressible rabbit and his friend, Rags the Tiger.

19. *Dick Tracy.* A live-action detective series based on the famous comic strip character.

20. *Ding Dong School.* Aimed at preschoolers, this show had a "teacher" and a bunch of kids who pretended to be in school. There were games, songs, craft projects, and lots of discussion about being good.

21. *Flash Gordon.* Science fiction set in the 21st century and based on the comic strip character.

22. *Fury.* The adventures of a boy and his horse stressed good health, fair play, and good citizenship. Not as boring as you might think.

23. *The Gumby Show.* We're happy to know that Gumby is alive and well today. A character named Pinky Lee was the host of the show. He sang a ridiculous theme song that everyone loved!

24. *The Heckle and Jeckle Cartoon Show.* Starring two magpies and their pals, Dinky Duck, Gandy Goose, Little Roque-fort, and others.

25. *Hopalong Cassidy.* More western fun starring "Hoppy" and his horse, Topper.

26. *Howdy Doody.* "Buffalo" Bob Smith hosted the most popular children's show of the time. Howdy, a boy mari-onette, and his "father" told about their adventures in Doo-dyville. The show, which also had games, contests, and sing-alongs, had an audience of kids who were referred to as "the peanut gallery."

27. *Huckleberry Hound.* One of several Hanna-Barbera car-toon series starring the dumb but hardworking dog and his friends, Pixie and Dixie, Jinx, Hockey, and Yogi Bear, who eventually got his own show.

28. *The Incredible Hulk.* In 1978 Bill Bixby and body builder Lou Ferrigno starred in a version of this show. But before that, in 1966, it was a cartoon show.

29. *Jon Gnagy.* A 15-minute program that had an artist demonstrating drawing methods. There was a Jon Gnagy kit that you could buy that had all the same materials as those the artist used on TV and a step-by-step book that enabled you to reproduce Gnagy's "masterpieces" at home. You see lots of shows like this on cable channels now, but Jon Gnagy was the first!

30. *Kukla, Fran and Ollie.* Fran Allison first brought the Kuklapolitan players (puppets, that is) to TV in 1947. The cast included Beulah the Witch, Fletcher Rabbit, Madame Ophelia Ooglepuss, Colonel Cracky, and Clara Coo, among others.

31. *Land of the Giants.* An action adventure about a group of Earthlings stranded in a world of cranky giants.

32. *Lassie.* The famous collie performed heroic acts week after week, saving people from burning buildings, detaining criminals until the sheriff could make the arrests, and some-how always managing to communicate whatever was on her mind.

33. *The Little Rascals.* The Our Gang kids have been getting themselves into trouble on TV since 1954.

34. *The Lone Ranger.* The Masked Man, together with his horse, Silver, and his trusty Indian companion, Tonto, were in the longest-running western series.

35. *Looney Tunes.* This consisted of 191 different cartoons featuring Porky Pig, Daffy Duck, and the rest of the Warner Bros. crew. They're still around today, of course.

36. *The Mickey Mouse Club.* The Mouseketeers, a bunch of kids including Annette Funicello and others who went on to be pop stars and performers, helped host this show, which included cartoons, music, minidramas, and skits.

37. *My Friend Flicka.* Another boy-and-his-horse drama, this one set at the turn of the century. The show was based on the popular book by Mary O'Hara.

38. *The Paul Winchell and Jerry Mahoney Show.* Winchell, a ventriloquist, starred with his fairly funny dummies, Jerry Mahoney and Knucklehead Smith, who lived up to his name. This show had a studio audience, much like *Howdy Doody.*

39. *Quiz Kids.* This adaptation of a popular radio series had a group of pretty smart kids answering questions on different subjects. In 1980 Norman Lear revived the format in a show of the same name.

40. *Romper Room.* Still going strong, this one featured kids pretending to be in school. There were musical, instructional, patriotic, and entertainment segments and lots of ads for Romper Room toys.

41. *The Roy Rogers Show.* "The King of Cowboys," "Sheriff" Roy Rogers, and his wife, Dale Evans, maintained law and order in Mineral City.

42. *Sergeant Preston of the Yukon.* A Canadian Mountie, aided by his horse, Rex, and his dog, Yukon King, patrol the Northwest while hunting for his father's murderer.

43. *The Shari Lewis Show.* Shari Lewis, the famous ventriloquist, starred with her family of puppets: Lamb Chop, Hush Puppy, Charlie Horse, Mr. Goodfellow, and Jump Pup—and still charms us today. Let's face it: Nothing is cuter than Lamb Chop yawning!

44. *Sheena, Queen of the Jungle.* A young girl grows up in the jungle after surviving a plane crash and successfully defends herself and the natives using only a spear and lots of quick thinking.

45. *The Soupy Sales Show.* Comic madness with Soupy, the zany pie-throwing emcee and his puppet friends White Fang and Black Tooth (you only saw their paws), Pookie, and Marilyn Monwolf. Lots of weird humor here, which eventually led to the show's being canceled.

46. *Space Patrol.* Commander Buzz Cory and Cadet Happy battle evil forces in the 21st century in this sci-fi action series, which originally aired in 15-minute segments.

47. *The Three Stooges.* The original TV show, starring the inimitable Moe, Larry, and Curly, used recycled clips from their motion pictures.

48. *Watch Mr. Wizard.* This show taught you about science by demonstrating experiments. There'd be a scientist doing the stuff in the presence of kids who always acted surprised at the results.

49. *Winky Dink and You.* This show caused major problems in homes all across America. Here's how it worked: An adult host (Jack Barry) talked to cartoon characters Winky Dink and Woofer while drawing pictures of them on a screen. As Barry completed the pictures, the characters would come to life in animated cartoons. In the meantime, kids at home could draw on the same screen by first covering their TV screens with a plastic sheet and using special crayons that you could get for 50 cents. You didn't really need the kit; you could just as easily use cellophane and regular crayons. This show was really fun, but kids got in trouble for getting in the habit of writing on their TV screens *without* the plastic sheet!

50. *Wonderama.* This show had four different hosts, starting with Sandy Becker. It featured games, interviews, civic discussions, weather reports, cartoons, and even drawing lessons with Jon Gnagy. It was the first real variety show for kids.

11 TV COWBOYS AND THEIR HORSES
(Can you connect them?
See the answers below.)

1. Gene Autry
2. Hopalong Cassidy
3. The Cisco Kid
4. Dale Evans
5. The Lone Ranger
6. Tom Mix
7. Annie Oakley
8. Sgt. Preston
9. Roy Rogers
10. Tonto
11. Zorro

a. Rex
b. Silver
c. Blue
d. Topper
e. Scout, White Feller, Paint
f. Target
g. Buttermilk
h. Tornado, Phantom
i. Trigger
j. Diablo
k. Champion

Answers: 1k, 2d, 3j, 4g, 5b, 6c, 7f, 8a, 9i, 10e, 11h.

KING KONG'S DIMENSIONS

These are the big ape's statistics, according to RKO Pictures, which made the original movie.

Height: 50 feet
Face: 7 feet from forehead to chin
Nose: 2 feet long
Mouth: 6 feet from corner to corner
Eyes: 10 inches in diameter
Ears: 1 foot long
Chest: 60 feet around
Legs: 15 feet long
Arms: 23 feet long
Eyeteeth: 10 inches long, 4 inches wide

4 KIDS WHO HAVE WON ACADEMY AWARDS

		Age	Year
1.	Shirley Temple	6	1934
2.	Margaret O'Brien	7	1944
3.	Tatum O'Neal	10	1973
4.	Anna Paquin	11	1994

BUGS BUNNY'S 3 BEST FRIENDS

The most popular rabbit in the world, created by the great Chuck Jones, appeared in his first motion picture, *A Wild Hare,* in 1940. Since then, he has starred in 263 short films, 4 feature films, and 11 half-hour prime-time TV shows. In addition, Bugs Bunny cartoons have appeared on TV continuously for over 30 years in what has become the longest running show in TV history. It has been estimated that within a one-week period, over 100 million people tune in to Bugs and his pals, who include Porky Pig, Sylvester, Tweety, Road Runner, Speedy Gonzales, and, of course, these favorites.

1. Elmer Fudd. We frequently see Elmer, the little hunter, stalking Bugs as he tells us, "Be wery, wery quiet. I'm hunting wabbits! It's wabbit season!" But Bugs knows that Elmer is just an excitable little man who really means no harm. So he plays tricks on poor Elmer, who is always frustrated in the end. Bugs's favorite nicknames for Elmer are "Doc" and "Fudsy."

2. Yosemite Sam. Sam is the worst-tempered man in the world. He refers to Bugs as "that rackinfrackin' varmint" and continually announces, "I hates that rabbit!" Still, Bugs, who always enjoys a good chase scene, regards Sam as a friendly foe.

3. Daffy Duck. Daffy is a cowardly, selfish duck who

spends most of his time thinking up ways to become rich and famous. Of course, he's so daffy that he always loses his fights to Bugs and winds up spitting, "You're diss-picable!" Nevertheless, Bugs is amused by Daffy and secretly considers him a friend.

7 WAYS THAT POKÉMON IN THE U.S. IS DIFFERENT FROM THE JAPANESE VERSION

Pokémon is now the number-one children's TV program in America. Reshaping each Pokémon cartoon for American audiences takes up to three months and costs nearly $100,000. Is it worth it? Millions of American children say yes. But the Pokémon episodes that you see are nothing like the original Japanese versions.

1. In Japan 10-year-old Satoshi faces evildoers Musashi and Kojiro. In the U.S., children watch Ash fight the same battles against Jessie and James.

2. The sights, sounds, jokes, and sometimes even the storylines of Pokémon are different in Japan and the U.S.

3. Japanese street signs are given different names in the U.S. version.

4. Not one word remains the same in both versions. The English translations have to be changed so that the words match the lip movements of the characters, and every word must fit.

5. Puns are commonly used in Japanese scripts and have no English translation. So if a character is laughing, a new story has to be written to show why the character is laughing.

6. Pokémon in America features lively music throughout the entire episode. The Japanese cartoon uses music only occasionally.

7. Original Japanese characters become more loudmouthed when they become American. James, who is sober and sinister in the Japanese original, can be comically flashy in the American version. His pet Pokémon, Meowth, is considered something of an Eastern philosopher in Japan; in America, Meowth speaks clownishly, with a tough-guy New York accent.

10 THINGS YOU PROBABLY DIDN'T KNOW ABOUT SUPERMAN

1. Superman premiered as a comic book character in Action Comics, dated June 1938.

2. In the original legend, Superman's parents were named Jor-L and Lora. A later comic book changed their names to Jor-El and Lara. Similarly, *Daily Planet* editor George Taylor suddenly appeared one day as Perry White.

3. In 1940 Superman became the star of his own radio program, a serial drama that was on three days a week.

4. It was on the radio program—not in the comic book—that kryptonite, Superman's famous weakness, came into the story.

5. The "Superman" radio program was originally sponsored by Kellogg's.

6. In the early days, Superman appeared in 17 fully animated color cartoons that were shown in movie theaters.

7. The films starring Christopher Reeve as the Man of Steel were not the first Superman movies. In 1948 Columbia Pictures produced the first live-action Superman film, called *Superman,* and in 1950 it released *Atom Man Versus Superman.*

8. In 1951 a third film appeared, *Superman and the Mole Men,* which starred George Reeves, who also played Superman in the TV series.

9. There were 104 *Adventures of Superman* TV episodes, which were produced from 1952 to 1957. One of the first shows to be filmed in color, it immediately became one of the top kids' TV shows in the country.

10. George Reeves committed suicide in 1959, two years after *The Adventures of Superman* ceased production.

10 THINGS YOU PROBABLY DIDN'T KNOW ABOUT SHIRLEY TEMPLE

1. When Shirley began making films, she was the youngest person ever to appear on the cover of *Time* magazine. She was also the youngest person listed in *Who's Who*, and she was the youngest actress to receive an Academy Award.

2. Her insurance policy with Lloyd's of London stated that there would be no compensation if Shirley were either injured or killed while intoxicated.

3. She did not begin formal schooling until she was 13.

4. She became a Republican at the age of 10, after the Democratic mayor of Boston accidentally slammed a car door on her hand.

5. Shirley was made an honorary Kentucky colonel, honorary captain of the Texas Rangers, mascot of the Chilean navy, and honorary G-woman by J. Edgar Hoover, of the FBI.

6. In the film *Polly-tix in Washington,* Shirley played the role of a prostitute.

7. Her movies earned between $1 million and $2 million each in the days when the price of a movie ticket was 15 cents.

8. In 1938 Shirley's income was the seventh highest in America; she was making over $300,000 a year. Shortly thereafter, she started earning more than three times that amount annually.

9. She was given a weekly allowance of $4.25.

10. For her eighth birthday, Shirley received over 135,000 gifts, including a baby kangaroo from a fan in Australia and a calf from a group of schoolchildren in Oregon.

11 OF HALEY JOEL OSMENT'S FAVES

Haley Joel Osment is not only one of the most gifted child actors in Hollywood but one of the most gifted actors—period! He has starred in such films as *The Sixth Sense, Pay It Forward,* and *A.I. Artificial Intelligence.* You can write to him c/o Meredith Fine, Coast To Coast Talent Group, 3350 Barham Blvd., Los Angeles, CA 90068.

1. Favorite hobbies—horseback riding and singing; he likes to build stuff
2. Favorite classes—Science, History, and Math
3. Favorite band—R.E.M. (rock music in general)
3. Favorite sports—basketball, golf, baseball, and football
4. Favorite authors—J.R.R. Tolkien and Edgar Allan Poe
5. Favorite movie—*Alien*
6. Favorite food—Mostly vegetarian, but likes chicken and fish
7. Favorite junk food—Snickers
8. Hopes to go to Yale University
9. Wants to visit Legoland someday
10. Wants to work with dolphins
11. Wants to be in a movie like *The Blair Witch Project*

10 OF THE WORST SPACE FILMS OF ALL TIME

These are the worst space films, as listed by Harry and Michael Medved in their wonderful book, *The Golden Turkey Awards.* The Medveds are probably the best TV historians around.

1. *Cat Women of the Moon* (1953). A group of astronauts meets up with creatures on the moon—cat women, of course—in a story that has less depth than most TV commercials.

The star, Sonny Tufts, is especially awful in this one, which was originally shown in 3-D.

2. *Frankenstein Meets the Space Monster* (1965). One of the worst plots ever: A robot astronaut gone berserk battles an outer space queen and an army of midgets. Not intended as a comedy, but good for laughs anyway.

3. *The Green Slime* (1969). A Japanese rocket is attacked by tiny creatures that grow larger and slimier as they devour American and Italian astronauts. The title role is badly executed by a man in a slime suit. Very corny.

4. *Invasion of the Star Creatures* (1965). American soldiers are captured by female aliens who command an army of giant carrots (no kidding) who wear tights and potato sacks and have Ping-Pong balls for eyes.

5. *Message from Space* (1978). Japan's answer to *Star Wars*, and not nearly as much fun as *Godzilla*. Horrible special effects and one of the worst jobs of overdubbing ever.

6. *Plan Nine from Outer Space* (1959). Commonly considered one of the most awful movies ever made, mostly for having the most convoluted and ridiculous plot ever concocted. The special effects are so bad in this one that if you look closely, you can see that the "flying saucers" are really paper plates. For the closing battle, when one of the spaceships is supposed to blow up, they just set fire to one of the plates.

7. *Queen of Outer Space* (1958). The trouble with this one is twofold: a ridiculous plot (Venutian slave girl betrays her people for the love of a human astronaut) and the actress who plays the girl from Venus—with a Hungarian accent! (That's Zsa Zsa Gabor.)

8. *Robot Monster* (1953). The robot monsters are actually men in gorilla suits with divers' helmets on their heads. Public reaction to this one was so bad that the director, Phil Tucker, tried to kill himself.

9. *Starship Invasions* (1977). Coneheads in flying saucers try to invade Earth, but Robert Vaughn saves the day with only his pocket calculator to guide him in his second most embarrassing film. (*Teenage Caveman* was his first.)

10. *Teenagers from Outer Space* (1959). Outer space teenagers plot to take over Earth, but romance gets in the way. (Boys will be boys!)

WILLIAM SHATNER LISTS 3 THINGS ABOUT <u>STAR TREK</u> THAT HE WISHES WERE REAL

1. People of different races and beliefs working in harmony for the good of all.

2. If the transporter were real, we could all get around much faster, which would be great.

3. The adventure of being able to travel and explore the universe.

WILLIAM SHATNER LISTS 3 THINGS ABOUT <u>STAR TREK</u> THAT HE'S GLAD AREN'T REAL

William Shatner became known to millions as Captain Kirk, commander of the *Enterprise*, on *Star Trek*, one of TV's most enduring science fiction programs. He's also played the role in the *Star Trek* movie and its sequels. Off-camera, Shatner is quite content with reality and generously offered to share some of his thoughts about his career with our readers. Here are three reasons he gives for preferring reality to the world of Star Trek.

1. I'm glad that I do not have the tremendous responsibility that Captain Kirk has as commander of the *Enterprise*.

2. I'm glad the Klingons aren't real because they are not very nice and cause lots of trouble.

3. The boots that I wore on the show were too high and very uncomfortable, so I'm glad they're not real!

THAT'S EASY FOR YOU TO SING
20 Rock Songs with Sound Effects for Titles

If your parents (or grandparents) complain about the music you listen to, remind them that these were some of their favorites when they were kids.

1. "Bang-Shang-a-Lang," the Archies
2. "Be-Bop-A-Lula," Gene Vincent
3. "Bon-Doo-Wah," the Orlons
4. "Boo, Boo, Don't 'Cha Be Blue," Tommy James
5. "Boom-A-Dip-Dip," Stan Robinson
6. "Cha-Hua-Hua," Bobby Rydell
7. "Chee Chee-Oo-Chee," Perry Como
8. "Da Doo Ron Ron," the Crystals
9. "De Do Do Do, De Da Da Da Da," the Police
10. "Do Wah Diddy Diddy," Manfred Mann
11. "Dum Dum Dee Dum," Johnny Cymbal
12. "In-a-Gadda-da-Vida," Iron Butterfly
13. "I.O.I.O," the Bee Gees
14. "Ka-Ding-Dong," the Diamonds
15. "La La La La La La-La Means I Love You," the Delfonics
16. "Ooby Dooby," Roy Orbison
17. "The Oogum Boogum Song," Brenton Wood

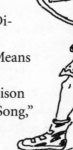

L.J.

18. "Ooh PooPah Doo, Part 11," Jessie Hill
19. "Papa Oom Mow Mow," the Rivingtons
20. "Sh-Boom," the Chords

STEVIE WONDER'S CHILDHOOD HOBBIES

Steveland Morris, better known as Stevie Wonder, is one of popular music's most successful and respected songwriters and musicians. He began his musical career at the age of 2 banging on pots and pans in time with the music and had his first number-one hit single at the age of 12. Stevie Wonder was blind at birth but never let his handicap stand in the way of his interests. Here are some of the numerous activities he was involved in as a kid.

1. Violin lessons
2. Piano lessons
3. String bass lessons
4. Swimming
5. Wrestling
6. Skating
7. Bowling
8. Tree climbing

6 OPERAS THAT KIDS ENJOY

1. *Aida,* by Giuseppe Verdi. Most people might not think *Aida* is an opera for kids, but I can't neglect this masterpiece —there are too many elements that kids will enjoy. The tunes are thrilling, the story is direct, and the "spectacle" of the piece is better than any circus I know (in fact, some big theaters even use horses and elephants when the hero returns in a triumphal march from winning a battle). The story is about an enslaved Ethiopian princess, Aida, who loves an Egyptian general, Radames, the enemy of her people. She persuades him to share military secrets that help her people escape, and

Radames is found guilty of treason. When he is sentenced, Aida stays to die with him instead of fleeing to Ethiopia. The opera is more than an ordinary love story, and the music is unforgettable.

2. *Amahl and the Night Visitors,* by GianCarlo Menotti. Amahl is a crippled boy who lives with his impoverished mother. They are ready to become beggars when the three Wise Men stop at their house on their way to visit the Christ child. While the kings are asleep, Amahl's mother tries to steal some of the gold they are bringing to present to Jesus. She is caught, and the guard makes a huge scene. After the kings describe who this Christ is, Amahl decides he wants to send the baby a present, too. All he has is his homemade crutch—and when he presents it, he is miraculously cured and can walk on his own. He decides to ride off with the kings to offer the gift in person. This was the first opera I had any contact with as a kid, and to me it remains one of the most touching Christmas stories I know.

3. *Carmen,* by Georges Bizet. The most popular question among kids when it comes to opera is, "Why are they always love stories?" But Carmen's flashy, daring personality makes the opera very exciting. Carmen lives with a group of Gypsies who dance and steal and tell fortunes. She falls in love with both a soldier and a bullfighter. The different settings that arise make for a most colorful opera. The character of Carmen has always appealed to me because she remains a heroine even though she is not particularly good. She is brave and strong, and it is those virtues that make us admire her. Again, in this opera many of the tunes will be familiar, and the music always maintains the excitement of the story.

4. *L'Enfant et les Sortilèges* (*The Child and the Magic Spells*), by Maurice Ravel. No matter what the definition of "kid" is, this beautiful magical tale after a story by the French writer Colette is one of my favorites for any age. The hero of the story is a boy (although sung by a mezzo-soprano) who is sent off without his supper. Locked away in his room, he throws a tantrum and almost destroys the nursery. Then the magic starts: His toys come to life and complain, and even the shards of a Chinese teacup chase him into the garden. There, the magic turns to nightmare when all the animals outside threaten him. But when they realize he is afraid and truly sorry for being bad, they all rally to his side and lead him home to plead his defense to his mother.

5. *Gianni Schicchi,* by Giacomo Puccini. One theme I always enjoyed when I was a kid was watching adults make fools of themselves. The Donati family does exactly that in *Gianni Schicchi.* They meet to mourn the death of their rich uncle, but after they read the will and realize they have all been left out, their real tears start. They hire Gianni to impersonate their uncle so he can change the will and then conveniently "die." Gianni is more clever than any of them realize, though, for when he changes his will, he bequeaths the money to himself and teaches all of them a lesson. This is a short opera and contains some of Puccini's most beautiful melodies.

6. *Die Zauberflöte (The Magic Flute),* by Wolfgang Amadeus Mozart. This is, and will always be, one of my favorite operas. It contains everything a kid could want in an opera: magic bells and flute, a dragon, enchanted animals, a wicked queen, a Prince Charming, and great music. It follows Prince Tamino's search to rescue Pamina, who is being held captive by her father, Sarastro. Tamino is misled and given many trials, but all of his adventures only prove his love and devotion. This opera does get a little long for kids who aren't used to sitting in a theater, but there are perfect moments in Sarastro's temple when you can catch a quick nap.

11 CLASSICAL MUSICIANS AND THE AGES AT WHICH THEY BEGAN TO PLAY MUSICAL INSTRUMENTS

1. Johann Sebastian Bach first played the violin at the age of 4.

2. Wolfgang Amadeus Mozart could play melodies on the harpsichord at 3.

3. Ludwig van Beethoven was taking piano lessons at the age of 3.

4. Franz Schubert started taking music lessons at the age of 7 but studied piano on his own before that.

5. Frédéric Chopin played melodies on the piano at 5—before anyone had shown him how.

6. Giuseppe Verdi started playing the piano at 7.

7. At 5, Johannes Brahms was playing the viola, the violin, and the piano and was already beginning to compose music.

8. Peter Ilich Tchaikovsky was able to play the piano at 4, but it was not until he was 23 that he began studying music seriously for the first time in his life.

9. By the time he was 2, Stephen Foster was playing the guitar and the organ and singing songs.

10. Jerome Kern taught himself to play the piano at the age of 4.

11. George Gershwin was able to play a song on the piano the first time he ever tried to play at all. He was 10 years old.

OUR TOP 20 WEIRD AL YANKOVIC SONG TITLES

1. "Another One Rides the Bus"

2. "Attack of the Radioactive Hamsters from a Planet Near Mars"

 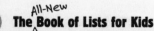

3. "The Biggest Ball of Twine in Minnesota"
4. "Dare to Be Stupid"
5. "Fat"
6. "Girls Just Want to Have Lunch"
7. "I Just Want a New Duck"
8. "I Lost on Jeopardy"
9. "Let Me Be Your Hog"
10. "Like a Surgeon"
11. "Mr. Frump in the Iron Lung"
12. "My Bologna"
13. "Slime Creatures from Out of Space"
14. "Smells Like Nirvana"
15. "Spam"
16. "Spatula City"
17. "Stop Draggin' My Car Around"
18. "Stuck in a Closet with Vanna White"
19. "(This Song's Just) Six Words Long"
20. "Toothless People"

THE 7 WORST THINGS ABOUT MUSIC TELEVISION

1. The hype and advertising can get to be too much. The stations are, after all, 24-hour commercials for music, movies, fashion, and the program itself. Ever get the feeling they're trying to tell you how to *think?*

2. You get to see lots of videos, but you don't get to see the ones that the producers don't think are "appropriate" for kids. They especially censor many rap groups and metal bands.

3. Because the largest portion of the music video audience is made up of young men, women are often treated unfairly. For instance, boys are made to believe that only girls who look like Cindy Crawford and Christie Brinkley are worth looking at.

4. Since getting a video shown on a music channel is so

important in selling records, some great musicians can't get record contracts just because they wouldn't look good in a video.

5. Watching the channels for a long time can be addictive. You're mesmerized by what you see, and this can numb your brain.

6. Everything happens very fast on these channels, so kids who watch a lot often wind up with short attention spans. This has been a real problem for educators.

7. Everyone looks so happy that you start thinking their lives are much better than yours.

8 GREAT THINGS ABOUT MUSIC TELEVISION

1. You can see rap and hip-hop entertainment that you don't often see anywhere else. The multicultural stuff that goes on is truly exciting.

2. News programs tell you lots about what's going on in the world—and not just in the world of music. News reports are often more honest than those you'll find on other news channels.

3. The award shows are sometimes lots of fun, and you get to see many of your favorite musicians performing.

4. The channels have aired specials on topics from racism and politics to environmental issues. President Clinton's appearances on MTV gave young people a chance to get involved in discussions that they aren't always included in.

5. MTV urges people to vote. Very Important!

6. The video countdown lets you know what's hot in the world of videos.

7. The TV graphics are more creative and exciting than on most TV commercials.

8. *MTV Unplugged* gives you a chance to see artists bring a new and sometimes very different approach to their own music.

SHARI LEWIS TELLS WHY IT'S IMPORTANT TO PLAY A MUSICAL INSTRUMENT

Our favorite puppeteer started every job interview by asking the applicant, "Did you ever study a musical instrument?" According to Lewis, studies have been done showing that people who are taught to read and play music are deeply affected by it, no matter how well or poorly they played. As her mother used to tell her, "Wouldn't the woods be silent if only the best birds sang?"

1. Musical training teaches you that if you stick to what you're doing, you'll "get it."

2. People who have learned to play instruments know that you can start out knowing nothing and, with effort, accomplish whatever you set your mind to.

3. People who study music are better at solving math problems.

4. They have better posture.

5. They show up for work more regularly and on time.

8 MUSICAL INSTRUMENTS YOU CAN MAKE AT HOME

Decorate these with sequins, beads, glitter, and fancy ribbons. Make a joyful noise!

1. Tambourine: Staple two stiff paper plates together, "food" sides facing each other. Use a hole punch to make eight holes evenly spaced around the edges of the plates. Use ribbon to tie a few jingle bells through each hole.

2. Drum: An empty oatmeal container or a coffee can works well. Any box or surface that makes an interesting sound when you hit it is a good drum. Use pencils, chopsticks, or your hands to beat out the rhythm.

3. Chimes: Hold a ruler horizontally, and at each inch mark, tie different metal objects to the ruler with string. The metal objects can be pieces of hardware such as washers, old toy parts, or even empty soda cans. Strike the objects with a spoon to make music.

4. Horn: Cover one end of a cardboard paper towel tube with wax paper, using a rubber band to hold it in place. Punch a row of holes along one side of the tube. Sing or hum into the open end of the tube.

5. Cymbals: Two matching pot covers do the trick.

6. Kazoo: Fold a piece of tissue paper around the comb side of a pocket comb and hum through the tissue paper.

7. Guitar: Stretch six large rubber bands horizontally around an open shoebox. Pluck the "strings" with your fingers to play.

8. Maracas: Put some unpopped popcorn or beans in an empty soda bottle or a coffee can.

7

It's a Fact

10 BASIC RIGHTS OF ALL CHILDREN

In 1959 the United Nations declared that all children all over the world have the following rights. These were listed as the Declaration of the Rights of the Child.

1. To enjoy the rights listed regardless of race, color, religion, or nationality.

2. To be able to grow in a healthy, normal way, free and dignified. Children should be specially protected and should be given special opportunities to grow.

3. To name and nationality.

4. To social security. This includes a decent place to live, good food, health care, and opportunities to play.

5. To special treatment, schooling, and care if handicapped.

6. To love and understanding. Children should be raised so that they feel secure and loved and live with their parents, if possible.

7. To free schooling and an equal opportunity to become everything they can be.

8. To prompt protection and relief in times of disaster.

9. To protection against all kinds of neglect, cruelty, and abuse from others.

10. To protection from any kind of unfair treatment because of race or religion.

YOUR LEGAL RIGHTS

Being young doesn't mean you're not a citizen with rights. The following are not all written laws, but based on the judges' decisions in cases that have involved kids, this is pretty much what you can expect from our judicial system. However, keep in mind that legal trends do change from state to state.

1. Within limits, you have the right to dress and wear your hair any way you and your parents wish when you go to school. If school authorities want to challenge you, they must show that your clothing or hairstyle interferes with the educational process or that it is disruptive.

2. You have the constitutional right to demonstrate in an orderly fashion within the school as long as the demonstration is not disruptive or violent.

3. If you have a job, you are entitled to the same minimum wage as adults earn, but your salary can be limited based on your lack of experience.

4. Girls must receive the same salary as boys for doing the same work.

5. As a minor, no contract you sign is valid unless your parent or guardian signs it, too.

12 RULES OF CONDUCT FOR TEACHERS, 1915

The following rules of conduct applied to teachers in a town in West Virginia in 1915, but they are very much like the rules that all teachers in the U.S. had to follow at the time.

1. A female teacher was not allowed to date men.

2. A teacher was not allowed to get married during the school term.

3. Unless they were at a school function, all teachers had to be at home between the hours of 8:00 P.M. and 6:00 A.M.

4. Teachers were not allowed to loiter at downtown ice cream parlors.

5. They were not allowed to travel outside the city limits unless they had special permission from the school board.

6. A female teacher could not ride in a carriage or automobile with a man other than her brother or father.

7. Smoking was not allowed.

8. Teachers could not wear brightly colored clothing.

9. Teachers were not allowed to dye their hair.

10. A female teacher had to wear at least two petticoats.

11. Dresses had to be worn no shorter than 3 inches above the ankle.

12. Teachers had to keep the schoolroom neat and clean. Each day the floor had to be swept and scrubbed with hot, soapy water and the blackboards had to be cleaned. The teacher also had to start a hearth fire by 7:00 A.M. in winter so that the room would be warm by 8:00 A.M., when the kids showed up for school.

HOW THE WORLD IS LIKELY TO CHANGE BY THE TIME YOU GROW UP
And Other Predictions

Here's a rundown of what scientists think your life will be like in about 20 years. But be careful about predictions; in 1948 a pioneer in the field of radio development claimed that TV would never last, and in 1899 the director of the U.S. Patent Office claimed that there was nothing new left for anyone to invent. You'll find "10 Predictions That Didn't Come True (And Which Aren't Likely To)" on page 343.

1. For one thing, you might become one of over 2,000 people who live and work on the moon, although your chances are greater if you're male, since women will make up only a small percentage of those who get to go. Back on Earth, things won't look so rosy. According to the United Nations, over 600 million people will be living in poverty.

2. You won't have to worry about carrying books to school, since reference books and those with lots of pictures will be too expensive to reproduce. Instead, when you need information, you'll get it from your computer, videodisc system, or e-book.

3. You'll still be able to dance to pop music, but most of it will be generated by synthesizers and computers instead of real people and real instruments.

4. We'll have test-tube dogs.

5. Lifespans will increase; an American born in 2020 can expect to live for 120 years.

6. The typical family room in the American household will be replaced by a "video environment." At the touch of a button on your computerized entertainment system, you'll be able to surround yourself with a tropical rain forest or a Saturnian landscape. Of course, you'll still be able to tune in your favorite movie — on your 360° movie screen!

7. Genetic engineers will enable parents to pick and choose the traits they want their babies to have. You'll be able to order blue eyes, good singing voices, and blond hair. It is also likely that such practices will be the center of legal and moral disputes.

8. Scientists may begin a process called "terraforming," in which outer space environments are made fit for human occupation. This may well lead to a colony of humans living on Mars.

9. The clothing you wear will probably be made from thin fabric of great durability. More important, the warmth that it provides will be controlled by pushing a button on a special power belt. That is, you'll wear the same clothing in summer as you do in winter; you'll just "program" it differently depending on the weather.

10. By 2050, it is expected that the population of outer space will exceed 7,500.

11. There will be 50% more automobiles on the road than there are now, but air pollution will have dropped, since all cars will run on electricity.

7 FACTS ABOUT KIDS AND GUNS

For information about handgun control and safety, write to the Center to Prevent Handgun Violence, 1225 Eye St., NW, Suite 1100, Washington, DC 20005. Here are some things you should know:

1. Every day twelve children aged 19 and under are shot and killed.

2. One out of six pediatricians nationwide has treated a child who was shot.

3. Gunshot wounds are the leading cause of death for both black and white teenage boys in America.

4. Every six hours a youth aged 10–19 commits suicide with a gun.

5. About 100,000 students take guns to school every day.

6. A gun in the home is more likely to be used to kill a family member or friend than a criminal.

7. A third of all high school students say they can get a gun whenever they want it.

22 SPORTS REPRESENTED IN THE SPECIAL OLYMPICS

We all have a lot to learn from the people who run and participate in the Special Olympics, which holds competitions in different categories for children and adults who are mentally retarded. Their motto is especially notable: "Let me win, but if I cannot win, let me be brave in the attempt." If you want to participate in any way at all, contact Special Olympics International Headquarters, 1350 New York Ave., NW, Suite 500, Washington, DC 20005 (202-628-3630).

1. Alpine skiing

2. Aquatics

3. Athletics

4. Badminton

5. Basketball

6. Bowling

7. Cycling
8. Equestrian
9. Figure skating
10. Floor hockey
11. Football (soccer)
12. Golf
13. Gymnastics
14. Poly hockey

15. Powerlifting
16. Roller skating
17. Softball
18. Speed skating
19. Table tennis
20. Team handball
21. Tennis
22. Volleyball

10 PROBLEMS LEFTIES HAVE

Did you know that polar bears are left-handed? Or that over 2,500 left-handed people die each year trying to use products made for right-handed people? Read this list even if you're right-handed. We bet you didn't know that your left-handed pal has to deal with these problems day in and day out. If you find any of them confusing, try performing these tasks "switching hands" and see what happens.

1. In school, penmanship lessons are taught as though everybody were right-handed. Lefties are often made to feel like there's something wrong with them because they're not able to write if they follow the same posture guidelines as the others. *If you're a lefty (or you think you are), make sure you let your parents and teachers know.*

2. Chairs that come with writing arms attached are almost always designed for righties, so lefties have to twist their bodies awkwardly in order to lean on the desk.

3. When a left-handed person tries to use ordinary scissors, the blades wind up in the wrong position. There *are* scissors made for lefties, but they are expensive.

4. If a lefty tries to draw a straight line using a ruler, he holds the ruler down with his right hand and then has to cross his left hand *over* the right to draw the line, which he would start at the left. Whew! To make matters worse, teachers show students how to use rulers assuming that everyone is right-handed.

5. Left-handed kids have trouble learning to set the table, which is "properly" set up for righties.

6. A left-handed person sitting next to a right-handed person at the dinner table is going to bump elbows with her neighbor if she cuts her food with the knife in her right hand. A lefty is better off sitting at the corner of a table, so that her left hand can remain free.

7. Left-handed people have to remember that the proper way to shake hands with someone is with your *right* hand.

8. Some left-handed people have to change the order of strings on a guitar in order to play it.

9. Public telephones are designed for righties.

10. Barbers, gardeners, doctors, dentists, cooks, and knitters all must use "standard" equipment designed for right-handed people.

TO PEE OR NOT TO PEE

Any way you say it, when you gotta go, you gotta go.

1. Take a leak
2. Tinkle
3. Go pee-pee
4. Take a whiz
5. Drain the lizard
6. Visit the golden arches
7. Powder your nose
8. Go to the john
9. Visit the little girls' room
10. Make number one
11. Urinate
12. Micturate
13. Eliminate
14. "Nature calls"

THE BEST ROLLER COASTERS

In 1920 there were over 1,500 roller coasters in the U.S. These days we're down to under 400. But look at the bright side: Back in 1920, you couldn't ride at 80 miles per hour. You can now!

1. The Steel Phantom in West Mifflin, Pennsylvania, is the fastest roller coaster, traveling at 80 miles an hour.

2. The Riverside Cyclone in Agawam, Massachusetts, has the roughest ride of them all. The first drop takes you from 0 to 60 miles per hour in just 3 seconds.

3. The Yankee Cannonball in Salem, New Hampshire, has the smoothest ride, which takes 2 minutes and covers 2,000 feet.

4. The Twister in Denver, Colorado, is the scariest. It has a 65-mile-an-hour plunge into a tunnel that has a high-banked curve.

5. The Dragon Coaster at Rye Playland in Rye, New York, is perhaps the oddest of all the coasters. It has a 2-minute ride through the mouth of a dragon.

6. The Beast in King Island, Ohio, has the longest ride — just slightly over 4 minutes.

7. The Tidal Wave in Santa Clara, California, has the shortest ride — just 36 seconds. This may seem like a waste of time, but consider that you get hurled from 0 to 55 miles per hour in just 4.2 seconds.

22 FAMOUS DYSLEXICS

1. Muhammad Ali, boxer
2. Hans Christian Andersen, writer
3. Erin Brockovich, political activist
4. Cher, pop singer
5. Winston Churchill, statesman

6. Tom Cruise, actor
7. Leonardo da Vinci, artist
8. Walt Disney, entertainment mogul
9. Thomas Edison, inventor
10. Albert Einstein, scientist
11. Harrison Ford, actor
12. Henry Ford, inventor
13. Whoopi Goldberg, actress
14. Thomas Jefferson, statesman
15. Magic Johnson, basketball player
16. John Lennon, musician
17. Pablo Picasso, artist
18. Nolan Ryan, baseball player
19. Ted Turner, media mogul
20. George Washington, statesman
21. Robin Williams, actor
22. Woodrow Wilson, statesman

LITTLE LEAGUE WORLD SERIES CHAMPS

Little League baseball has grown a lot since it began in 1947, when the first championship took place and the Maynard team from Williamsport, Pennsylvania, won first place in Hammonton, New Jersey. The first World Series of Little League Baseball was held in 1953, and by 1978, the league included more than 6,500 programs for 9- to 12-year-olds. In 1998 the Little League World Series was held before a crowd of over 41,200 fans at Lamade Stadium in Williamsport. And by 1999 the number of countries with Little League programs hit 100.

1947. Maynard, Williamsport, Pennsylvania
1948. Lock Haven, Lock Haven, Pennsylvania
1949. Little Big League, Hammonton, New Jersey

1950. National, Houston, Texas
1951. Stamford, Stamford, Connecticut
1952. National, Norwalk, Connecticut
1953. Southside, Birmingham, Alabama
1954. National, Schenectady, New York
1955. Morrisville, Morrisville, Pennsylvania
1956. Hondo Lions, Roswell, New Mexico
1957. Industrial, Monterrey, Mexico
1958. Industrial, Monterrey, Mexico
1959. National, Hamtramck, Michigan
1960. American, Levittown, Pennsylvania
1961. Northern, El Cajon/La Mesa, California
1962. Moreland District, San Jose, California
1963. National, Granada Hills, California
1964. Mid Island, Staten Island, New York
1965. Windsor Locks, Windsor Locks, Connecticut
1966. Westbury, Houston, Texas
1967. West Tokyo, Tokyo, Japan
1968. Wakayama, Wakayama, Japan
1969. Taipei, Chinese Taipei
1970. Wayne, Wayne, New Jersey
1971. Tainan, Chinese Taipei
1972. Taipei, Chinese Taipei
1973. Tainan, Chinese Taipei
1974. Kao Ksiung, Chinese Taipei
1975. Lakewood, Lakewood, New Jersey
1976. Chofu, Tokyo, Japan
1977. Li, The, Chinese Taipei
1978. Pin, Kuang, Chinese Taipei
1979. Pu, Tzu Town, Chinese Taipei
1980. Hua Lian, Chinese Taipei
1981. Tai-Ping Little League, Chinese Taipei
1982. Kirkland National, Kirkland, Washington
1983. East Marietta National, Marietta, Georgia
1984. Seoul, Seoul, Korea
1985. Seoul, Seoul, Korea

1986. Tainan Park, Chinese Taipei
1987. Hua Lian, Chinese Taipei
1988. Tai Chung, Chinese Taipei
1989. National, Trumbull, Connecticut
1990. San, Hua, Chinese Taipei
1991. Hsi Nan, Chinese Taipei
1992. Long Beach, Long Beach, California
1993. Long Beach, Long Beach, California
1994. Coquivacoa, Maracaibo, Venezuela
1995. Shan-Hua, Chinese Taipei
1996. Fu-Hsing, Chinese Taipei
1997. Linda Vista, Guadalupe, Mexico
1998. Toms River, New Jersey
1999. Hirakata, Osaka, Japan
2000. Sierra Maestra, Maracaibo, Venezuela
2001. Tokyo, Kitasuna, Tokyo

GIRLS LITTLE LEAGUE SOFTBALL WORLD SERIES WINNERS

In 1974 the Little League and Senior Little League Softball programs were created, giving girls the chance to participate for the first time.

1974. Wellswood, Tampa, Florida
1975. National, Medford, Oregon
1976. Salinas, Salinas, California
1977. American, Salinas, California
1978. Shippensburg, Shippensburg, Pennsylvania
1979. North Providence West, North Providence, Rhode Island
1980. Glendale, Glendale, California
1981. Gresham, Gresham, Oregon
1982. 76er, Glendale, California

1983. Greater Naples, Naples, Florida
1984. Albuquerque, Albuquerque, New Mexico
1985. National, Brookfield, Illinois
1986. Tampa Bay, Tampa, Florida
1987. Tampa Bay, Tampa, Florida
1988. Greater Naples, Naples, Florida
1989. Greater Naples, Naples, Florida
1990. Foothill, Glendale, California
1991. Greater Naples, Naples, Florida
1992. Midway, Waco, Texas
1993. Midway, Waco, Texas
1994. Midway, Waco, Texas
1995. Midway, Waco, Texas
1996. Countryside, Clearwater, Florida
1997. Midway, Waco, Texas
1998. Midway, Waco, Texas
1999. Midway, Waco, Texas
2000. Midway, Waco, Texas
2001. Rosario Paoli, Maunabo, Puerto Rico

8 KIDNAPPINGS WITH HAPPY ENDINGS

In 1874, 4-year-old Charles Brewster "Charley" Ross became the first victim of a sensational kidnapping in American history. Little Charley was told that he could have firecrackers and balloons if he went along with the two men who made the offer. Although the kidnappers were captured months later, little Charley was never heard from again. Throughout the years, there have been horrible stories of kidnappings that have ended in tragedy. A lucky few, however, were able to live through the ordeal. Here are eight of them.

1. Edward A. Cudahy, Jr., the son of a rich meatpacker, was

15 when he was approached by two men on the street who said they were detectives and that they needed Edward to come with them. Eddie was held for two days, until his father paid a $25,000 ransom. The kidnapper, Pat Crowe, must have had second thoughts about what he'd done, even though Edward had not been harmed. He sent Christmas cards to his little victim years after the kidnapping, and finally, in 1906, six years after the crime, he returned the money and confessed. Crowe was acquitted.

2. Eight-year-old Willie Whitla, the son of a rich lawyer, was kidnapped from his boarding school in 1909 when a man and a woman told him that they were taking him to visit his parents. They demanded a ransom of $10,000 and got it, and Willie was released. But a while later, as the kidnappers were celebrating their victory in a Cleveland bar, they were picked up by the police. The ransom money was recovered, and the criminals, Helen and James Bogle, were given long jail sentences.

3. When 9-year-old George Weyerhaeuser was abducted from the home of his wealthy family in Tacoma, Washington, in 1935, his $200,000 ransom was paid with bills that the police had specially marked. George was returned safely home after a week, but when a department store clerk recognized the bills (which the kidnapper was using to make a purchase), he called the police. William Mahon, the kidnapper, was given 60 years in prison.

4. Lee Crary was 8 when he was kidnapped in 1957 from his home in Everett, Washington. George E. Collins, Jr., the kidnapper, demanded $10,000 for the child's return, but before it could be paid, little Lee escaped and led police to Collins's hideout. Collins got a life sentence in prison.

5. In 1960 Eric Peugeot, the son of the famous car manufacturer, was kidnapped from a playground at a golf course in Paris by a group of men. The $300,000 ransom was paid, and Eric was released a few days later. Only two of the kidnappers were ever found, and they were sent to prison.

6. Eleven-year-old Kenneth King was kidnapped in 1967 from his home in California. His kidnapper demanded and got $250,000 for the boy's safe return three days later. The kidnapper was never found.

7. The kidnapping of John Paul Getty III in June of 1973 was one of the most publicized ever, since he was the grandson of J. Paul Getty, who was, at the time, the richest man in the world. The young Getty was 16 when four men seized him and drove off with him. But Getty's grandfather refused for many months to pay the ransom, thinking that it was just a trick that had been set up by his grandson to get money. Finally, in October, the brutal kidnappers sent one of the boy's ears (and a photo of his head) to Getty, threatening to do worse if the $2.9 million ransom was not paid. Young Getty was released, but the kidnappers were never found.

8. In July 1976 one of the most horrible kidnappings ever occurred. Three kidnappers captured a school bus containing 26 children and a driver and forced it into a large hole, which they had dug. The bus and its riders were buried in the hole with just enough air to allow them to breathe. The kidnappers, James and Richard Schoenfeld and Fred Woods, demanded a $5 million ransom, but they were apprehended before the sum was paid, and they led police to the buried bus. All the children and the driver were rescued after having been buried for 30 hours. The kidnappers were sent to prison for life.

10 PREDICTIONS THAT DIDN'T COME TRUE
And Which Aren't Likely To

A playwright named Eugène Ionesco once said, "You can predict things only after they've happened." The following list of some of the worst predictions ever made proves he was right.

1. "Man won't fly for a thousand years," said Wilbur Wright to his brother Orville in 1901.

2. Edward Welsh, former executive secretary of NASA, predicted that by 1982 there would be one or more permanent bases on the moon.

3. *Life* magazine predicted, in 1970, that instead of having family cars, the average family would soon own helicopters.

4. *U.S. News and World Report* disagreed; in 1969 it predicted that families would still own cars but that each family would own about four or five of them.

5. That same year, Harold and June Shane, professors of education, predicted that kids would soon start school at the age of 2.

6. "Three-dimensional color television, with smell, touch, and taste added, may be available by the 1990s," predicted scientist and mathematician Desmond King-Hele.

7. In 1904 Lord Kelvin, an engineer and physicist, said, "Radio has no future."

8. Waldemar Kaempffert wasn't too optimistic about the future of robots. In 1927 he said that they would never exist because "even the most ingenious technologist cannot make a collection of wheels, shafts, magnets, and wires think."

9. "The Beatles are just a passing phase," said the Reverend Billy Graham in 1964.

10. In 1990 John Elfreth Watkins, Jr., predicted that by the year 2001 the letters C, X, and Q would be dropped from the alphabet.

7 WHITE HOUSE GHOSTS

According to "official government records," the following ghosts have all been detected in the White House.

1. The ghost of Abigail Adams, wife of the second president, John Adams, has been seen in the East Room, where she used to hang laundry.

2. The ghost of Dolley Madison, wife of the fourth president, James Madison, shows up each year at the White House to see the roses she planted in the garden long ago.

3. Thomas Jefferson has been heard playing his violin.

4. Andrew Jackson has occasionally haunted the White House.

5. Abraham Lincoln is the most famous White House ghost, and Eleanor Roosevelt's maid claimed to have seen him. Rumor has it that just before something awful happens in the country, Lincoln shows up and paces the floors of the mansion.

6. The ghost of the original owner of the land on which the White House was built is occasionally heard (but never seen) greeting White House guests.

7. The ghost of an old janitor has been seen roaming the halls, dusting the place.

10 CITIES OF LOVE

1. Love, Mississippi
2. Love, Saskatchewan
3. Love Point, Maryland
4. Lovejoy, Illinois
5. Lovelady, Texas
6. Loveland, Colorado
7. Loveland, Iowa
8. Loveland, Ohio
9. Loveland, Oklahoma
10. Lovelock, Nevada

THE 36 AMERICAN CITIES WITH THE WEIRDEST NAMES

1. Bummerville, California
2. Cabbage Patch, Illinois
3. Constant Friendship, Maryland
4. Disco, Illinois
5. Do Stop, Kentucky
6. Dreamworld, Florida
7. Frog Jump, Tennessee
8. Puddle Town, Connecticut
9. Fugit, Indiana

10. Fussville, Wisconsin
11. Good Luck, Tennessee
12. Goofy Ridge, Illinois
13. Goose Pimple Junction, Virginia
14. Hoo Hoo, West Virginia
15. Jolly Dump, South Dakota
16. Mosquitoville, Vermont
17. Muck City, Alabama
18. Nameless, Tennessee
19. Oddville, Kentucky
20. Only, Tennessee
21. Oz, Kentucky
22. Puddle Town, Connecticut
23. Roaches, Illinois
24. Shortly, Delaware
25. Snowball, Alaska
26. Sweet Lips, Tennessee
27. Tight Squeeze, Virginia
28. Two Egg, Florida
29. Wham, Louisiana
30. What Cheer, Iowa
31. Who'd a Thought It, Alabama
32. Why, Arizona
33. Whynot, Mississippi
34. Wigwam, California
35. Zip City, Alabama
36. Zzyzx, California

1 REAL MONSTER THAT WAS REPORTED KILLED

(And 10 That Are Still Believed To Be Alive Today!)

1. Mo-Mo. As recently as 1972, residents of Louisiana panicked at repeated reports of an apelike monster with long, dangling hairy arms.

2. The Abominable Snowman. For over 100 years, this monster, reported to be a large, hairy humanoid creature that lurks in the icy Himalayan region, has been sighted and sometimes even photographed. It is still believed to be alive today.

3. Alma. The Russian version of the Abominable Snowman was described in 1957 by one witness as having "hairy arms longer that the ordinary man" and being covered all over with reddish-gray hair.

4. Goatman. Known as the Monster of Lover's Lane,

Goatman roams Prince George's County in Virginia. He is popularly believed once to have been a scientist whose experiments with goats went awry.

5. The Giant Sloth. A gigantic armadillo seen in Patagonia, Argentina, seemed to be resistant to the bullets and arrows that were shot at him. It is believed that he has become extinct since his last sighting in the 19th century.

6. The Beast of Le Gevaudan. A strange wolflike creature with short ears and hooflike feet was killed in France in 1767 after murdering numerous young children. He was finally shot by a hunter with silver bullets, and his carcass was displayed as proof of his death.

7. Mngwa. Mngwa is described by witnesses as a catlike animal that will mutilate any human who confronts it in the Central African jungle where it dwells. Attempts have been made to capture the beast, but none has been successful.

8. The Berkeley Square Horror. If you travel to 50 Berkeley Square in London, England, you'll only find a bookstore there. But legend has it that long ago the house that stood there was occupied by a gruesome, slimy, slithering thing that had crawled up from the sewers and came to occupy the top floor of the building. Anyone who tried to spend a night in the room—as a few unfortunate souls reportedly did—was found dead by morning, a frozen look of horror upon his or her face.

9. Hairy Hands. A surprising number of gruesome accidents have been reported on a stretch of road between the villages of Postbridge and Two Bridges in the Dartmoor region of England. Those who have lived through the ordeal (some never made it) swear that a pair of large, hairy hands have reached out from the darkness to claim their victims. The last account of an attack dates back to 1921, but some residents claim that the thing—whatever it is—still dwells there.

10. The Beast of 'Busco. Each year the people of Churubusco, Indiana, hold a festival known as Turtle Days, during which they honor their local monster, a 200-pound snapping turtle called the Beast of 'Busco. The thing is said nearly to have been captured in 1948 by hunters, but Oscar, as he is sometimes known, finally slipped back into the murky waters of the local pond, where many claim he hides today, waiting to surface again.

11. Slimy Slim. In 1941 a man named Thomas L. Rogers, of Boise, Idaho, reported seeing a "serpent about 50 feet long" with a head that resembled "a snub-nosed crocodile." But Rogers wasn't the only one. After a number of other residents also reported seeing the monster, all agreeing on its description, it was given the nickname Slimy Slim. It has not been seen since 1941, nor has anyone reported its death.

(How to Remember the Names of) THE SEVEN DWARFS

You can memorize their names by remembering that two start with D, two start with S, and three of them are named after emotions.

1. Doc	**5.** Bashful
2. Dopey	**6.** Happy
3. Sleepy	**7.** Grumpy
4. Sneezy	

SANTA'S REINDEER

Note that Rudolph was not one of the original eight.

1. Dasher	**5.** Comet
2. Prancer	**6.** Cupid
3. Donder	**7.** Dancer
4. Blitzen	**8.** Vixen

All-New
^

SANTA'S HOMETOWN

Some say Santa spends his time at the North Pole, but there are those who would argue that Mistletoe, Kentucky, or Rudolph, Ohio, is really the home of St. Nick. Consider also the following list of "Christmas cities." You might be interested in knowing that you can have your Christmas cards postmarked in any one of them just by sending all your cards in one package—stamped, of course, to the postmaster there. Write "Postmark Request" clearly in the lower-left-hand corner of the front of the package.

1. Bethlehem, GA 30620
2. Christmas, FL 37209
3. Mistletoe, KY 41351
4. Nazareth, MI 49074
5. Noel, MO 64854
6. North Pole, AK 99706
7. Rudolph, OH 43462
8. Santa Claus, IN 47579
9. Silver Star, MT 59751
10. Wiseman, AR 72587

11 NAMES FOR SANTA CLAUS

1. *Babbo Natale,* Italian
2. *Jul emanded,* Danish
3. *Jultomten,* Swedish
4. *Kriss Kringle,* Hungarian
5. *Papa Noel,* Brazilian
6. *Le Père Noël,* French
7. *St. Nicholas,* German
8. *Saint Nikkolo,* Austrian
9. *Shen Tan Lao Jen,* Chinese
10. *Sinter Klaas,* Dutch
11. *Ukko,* Finnish

GO TO THE HEAD OF THE CLASS
I.Q. Classifications

Intelligence Quotients—or I.Q.'s, as they're commonly called—used to mean a whole lot more years back when your parents went to school. These days, many educators regard them as irrelevant, saying that the tests on which I.Q.'s were based were never really fair to begin with and that a student's performance, rather than potential—which is what the I.Q. really measured—is what counts. In any case, Terman's Classification (one system for labeling I.Q. ranges) assigned the following labels for I.Q.'s.

Genius	above 140
Very Superior	120–140
Superior	110–120
Normal	90–110
Dull	80–90
Borderline	70–80
Moron	50–70
Imbecile	25–50
Idiot	below 25

12 REAL JOBS YOU PROBABLY NEVER KNEW EXISTED

Hate school? Here are some jobs that await you if you don't get over it.

1. Airplane coverer
2. Artery pumper
3. Banana ripener
4. Beer sampler
5. Carrot washer
6. Denture waxer
7. Egg breaker
8. Fur blower
9. Glove pairer
10. Hairnet knotter
11. Oyster washer
12. Sap collector

10 BEST KIDS' ATTRACTIONS IN EUROPE

If you think Disney has it all, think again.

1. De Efteling Amusement Park, Kaatsheuvel, the Netherlands. This is the place for you if scary rides are your thing. This amusement park has one of Europe's largest roller coasters as well as a whole slew of other stupefying attractions, including the Piranha (a swirling water ride) and the Half Moon (a lurching, swinging pirate ship), both of which have you hanging on for dear life. There's a truly enchanting fairy tale forest with animated models of Sleeping Beauty and Arabs on flying carpets, plus a steam railway, a puppet theater, and a playground. There's a great haunted house that you shouldn't miss as well as lots of other interesting points, like a trash can that says "Thank you" when you throw something into it, a swimming pool, a paddling pool, and a life-size model of an elephant that shoots water from its trunk.

2. The German Museum of Masterworks of Natural Science and Technology, The Deutsches Museum, Munich, Germany. Here is truly one of the most amazing museums in the world, for it brings education to life. It is the largest technological museum in the world, covering six floors and consisting of 300 rooms filled with 45,000 exhibits along 10 miles of corridor! But aside from the size, the exhibits themselves are wonderful. Here you'll find model coal mines, salt mines, iron mines, cars, airplanes, rocket ships, an Alpine chalet, musical instruments, oceangoing ships, and the first diesel engine. Many of the displays have buttons you can push or handles you can crank to make the models move. Learning has never been this much fun.

3. Hamleys, the Biggest Toy Store in the World, London, England. Hamleys Toy Store in London, founded in 1760, is the biggest in the world, and around Christmastime it must be the most crowded place in the world as well. Spread over six floors in the heart of London, it contains every kind of toy you can imagine, from tiny tin soldiers to superhuge stuffed animals. There are books, models, puppets, computer and video games, some really terrific train sets, dolls and dollhouses, and lots more. You'll be familiar with a lot of the stuff already — Fisher Price and Mattel toys, for instance, are as popular in Europe as they are in America — but there are also tens of thousands of toys from Britain and the rest of the world that you won't find gathered together anywhere else, like life-size models of movie characters and a 4-foot-long motorized replica of a Rolls-Royce.

4. The Historical-Archaeological Experimental Center, in Lejre, Denmark. The name may be a mouthful, but this is really an exciting place. If you've ever wondered what life was really like in the Stone Age, here's where you can find out. There are farms, workshops, and dwellings inhabited by volunteers who live, work, dress, and even eat as people really did from prehistoric times up to the 19th century. You can find out how roads were built, crops were cultivated, animals tamed, and food cooked. There's a stone field in which you can watch experiments designed to discover how primitive tools could be used to build the vast European monuments like Stonehenge, and you can participate in fire experiments in Fire Valley—under supervision, of course. If you go during the summer months, you'll be treated to weaving, pottery, and flint-working demonstrations.

5. Legoland, near Billund, Denmark. If you've ever built anything with Legos—those plastic toy bricks—or even if you haven't, you'll be fascinated by Legoland, one of the most unusual attractions in all of Europe. It's built entirely of Legos! It began as a model village in which dozens of the world's most famous structures—the Taj Mahal, Mount Rushmore, the Acropolis—were reproduced using Legos. But eventually the park grew to include rides, a marionette theater, a western town called Legoredo, a wonderful collection of antique dolls, and a long list of educational exhibits.

6. Madurodam, the Miniature Village, The Hague, the Netherlands. Europe is filled with dozens of miniature villages, where you'll feel like a giant no matter how short you are. The best of these is Madurodam, which was built by a Dutch couple as a memorial after their son was killed at war. It's a complete Dutch town, built $1/25$th of the size of a real one, with castles, churches, shops, windmills, houses, and even canals, just like a real Dutch town. A two-mile model railway runs through the farms and factories, and many parts of the transportation system really move: Ships glide on the tiny waterways, small airplanes taxi on a runway, and a miniature band plays music at a country fair. The scene is especially exciting at night, when 50,000 tiny lights come on at the windows and along the little streets. Altogether, the place is magical.

7. Maihaugen Museum, Lillehammer, Norway. All over Scandinavia there are dozens of open-air museums where ancient buildings have been gathered to give spectators an idea of what life was like in olden times. Maihaugen is one of the best of them. It was started by a 19th-century dentist named Anders Sandvig. Since his patients were sometimes too poor to pay him, they gave him whatever objects they could spare — a spoon or a small piece of furniture — instead. Now these old objects are assembled here to illustrate what life was like for the Norwegian people from the 11th through the 19th century. Assembled around a large, shady park, there are cottages, a complete manor farm, over 30,000 period pieces, a modern gunsmith's, and other craftspeople at work.

8. Phantasialand, Bruhl, Germany. You'll definitely want to spend a whole day at Phantasialand, the largest amusement park in Europe. Here you'll find Viking ships and pirate ships that you can really ride on, an exciting water flume ride, and a monorail that circles the entire park. You'll also visit a full-size Polynesian village, a Chinatown, a fairy tale park, a Wild West town called Silverstone City, and an area called Old Berlin, which shows what life was like there in 1900. When you get tired of touring the place, you can sit and watch the performing dolphins and seals or the chimpanzee jazz band, the only one of its kind.

9. Potter's Museum of Curiosity, Arundel, West Sussex, England. Potter's Museum of Curiosity is quite simply one of the most amazing places you could ever hope to spend a rainy afternoon. Walter Potter, who started the museum in

1862, was a taxidermist—he stuffed animals—with a very weird approach to his work. While most taxidermists just stuffed owls or squirrels and put them under glass domes for people to look at, Potter dressed up his stuffed creations and put them in elaborate scenes. There is, for instance, a kitten's tea party in which 37 cats are dressed up for a croquet match as others have tea on the lawn of a country house. The Rabbits School has 20 young rabbits sitting at school desks doing their arithmetic and learning to read. There's a two-headed lamb and a great goat with six legs. The effect is like wandering though the attic of some demented old man—terrific!

10. The Torture Museum, The Hague, the Netherlands. Here's one of Europe's spookier attractions. It's a museum of torture displaying almost everything that was used to get confessions out of people—and inflict pain—from the 15th to the 19th century, and it's spread over four awesome floors. All the devices are appropriately displayed here, since the building was actually a real prison until 1828.

THE 19 LANGUAGES MOST COMMONLY SPOKEN AT HOME IN THE U.S.

Some 31.8 million Americans speak something other than English at home. In fact, Americans speak over 300 languages in their households. Friends are most likely to know, in order of popularity:

1. Spanish
2. French
3. German
4. Italian
5. Chinese
6. Tagalog
7. Polish
8. Korean
9. Vietnamese
10. Portuguese
11. Greek
12. Arabic
13. Hindi
14. Russian
15. Yiddish
16. Thai/Lao
17. Persian
18. Creole
19. Armenian

10 KIDS WHO INVENTED THINGS

1. Louis Braille, a blind boy from France, invented a "language" of raised dots that could be "read" by blind people when he was 17.

2. Chester Greenwood loved ice skating but hated the fact that his ears got cold. So when he was 15 years old, he invented earmuffs.

3. Robert Patch is the youngest inventor ever. In 1962, when he was only 5, he designed a toy truck that could be taken apart and put back together.

4. Eric Van Paris, from Belgium, was 14 when he invented a "cooling fork" that blew air onto hot food so that kids could eat more easily.

5. Becky Schroeder received a patent at the age of 14 for creating a way of reading and writing in the dark. She used phosphorescent paint on paper underneath her writing paper so that she could write in the dark. Doctors now use it in hospitals to read patients' charts at night without waking them. Astronauts use this same technology when their electrical systems are turned down for recharging. She was named an Ohio Inventor of the Year and was inducted into the Ohio Inventors Hall of Fame.

6. Eight-year-old Theresa Thompson and her 9-year-old sister, Mary, were the youngest sisters to ever receive a U.S. patent. They invented a device that they called a Wigwam—a tepee which was warmed by solar energy.

7. When Matt Balick and Justin Lewis were only 8 years old, they had an idea for turning the little plastic stands used in pizza boxes into little toys called Flip-Itz. They sold their idea to a toy company, which expects to make $5 million in one year alone.

8. At age 9, Margaret Knight invented a safety device used in cotton mills that protected workers from injury. She began working in a cotton mill, where she saw a steel-tipped shuttle fly out of a loom and hit a nearby worker. She went on to invent the machine that makes the square-bottom paper bags we still use for groceries today. That machine was patented in 1871.

9. Chelsea Lannon at the age of 8 received a patent for her "pocket diaper," a diaper that has a pocket that holds a baby wipe and baby powder puff.

10. When Suzanna Goodin was 6, she got tired of having to clean the cat food spoon. Her solution was an edible, spoon-shaped cracker.

10 REASONS WHY GIRLS ARE BETTER THAN BOYS

You boys out there may not like these, but they're true, according to Jacqueline Shannon's book of surprising facts, *Why It's Great to Be a Girl* (Warner, 1994).

1. Girls see better in the dark.

2. Girls start talking earlier than boys.

3. They make better astronauts (they're smaller, weigh less, require less food and oxygen).

4. Girls handle pain better than boys.

5. Females have better hearing.

6. Girls get fewer viral and bacterial illnesses than boys.

7. They don't get as many zits as boys.

8. Girls don't get hiccups as often as boys do.

9. They handle extreme weather conditions—hot and cold—better than boys.

10. Girls have longer attention spans than boys.

8 ITEMS OF CLOTHING THAT HAVE BEEN BANNED IN SCHOOLS

1. Baggy jeans. Banned because of the large pockets, which make good hiding places.

2. Bandannas. Outlawed in some schools because they are considered gang garb.

3. Gold jewelry. Considered a reason to start fights and therefore against the law in some schools.

4. Net blouses. Cause problems in the summer, when some girls wear them with nothing underneath.

5. Leggings. At the Bates Academy in Detroit, girls are forbidden to wear anything "form-fitting, suggestive, or cut out too much."

6. Underwear. Sticking out of the top of your pants, like Marky Mark wore.

7. Baseball caps. Many public schools have outlawed them, since they can hide small handguns and knives.

8. T-shirts with drug logos on them. They violate the drug-free lifestyle that schools are supposed to be teaching.

20 WEIRD LAWS YOU SHOULD KNOW ABOUT

If you like putting pennies in your ears, don't go to Hawaii — it's illegal there. And did you know that it's illegal to fish while sitting on a horse in Washington, D.C.? There are actually hundreds of laws that made sense when they were passed (at least to someone) but now sound ridiculous. Still, they're real laws, so you should obey them, right?

1. No one in Hanford, California, can stop a child from jumping over a puddle.

2. It is illegal to give a child a cup of coffee in Lynn, Massachusetts.

3. Restaurants serving ice cream on a piece of cherry pie in Kansas are breaking the law.

4. You are not allowed to roller-skate on the streets of Quincy, Massachusetts.

5. It is illegal for a baby-sitter in Altoona, Pennsylvania, to eat the entire contents of the employer's refrigerator.

6. A person living in Saco, Missouri, is not allowed to wear a hat that can frighten a child.

7. Sheep are not allowed to run wild in schoolyards in Vermont.

8. It's against the law to pretend your parents are rich in the state of Washington.

9. It's illegal for youngsters in Mesquite, Texas, to have unusual haircuts.

10. In Indiana, it is against the law for a parent to drink beer if his or her child is present.

11. It is illegal to wear a fake mustache that causes laughter in a church in Alabama.

12. In Dyersburg, Tennessee, it is illegal for a girl to telephone a boy and ask for a date. And, girls, whatever you do, don't propose marriage to your boyfriend in Whitesville, Delaware. It's against the law!

13. In Oklahoma, people who make faces at dogs are breaking the law.

14. In Muskogee, Oklahoma, it is against the law for any member of a ball team to hit a ball over a fence or out of a park. (Could this be the reason Muskogee has no baseball team? Duh.)

15. Don't fish in your pajamas in Chicago.

16. You can't play hopscotch on the sidewalk in Missouri.

17. You can't use a lasso to catch a fish in Tennessee. (You probably can't do it anywhere, but if you succeed in Tennessee, you're breaking the law.)

18. Hollering "snake" within the city limits of Flowery Branch, Georgia, is against the law.

19. You can't slurp your soup in public in New Jersey.

20. It's illegal to remove your shoes if your feet smell while you're in a theater in Winnetka, Illinois. (This one actually makes sense.)

8 STUPENDOUS, SHOWSTOPPING STATISTICS ABOUT "THE GREATEST SHOW ON EARTH"

In 1870 P. T. Barnum's Museum, Menagerie, Caravan and Hippodrome was founded. That same year the seven Ringling brothers presented their "backyard circus" for the first time. It wasn't until 1919 that both circuses joined to form what is now known as the Ringling Bros. and Barnum & Bailey Circus. Here are some amazing facts about "the Greatest Show on Earth."

1. There are actually two different circus units that tour each year.

2. These circuses entertain 25 million people in 97 countries each year.

3. The circus has more than 1,000 costumes.

4. It takes about 8 hours to set up all the rigging before a performance.

5. The animals are fed 364 tons of hay, 46,800 pounds of meat, 62,400 pounds of carrots, 39,000 pounds of apples, and 15,288 loaves of bread each year.

6. The circus owns 42 elephants, 10 lions, 14 tigers, 6 bears, 33 horses, 2 camels, 2 llamas, and 4 zebras. (And a partridge in a pear tree.)

7. Approximately 1,075 performances are given each year.

8. When the circus train of 53 cars is fully loaded, it weighs 1½ billion pounds.

10 FAMOUS PEOPLE WHO NEVER GRADUATED FROM GRADE SCHOOL

1. Andrew Carnegie, U.S. industrialist
2. Charlie Chaplin, British actor
3. Charles Dickens, British writer
4. Isadora Duncan, American dancer
5. Thomas Edison, American inventor (Deaf from the time he was 12, Edison spent just three months in public schools.)
6. Claude Monet, French painter
7. Sean O'Casey, Irish playwright
8. Alfred E. Smith, American politician
9. John Philip Sousa, American composer
10. Mark Twain, American writer

HOW TO BE POLITE IN 6 LANGUAGES

Here's how to say "hello," "good-bye," please," and "thank you" in six languages.

Esperanto
Hello: bonan matenon (BOH-nahn mah-TEH-nohn)
Good-bye: adiau (ah-DEE-ow)
Please: bonvole (bohn-VOH-leh)
Thank you: dankon (DAHN-kohn)

French
Hello: bonjour (bohn-ZHOOR)
Good-bye: au revoir (OH ruh-VWAHR)
Please: s'il vous plait (seel voo PLAY)
Thank you: merci (merh-SEE)

All-New
^

Italian

Hello: buon giorno (BWAN JOHR-noh)
Good-bye: arrivederci (ah-ree-vay-DAYR-chee)
Please: per favore (payr fah-VOH-ray)
Thank you: grazie (GRAH-tsyay)

Japanese

Hello: ohayo (Oh-hah-YOH)
Good-bye: sayonara (sah-yoh-nah-ra)
Please: kudasai (koo-dah-sahee)
Thank you: arigato (ah-rih-gah-toh)

Russian

Hello: zdravstvuite (ZDRAH-st'eh)
Good-bye: do svidanya (duh sv'i-DAH-n'uh)
Please: pozhaluista (puh-SHAL-stuh)
Thank you: blagodaryu (bluh-guh-duh-R'OO)

Spanish

Hello: buenos dias (BWEN-nohs DEE-ahs)
Good-bye: adios (ah-dee-OHS)
Please: por favor (POHR fa-VOHR)
Thank you: gracias (GRAH-see-uhs)

WHEN YOU GOTTA GO, YOU GOTTA GO
14 Words for "Bathroom"

1. Toilet
2. Potty
3. W.C. (for "water closet," which is what toilets were once called and are still called in England)
4. John
5. Jane
6. Powder room
7. Loo
8. Commode
9. Can

10. Hopper
11. Throne room
12. Toidy

13. The little girls' (or little boys') room
14. The smallest room in the house

HOW TO SAY "I HAVE TO GO TO THE BATHROOM" IN 9 LANGUAGES

It would be pretty hard to memorize how to say "I have to go to the bathroom" in 9 languages. So here are the words for "bathroom." Chances are, if you say this with the right expression of urgency, they'll know what you mean, and you'll be directed to the nearest john, loo, hopper—whatever you want to call it. If this doesn't work, you can always try grabbing your privates and jumping up and down on one foot!

Language	Word	How to Pronounce It
1. Esperanto	traduku	trad OO koo
2. French	le toilette	lah TWA let
3. German	Bad	bod
4. Hawaiian	lumi au au lua	LUmi oh oh LUwa
5. Italian	bagno	BON yo
6. Korean	hwa jang shil	WHA jang shil
7. Polish	lazienka	
8. Spanish	cuarto de bano	KWAR to day BONyo
9. Tagalog	banyo	BONyo

46 PHOBIAS

Everyone is afraid of *something*. Here are some fancy names for fears of some ordinary things.

1. Pogonoophobia: fear of beards
2. Amychophobia: fear of being scratched

3. Ereuthophobia: fear of blushing
4. Bibliophobia: fear of books
5. Mysophobia: fear of dirt
6. Cynophobia: fear of dogs
7. Pediophobia: fear of dolls
8. Paraskavedekatriaphobia: fear of Friday the 13th
9. Clinophobia: fear of going to bed
10. Shamhainophobia: fear of Halloween
11. Trypanophobia: fear of injections
12. Astrapophobia: fear of lightning
13. Gymnophobia: fear of being naked
14. Arachiutyrophobia: fear of peanut butter sticking to the roof of your mouth
15. Ombrophobia: fear of rain
16. Batrachophobia: fear of reptiles
17. Scholionophobia: fear of school
18. Hypnophobia: fear of going to sleep
19. Blennophobia: fear of slime
20. Chionophobia: fear of snow
21. Phonophobia: fear of speaking aloud
22. Topophobia: stagefright
23. Triskaidekaphobia: fear of the number 13
24. Wicaphobia: fear of witches
25. Ergasiophobia: fear of work
26. Helminthophobia: fear of worms
27. Zoophobia: fear of animals
28. Automysophobia: fear of being dirty
29. Scopophobia: fear of being stared at
30. Gephydrophobia: fear of crossing a bridge
31. Pantophobia: fear of everything
32. Pyrophobia: fear of fire
33. Sitophobia: fear of food
34. Phasmophobia: fear of ghosts
35. Acrophobia: fear of heights
36. Musophobia: fear of mice
37. Eisoptrophobia: fear of mirrors

38. Teratophobia: fear of monsters
39. Nyctophobia: fear of night
40. Poinephobia: fear of punishment
41. Scholionophobia: fear of school
42. Sciophobia: fear of shadows
43. Pnigerphobia: fear of smothering
44. Xenophobia: fear of strangers
45. Tonitrophobia: fear of thunder
46. Hydrophobia: fear of water

6 FANCY WORDS FOR GROSS SOUNDS THAT EVERYBODY MAKES

Don't make a big deal out of these, whether they're yours or someone else's.

1. Borborgymus: when your stomach "growls." The sound your stomach muscles make when your stomach is empty. Your stomach also "growls" as you digest food.

2. Eructation: burping. It happens when your stomach releases air that you swallowed while you were eating. If you eat slowly, it happens less.

3. Flatulence: the dreaded *F* word, fart. If you swallowed air and didn't burp, it'll come out the other end. Lots of fun at bathtime.

4. Pandiculation: yawning. The body's way of trying to get more oxygen as you get tired, although the exact cause is not completely understood.

5. Singulthus: caused when your diaphragm has a spasm, throwing off the rhythm of the air going into your lungs. In the meantime, as you breathe more air, it gets stuck in the back of your throat, resulting in a hiccup.

6. Stenutation: a big word for a sneeze. Your nose automatically cleans out dust, mucus, or certain smells.

76 IDIOMS YOU'RE LIKELY TO COME ACROSS

An idiom is an expression that does not mean exactly what it sounds like. "Lend us your ears" means *listen.* a friend who "looks down his nose at you" is *acting like a snob.* Here are 76 more idioms you're likely to come across in your travels as a kid.

1. Down in the dumps: depressed

2. A good head on your shoulders: smart and sensible

3. Frozen with fear: petrified

4. Lose your voice: laryngitis

5. The walls have ears: Someone might hear you, even if you think they can't.

6. The cat got your tongue: you're not speaking

7. Bite off more than you can chew: take on too big a project

8. Spill the beans: tell a secret

9. Go fly a kite!: Get out of here!

10. Fill the queen's shoes: be able to take over someone's responsibilities and do the work just as well

11. I'm all ears: I'm listening.

12. Travel light: with little luggage

13. Heart of gold: genuinely kind

14. Cost a pretty penny: expensive

15. Hold your horses!: Be patient!

16. On your toes: alert

17. Covered his tracks: didn't leave evidence of what he did

18. See red: enraged

19. Rose-colored glasses: sees only the good

20. Be in hot water: get into really big trouble

21. Time flies: time seems to be passing quickly

22. Clean as a whistle: immaculate

23. Hot under the collar: angry

24. Make quite a splash: really impress people

25. Have the last laugh: be the winner in a prank

26. Piece of cake: easy to do

27. A photographic memory: ability to memorize lots of information easily

28. Cut corners: do something in the least expensive way

29. Make tracks: hurry

30. A needle in a haystack: impossible to find

31. Keep it under your hat: keep a secret

32. His bark is worse than his bite: He doesn't behave as badly as he talks.

33. A horse of a different color: a completely different situation

34. Life in the fast lane: the difference between training wheels and roller blades

35. Suits me to a *T:* just right

36. A green thumb: a good gardener

37. Nothing to sneeze at: something that should be taken seriously

38. That's it in a nutshell: an abbreviated version of a story

39. Lying down on the job: refusing to work

40. Royal treatment: the best treatment available

41. Our neck of the woods: our area

42. Playing with a full deck: your brain is working well

43. Fit as a fiddle: in perfect health

44. Pulling my leg: teasing

45. Change your tune: change your mind

46. Face the music: do something that's hard to do, like telling your parents about a rotten report card

47. Music to my ears: good news

48. Until the cows come home: forever

49. Run of the mill: ordinary

50. Take a crack at: try

51. White elephant: a thing of little value

52. Dust bunnies: Look under your bed for an example!

53. Thumbs down: disapproval or dislike

54. Hit the deck: get down

55. You took the words right out of my mouth: You said what I planned to say.

56. Lucky dog: someone who just had good luck

57. Born yesterday: stupid

58. Fishing for compliments: hinting for someone to say something nice about you

59. Head in the clouds: dazed and confused

60. Out of this world: extraordinary

61. Hit the roof: outraged

62. Wet behind the ears: inexperienced

63. Wet our whistles: take a drink

64. Big cheese: someone very important

65. Fruits of our labor: the results of work

66. Clotheshorse: someone who loves buying clothes

67. Doggy bag: leftovers from a restaurant meal

68. Copy cat: someone who imitates others

69. Burst your bubble: disappoint

70. Left no stone unturned: looked everywhere

71. A lemon: something of poor quality

72. Wipe the slate clean: start all over

73. In the doghouse: in trouble

74. Barking up the wrong tree: looking in the wrong place for what you want

75. In your dreams: wishful thinking

76. Jumping to conclusions: thinking you know what's going on before you really have all the facts

7 WAYS TO IMPRESS A FLIGHT ATTENDANT

Try using these insider slang phrases to suggest you're a world-class traveler.

1. Blue room: bathroom
2. Bug smasher: a small private plane
3. Dogs: passengers
4. Hawk or vulture: a passenger who causes trouble
5. PAX: passenger
6. Pit: the storage area on the plane
7. Red-eye: a late-night flight

NATIONAL SPELLING BEE WINNERS AND THEIR WINNING WORDS

You may want someone else to read you this list so you can see if you could have spelled these words correctly. Some are easy, and some will give you a headache. Of course, we expect you to look up the meanings of all the words you don't know.

1980. Jacques Bailly: elucubrate
1981. Paige Pipkin: sarcophagus
1982. Molly Dieveney: psoriasis
1983. Blake Giddens: Purim
1984. Daniel Greenblatt: luge
1985. Balu Natarajan: milieu
1986. Jon Pennington: odontalgia
1987. Stephanie Petit: staphylococci
1988. Rageshree Ramachandran: elegiacal
1989. Scott Isaacs: spoliator
1990. Amy Marie Dimak: fibranne
1991. Joanne Lagatta: antipyretic
1992. Amanda Goad: lyceum
1993. Geoff Hooper: kamikaze
1994. Ned G. Andrews: antediluvian

1995. Justin Tyler Carroll: xanthosis
1996. Wendy Guey: vivisepulture
1997. Rebecca Sealfon: euonym
1998. Jody-Anne Maxwell: chiaroscurist
1999. Nupur Lala: logorrhea
2000. George Abraham Thampy: demarche
2001. Sean Conley: succedaneum

71 TWO-LETTER WORDS

Two-letter words may not seem important to know, but the next time you do a crossword puzzle or play a game of Scrabble, they'll probably come in very handy. These are all legitimate words; they appear in *Funk & Wagnalls Standard College Dictionary*.

1. aa	**19.** eh	**37.** ka	**55.** os
2. ad	**20.** el	**38.** la	**56.** ox
3. ae	**21.** em	**39.** li	**57.** pa
4. ah	**22.** en	**40.** lo	**58.** pe
5. ai	**23.** et	**41.** ma	**59.** pi
6. am	**24.** fa	**42.** mi	**60.** re
7. an	**25.** go	**43.** mo	**61.** si
8. ar	**26.** ha	**44.** mu	**62.** so
9. as	**27.** he	**45.** my	**63.** ti
10. at	**28.** hi	**46.** na	**64.** to
11. ax	**29.** ho	**47.** no	**65.** up
12. ay	**30.** id	**48.** nu	**66.** us
13. ba	**31.** if	**49.** od	**67.** ut
14. be	**32.** in	**50.** of	**68.** we
15. bi	**33.** is	**51.** oh	**69.** wo
16. by	**34.** it	**52.** on	**70.** xi
17. de	**35.** ja	**53.** op	**71.** ye
18. do	**36.** jo	**54.** or	

THE 3 LONGEST WORDS IN THE ENGLISH LANGUAGE

1. If you're looking in *The Oxford English Dictionary,* the longest word will be **supercalifragilisticexpialidocious.**

2. In *Webster's Third International Dictionary,* the longest word is the 47-letter plural of a lung disease called **pneumonoultramicroscopicsilicovolcanoconiosises.**

3. In the novel *Finnegans Wake,* by James Joyce, the longest word is the term for a chemical formula. It has 1,913 letters. If you're ever truly bored and can't think of anything to do, count the letters. If they are wrong, write to us and let us know. No cash awards given. The word is: **Methionylglutaminylarginyltyrosylglutamylserylleucylphenylalanylalanylglutaminylleucyllysylglutamylarginyllysyglutamylgycylalanylphenylalanylvalylprolylphenylalanylvalylthreonylleucylglycylaspartprolylglycyllisoleucylglutamylglutaminylserylleucyllysylisoleucylaspartylthreonylleucylisoleucylglutamylalanylglycylalanylaspartylalanylleucylglutamylleucylglycylisoleucylprolylphenylalanylserylaspartylprolylleucylalanylaspartylglycylprolylthreonylisoleucylglutaminylasparaginylalanylthreonylleucylarginylalanylphenylalanylalanylalanylglycylvalylthreonylprolylalanylglutaminylcysteinylphenylalanylglutamylmethionylleucylalanylleucylisoleucylarginylglutaminyllysylhistidylprolylthreonylisoleucylprolylisoleucylglycylleucylleucylmethionyltyrosylalanylasparaginylleucylvalylphenylalanylasparaginyllysylglycylisoleucylaspartylglutamylphenylalanyltyrosylalanylglutaminylcysteinylglutamyllysylvalylglycylvalylaspartylsrylvalylleucylvalylalanylaspartylvalylprolylvalylglutaminylglutamylserylalanylprolylphenylalanylarginylglutaminylalanylalanylleucylarginylhistidylasparaginylvalylalanylprolylisoleucylphenylalanylisoleucylcysteinylprolylprolylaspartylalanylaspartylaspartylaspartylleucylleucylarginyl-**

glutaminylisoleucylalanylseryltyrosylglycylarginylglycyltyrosylthreonyltyrosylleucylleucylserylarginylalanylglycylvalylthreonylglycylalanylglutamylasparaginylarginylalanylalanylleucylleucyllysylglutamyltyrosylasparaginylalanylalanylprolylprolylleucylglutaminylglycylphenylalanylglysylisoleucylserylalanylprolylaspartylglutaminylvalyllysylalanylalanylisoleucylaspartylalanylglycylalanylalanylglyclalanylisoleucylserylglycylserylalanylisoleucylvalyllysylisoleucylisoleucylglutamylglutaminylhistidylasparaginylisoleucylglutamylprolylglutamyllysylmethionylleucylalanylalanylleucyllysylvalylphenylalanylvalylglutaminylprolylmethionyllysylalanylalanylthreonylarginylserine.

23 FACTS THAT NO ONE NEEDS TO KNOW

1. Most lipstick contains fish scales.

2. The first product to have a bar code was Wrigley's gum.

3. No piece of square dry paper can be folded more than seven times.

4. Pinocchio is Italian for "pine eye."

5. The average lifespan of a major league baseball is five to seven pitches.

6. The electric chair was invented by a dentist.

7. There is one-tenth of a calorie in the glue on a postage stamp.

8. The glue on an Israeli postage stamp is kosher.

9. The average person has 1,460 dreams a year.

10. One in every four Americans has appeared on TV.

11. No NFL team that plays its home games in a domed stadium has ever won a Super Bowl.

12. The first toilet ever seen on TV was on *Leave It to Beaver*.

13. The Sesame Street characters Bert and Ernie were

named after the cop and taxi driver in the movie *It's a Wonderful Life*.

14. A statue of a person on a horse with both front legs in the air honors a person who died in battle. If only one leg is in the air, the person died as a result of wounds received in battle. If all four legs are on the ground, the person died of natural causes.

15. There are an average of 178 sesame seeds on a McDonald's Big Mac bun.

16. When ketchup leaves the bottle, it travels at a speed of 25 miles per hour. (Note: If it comes out slower or not at all, stick a straw into the bottle; the ketchup will flow a lot faster.)

17. Months that begin on a Sunday always have a Friday the thirteenth.

18. Chewing gum while peeling onions will keep you from crying.

19. The most common name in the world is Mohammed.

20. The strongest muscle in the body is the tongue.

21. More Monopoly money is printed every year than real money throughout the world.

22. When you put a seashell up to your ear, you're not hearing the ocean. You're hearing the echo of your own blood pulsing.

23. Gilligan of *Gilligan's Island* did have a first name, but it was used only once — on an episode that was never aired. His name was Willy. The Skipper's real name was Jonas Grumby; it, too, was mentioned only once — on the first episode, when there was a radio newscast about the shipwreck.

8

Just for Fun

14 QUESTIONS YOU WOULD BE ASKED IF YOU WENT TO CLOWN COLLEGE

Since 1968, during the winter, the Ringling Bros. and Barnum & Bailey circus held a clown college, where applicants were trained to look like clowns, dress like them, juggle, walk on stilts, and do all the other things you've seen circus clowns do. Anyone over 17 could apply, and tuition was free. In 2001 they sadly announced that they would discontinue the program after training more than 1,400 clowns. Here are some of the questions you would have been asked if you had applied to clown college.

1. What was your very first job for money?

2. What has given you the most pleasure during the past year?

3. Describe your first accomplishment.

4. If you could be someone else, who would you be, and why?

5. What character trait in yourself would you most like to change?

6. What is your worst hang-up?

7. What is the most important lesson you have learned?

8. Describe memorable turning points in your life.

9. Rate your anger "boiling point" from 1 to 10.

10. Name three favorite musical groups and several of their recordings that you consider outstanding.

11. Name your favorite foods.

12. List your all-time-favorite movies.

13. When was the last time you cried?

14. What does being a clown mean to you?

5 SONGS TO PLAY ON YOUR PUSH-BUTTON TELEPHONE

Before you begin your career as a "telephonist," you'll need to remember that if you just sit down to play these songs, pushing buttons right and left, you're liable to find yourself connected to someone in Hawaii or even Europe. To avoid the whopping phone bill that you'd get as a result, just call someone who lives close by and play the songs for them. You won't disconnect the call in the course of playing the songs, and the two of you can enjoy the concert.

1. **"Here We Go Round the Mulberry Bush"**
Here we go round the Mul- ber- ry bush,
  4 4 4 2   2 6   6 2 4
The mul- ber- ry bush, the mul- ber- ry bush,
  4 8 8 8 8 6 2   4 4 4
Here we go round the mul- ber- ry bush
  4 4 4 2   4 4 8 8 4
So ear- ly in the mor- ning.
  4 8 8 6 8   4   4

2. **"Mary Had a Little Lamb"**
Ma- ry had a lit- tle lamb
  6 0 4 0 6 6   6
lit- tle lamb, lit- tle lamb
  2 2 2   6 6   6
Ma- ry had a lit- tle lamb
  6 0 4 0 6 6 6
Its fleece was white as snow.
  6 8 8   6 8 4

3. **"Jingle Bells"**
Jin- gle bells, jin- gle bells
  6 6 6   6 6 6
Jin- gle all the way,
  6 # 7 8 6

Oh what fun it is to ride
9   9   9 9 9 5   5
In a one- horse o- pen sleigh
5 5 5   7 4 5 6

4. "Old MacDonald Had a Farm"
Old Mac- Don- ald had a farm, EE- I- EE- I- O!
 6   6   6   7 8 8 7   9 9 0 0 4
And on this farm he had some chicks, EE- I- EE- I- O!
 4 6 6   6 7 8 8   7   9 9 0 0 4
Here a chick, there a chick, ev- ery- where a chick chick,
 4 4 4   4 4 4   4 4   4 4 4   4
Old Mac- Don- ald had a farm, EE- I- EE- I- O!
 6   6   6   7 8 8 7   9 9 0 0 4

5. "Happy Birthday" (Leave this on someone's answering machine on his birthday.)
Hap- py Birth- day to you,
 1   1   2   1 # 6
Hap- py Birth- day to you,
 1   1   2   1 # 3
Hap- py Birth- day dear _____,
 1   1   #   # 8 4 ? 1
Hap- py Birth- day to you
 #   #   6   4 2 1

12 THINGS THAT ARE IMPOSSIBLE TO DO

1. Be in two places at once
2. Breathe water
3. Build castles in the air
4. Catch the wind in a sieve
5. Fall up
6. Find the secret of perpetual motion
7. Fix mercury so it won't move

8. Grow another foot
9. Live forever
10. Make parallel lines meet
11. Weave a rope of sand
12. Write on water

9 TONGUE TWISTERS

Tongue twisters were originally used in schools to teach children how to speak correctly. See if you can say each of the following three times fast.

1. The sixth sick sheik's sixth sheep's sick.
2. The swan swam out to sea. Swim, swan, swim!
3. A big black bug bit a big black bear and the big black bear bled blood.
4. The skunk sat on a stump; the skunk thunk the stump stunk, but the stump thunk the skunk stunk.
5. She's so selfish she could sell shellfish shells, but shells of shellfish seldom sell.
6. Three gay geese sat on the green grass grazing.
7. Some shun sunshine; do you shun sunshine?
8. How much wood would a woodchuck chuck if a woodchuck could chuck wood?
9. Peter Piper picked a peck of pickled peppers.

CAROLE KING LISTS "THINGS YOU SEE OUTSIDE YOUR WINDOW"

In the 1960s Carole King was one of the most popular songwriters, with hits such as "Will You Love Me Tomorrow?" and "Up on the Roof." Today she is one of the best-loved kids' performers, best known for *Really Rosie*, which she composed and performed. King's special talent for helping us appreciate life through her imaginative lyrics is as evident on her recording of that program as it is in this poem, which she wrote especially for this book.

Things You See Outside Your Window

Frost-covered trees like cotton balls;
Animal tracks that zigzag
Teardrops on telephone lines;
Vegetables looking like flowers;
Venus looking at Mars;
The past, the present, and the future;
Weaving among the stars;
City streets teeming with people;
Mountains covered in snow;
Other people at windows;
A whole world for you to know.

13 HORRIBLE NAMES TO CALL KIDS WHO WEAR BRACES

They've been called chain chompers, dentists' devils, tin tusks, foil fangs, snagglefangs, crumb catchers, cow catchers, tinker teeth, and pearly grates. By the time you get around to memorizing those names and the ones that follow, it will probably be time to get your braces off. Thanks to our friend (the amazing) Grace Townley for help with this one.

1. Metal Mouth
2. Tinsel Teeth
3. Fence Face
4. Shiny Smile
5. Tin Grin
6. Hi-Ho Silver
7. Foil Face
8. Brace Face
9. Bracket Bones
10. Rin Tin Tin
11. Tank Teeth
12. Tractor Mouth
13. Chew Chew Train

KERMIT THE FROG LISTS 7 GOOD THINGS ABOUT BEING A FROG

Born on a lilypad in a Mississippi swamp, Kermit the Frog was one of several thousand children. The most traumatic moment of young Kermit's brief youth came during his transformation from a pollywog to a frog; he literally lost his tail in the process. Displaying an early gift for music, Kermit learned to sing and play the banjo. With only his talent, his banjo, and a hope in his heart, Kermit, green but hopeful, left home in 1955 and headed for New York. On the way he stopped off in Washington, D.C., where he performed on television live for 5 minutes every night for eight years. Dressed up as a green lizard who denied he was a frog, Kermit became a capitol celebrity and won a local Emmy for Outstanding Television Entertainment. Then, in 1963, he made his debut on network television with an appearance on the Steve Allen *Tonight Show*. One of his biggest breaks came in 1969 with his invitation to be a featured player on *Sesame Street*. Then, in 1976, he became the international star of *The Muppet Show* —and the rest is history. The crowning experience for Kermit during *The Muppet Show* years was being presented to Queen Elizabeth II at a jubilee performance in London.

We are grateful for this list to Jim Henson, who passed away in 1990.

1. Being green
2. Sitting in the sun on a lilypad
3. Having thousands of brothers and sisters
4. Going to the hop
5. Playing leapfrog
6. Having bears and pigs and dogs and chickens as your friends
7. Getting kissed by princesses hoping to turn you into a handsome prince

13 TIMES TO MAKE A WISH

1. If a ladybug lands on you, make a wish just as it is leaving and then don't talk for three minutes.

2. If you see a duck, make a wish and then say "Quack!" If the duck quacks back, your wish will come true.

3. If you see three birds on a telephone wire, make a wish before they fly away.

4. Catch a firefly in your hand and start counting to 10. If the firefly flashes five times before you're finished counting, make a wish and let it go.

5. Wish on a new pair of shoes. By the time you have outgrown the shoes, your wish will come true.

6. If you find a turtle on its back, pick it up, turn it over, and you will get four wishes.

7. If you find a dandelion, make a wish and then blow off all the seed. If all the seeds blow away in one breath, your wish will come true.

8. Stick a watermelon seed on your forehead and make a wish. If the seed sticks until you've made your wish, the wish will come true.

9. Make a wish every time you eat a green M&M.

10. If you see a black cat with green eyes, pet it ten times and make a wish.

11. When you see a mail truck, cross your fingers and make a wish. Keep your fingers crossed until you see a dog.

12. If you can peel the silver foil from the wax paper on a gum wrapper without tearing it, make a wish and the wish will come true.

13. If the clasp on a necklace works its way to the front of your neck, make a wish while you move the clasp back to the back of your neck.

All-New
^

YOU FEEL LIKE ZIGGY WHEN . . .

Poor Ziggy! As one of America's best-loved cartoon characters, he's been making people laugh for years. We all have bad days, but Ziggy seems to get more than his share. You feel just like him when . . .

1. . . . all the mail you get is addressed to Occupant.

2. . . . your alphabet soup makes snide remarks.

3. . . . your clock-radio goes off in the morning and asks you what time it is.

4. . . . you have to pay an overdue fine at the library for a book entitled *How to Improve Your Memory*.

5. . . . opportunity knocks at the front door while you're out back, taking out the garbage.

6. . . . you know how to spell *bananas* but you don't know when to stop.

7. . . . you're an underachiever and your teacher is an over-expecter.

8. . . . your TV set breaks down on the same day your warranty expires.

9. . . . your palmist can't find your lifeline.

10. . . . you drop your open-faced peanut butter and jelly sandwich and it lands jelly side down.

20 SIGNS OF BAD LUCK

1. If you sing while you walk upstairs and don't finish the song by the time you get to the top.

2. If while riding over the railroad tracks in a car you don't pick up your feet.

3. If the initials of your name spell a word.

4. If your name has 13 letters.

5. If you play cards near a church.

6. If you cross the path of a black cat.

7. If you walk across a grave.

8. If you find a penny tails up.

9. If you spend a coin that you have found.

10. If you walk with one shoe on and one shoe off.

11. If you leave a house through a different door than the one you used to enter.

12. If you talk while riding over a bridge.

13. If you watch a friend who has been visiting you drive off.

14. If you hit something with your left foot while taking a walk.

15. If someone pinches your fourth finger and you scream.

16. If you cut your fingernails on Friday.

17. If a mouse leaves your house.

18. If you cut the part of the birthday cake with your name on it.

19. If you cry on your birthday.

20. If you walk under a ladder.

20 SIGNS OF GOOD LUCK

1. If your name has seven letters.

2. If you see three nuns riding in a car.

3. If you find a horseshoe.

4. If you sleep with a silver dollar under your mattress.

5. If you say "rabbit, rabbit," on the first day of a month as soon as you wake up.

6. If on the first day of a month you fill your mouth with water, turn around, walk down a flight of stairs backwards with your eyes closed, then, upon reaching the bottom of the stairs, you swallow the water, open your eyes, turn around, and kiss the first person you see.

7. If you cross your fingers when you see a mail truck and don't uncross them until you see another.

8. If you hold your breath and cross your fingers when you pass a graveyard.

9. If you point your thumbs up when passing a graveyard.

10. If you put on a piece of clothing inside out.

11. If you find a penny heads up.

12. If you find a stone with a hole in it.

13. If you eat an apple dipped in honey on New Year's Day.

14. If you tie a red bow on a new car.

15. If you pinch the person sitting next to you in a car just after you have seen an out-of-state license plate.

16. If you hit something with your right foot while taking a walk.

17. If you put your right shoe on first in the morning.

18. If June the 13th falls on a Friday.

19. If you eat figs for breakfast on your birthday.

20. If you tie your shoe with three loops for the bow instead of two.

7 CHARMS TO BRING YOU LUCK

Throughout history, people have practiced "magic," and for just as long, other people have been coming up with ways to counteract magic spells. All of the following are intended for that purpose.

1. To break a hex that has been placed on you, get a friend to read a Bible verse to you backwards, then fold the page, place a silver fork in it, and close the book. Before you go to sleep at night, put the Bible under your pillow and recite the Lord's Prayer backwards before lying down.

2. To protect yourself from evil spirits, cross your fingers tightly when passing a cemetery.

3. To prevent evil spirits from doing harm in your home, carry black pepper in your pockets.

4. You can change bad luck to good by tossing the hair of a black cat over your left shoulder.

5. An old broom hung over a door will supposedly keep disease away from the home.

6. If you pour champagne on all four corners of your property on a moonless night, you will have the help of good spirits when you need them.

7. Plant mustard seed at your front and back doors and you will have success and luck in everything you do.

27 EXAMPLES OF CIRCUS SLANG

1. Antipodist: a man or woman who juggles with his or her feet

2. Auguste: the clown who always gets it in the face when a pie is thrown or water is sprayed

3. Bender: the circus contortionist

4. Bull: an elephant

5. Cats: the wild animals, including tigers, lions, leopards, etc.

6. Cherry pie: extra work done by employees for extra pay

7. Denari: money

8. Diddy: a Gypsy

9. Dona: a woman

10. Ducat: a ticket to the circus

11. Flattie: a circus spectator

12. Jackpots: tall tales about the circus

13. Joey: a clown

14. Jonah's bad luck: when a circus wagon gets stuck in the mud

15. Josser: anyone who isn't in the circus business

16. Kicking sawdust: following the circus or being part of it

17. Kid show: the freak show

18. Letty: lodgings for circus performers

19. Little people: dwarfs or midgets

20. Lunge: the safety device used to keep performers from injuring themselves while doing difficult tricks

21. Missing a tip: missing a trick

22. Omney: a man

23. Run-in clown: the clown who runs out in between acts to perform while the next act is being set up

24. Shandy-man: the electrician

25. Star-backs: the most expensive seats in the audience

26. Turnaway: a sold-out show

27. Zanies: clowns

11 TERMS INVENTED BY THE HIPPIES IN THE 1960S

The next time your grandparents object to some of the strange terms that you and your friends use, remind them that back in the '60s, the hippies had a language of their own, too. Some of these terms are still in use today.

1. Crash pad: a place to spend the night

2. Different strokes for different folks: the idea that each person is entitled to his or her own likes, dislikes, and opinions. This term was popularized by a rock group called Sly & the Family Stone, who had a big hit with a song called "Different Strokes" in the late 1960s.

3. Drop out: to withdraw from something, like "dropping out of school"

4. Flower child: a hippie, or someone who tries to live in a natural environment, rejecting commercial values

5. Flower power: the idea of changing the world through peace and love

6. Freak out: to lose touch with reality; lose control

7. Freak: someone who is very involved with a certain thing, like a music freak or a food freak

8. Groovy: terrific; great

9. Hairy: frightening

10. Heavy: profound; meaningful

11. Hung up: unable to make a decision; bogged down with things to do, as in "I got hung up with chores and couldn't make it to the party."

GUMPS, GAZOOKS, AND GOOPS

If you've ever been told to stop calling your little brother Stupid, try any one of the following names instead, all of which have become part of the English language. If you haven't heard of all of them, there's no need for you to feel like a yap, though. Most of them haven't been used in years.

1. Addlebrain
2. Beetlebrain
3. Cabbagehead
4. Calabash
5. Chowderhead
6. Chucklehead
7. Dunderhead
8. Flibbertigibbet
9. Hockey puck
10. Jellybean
11. Jingle brain
12. Muff
13. Mushhead
14. Rattlehead
15. Sao
16. Yahoo
17. Yap
18. Yo-yo

10 WAYS TO SIGN YOUR NAME

Yours till . . .

1. the bed spreads
2. the sugar bowls
3. soda pops
4. the board walks
5. the pillowcase is solved
6. the banana peels
7. the bed springs
8. the kitchen sinks
9. ginger snaps
10. butter flies

HOW TO SIGN YOUR FRIEND'S AUTOGRAPH BOOK

Take the local,
Take the express,
Don't get off
Till you reach success.

Remember me,
When this you see,
And what good friends
We used to be.

You asked me to write
So what shall it be?
Two little words:
"Remember me."

2 nice
+ 2 be
* 4 gotten*

I love you bip
I love you bop
I love you more
Than a pig loves slop.

25 REASONS TO SKIP SCHOOL
Holidays Your Teacher Probably Never Heard Of

1. January 3, Sip-a-Drink-Through-a-Straw Day
2. January 11, Banana Boat Day
3. January 16, National Nothing Day
4. January 20, Hat Day

5. January 30, Swap-the-Brown-Bag-Lunch Day
6. March 1, National Pig Day
7. March 22, National Goof-off Day
8. April 15, National Gripers Day
9. May 8, Children-Should-Be-Seen-and-Not-Heard Day
10. June 15, Smile Power Day
11. June 18, International Picnic Day
12. June 22, National Fink Day
13. July 11, National Cheer-Up-the-Lonely Day
14. July 15, National Ice Cream Day
15. August 6, Summer-Is-Half-Over Day
16. August 13, International Left-Handers Day
17. August 15, National Failures Day
18. September 5, National Be-Late-for-Something Day
19. September 12, Snack-a-Pickle Day
20. September 30, Ask-a-Stupid-Question Day
21. October 15, National Grouch Day
22. November 17, Homemade Bread Day
23. November 23, Horror Movie Day
24. December 12, National Ding-a-Ling Day
25. December 21, Look-at-the-Bright-Side Day

7 REASONS TO WRITE TO THE AUTHORS OF THIS BOOK

Our address is: P.O. Box 74, Haworth, NJ 07641. Tell us what you think. Tell us if you hated some part of this book or if something in it made your day or if . . .

1. You have ideas for other lists that you'd like to see included in a future edition of this book.

2. You found something in the book that you think is wrong or stupid.

3. You have to use up the weird stationery that your aunt Ida gave you for your birthday last year. (Don't waste paper!)

4. You didn't understand something and you don't have anybody around who can explain it to you.

5. You like to write letters.

6. You like to lick stamps.

7. You like to get letters. (If you want us to write back, please enclose a stamped, self-addressed envelope.)

Contributors

Jim Abbate
American Cancer Society
Amnesty International
Ben and Jerry's
Gareth Branwyn at *Wired*
Bill Bryson
Kristen Carr
Sasha Carr
Casey Choron
D.A.R.E.
The Disney Channel
Mike Donner
Sandi Gelles-Cole
John Glenn
The Graduate School of
    Education at Northern
    Illinois University
Häagen-Dazs
Alexa Hamilton
Hasbro Toy Company
Jim Henson
Ice Skating Institute of America
International Paper Company
Chuck Jones
Jacqueline Kennedy Onassis
The Kids on the Block
Carole King
Lefthanders International
Shari Lewis
John Marr
Dave Marsh
Mattel
Fred Mayer of the International
    Wizard of Oz Club

National Association of the
    Deaf
National Association of Fan
    Clubs
Nickelodeon
North American Association
    of Ventriloquists
Omni Magazine
Bob Oskam
Peace Education Foundation
Pet Haven Cemetery
Public Broadcasting Service
Randi Reisfeld
Ringling Brothers and Barnum
    & Bailey Circus
Fred Rogers
Ellen Rosenberg
Paul Ruben
Carl Sagan
Ron Schaumburg
William Shatner
The Special Olympics
    Committee
Peter Stewart
Sally Struthers
Martha Thomases at D.C.
    Comics
Grace Townley
U.S.A. Gymnastics
Chris Warren of the Amuse-
    ment and Music Operators
    Association
Amy Wuhl
Ziggy

Bibliography

Ash, Russell. *The Top 10 of Everything*. Boston: Dorling Kindersley, 1994.

Barkin, Carol, and Elizabeth James. *Jobs for Kids*. New York: Lothrop, 1990.

Berg, Ariadne, and Arthur Bochner. *The Totally Awesome Money Book for Kids*. New York: Newmarket Press, 1993.

Bergstrom, Joan, and Craig Bergstrom. *All the Best Contests for Kids*. Berkeley: Ten Speed Press, 1993.

Berkeley Pop Culture Project. *The Whole Pop Catalog*. New York: Avon, 1991.

Bodner, Janet. *Kiplinger's Money-Smart Kids*. Washington, D.C.: Kiplinger, 1993.

Brainard, Beth, and Sheil Behr. *Soup Should Be Seen and Not Heard!* New York: Dell, 1990.

Caney, Stephen. *Stephen Caney's Kids' America*. New York: Workman, 1978.

Carrel, Annette. *It's the Law!* Volcano, Calif.: Volcano Press, 1994.

Chafetz, Michael. *Smart for Life*. New York: Penguin, 1992.

Child magazine, various issues.

Childress, Casey and Linda McKenzie. *A Kids' Guide to Collecting Baseball Cards*. Tucson, Ariz.: Harbinger House, 1994.

Coffey, Wayne. *303 of the World's Worst Predictions*. New York: Tribeca, 1983.

Dacyczyn, Amy. *The Tightwad Gazette*. New York: Villard, 1992.

Dickson, Paul. *Slang!* New York: Dell, 1990.

Dossey, Donald. *Holiday Folklore, Phobias and Fun*. Asheville, N.C.: Outcomes Unlimited, 1992.

Drew, Bonnie, and Noel Drew. *Kid Biz*. Austin, Tex.: Eakin, 1990.

Dunn, Jerry, ed. *Tricks of the Trade*. Boston: Houghton Mifflin, 1991.

Earthworks Group. *Fifty Simple Things Kids Can Do to Recycle.* Kansas City, Mo.: Andrews and McMeel, 1991.

——. *Fifty Simple Things Kids Can Do to Save the Earth.* Kansas City, Mo.: Andrews and McMeel, 1990.

Editors of *Prevention* magazine health books. *The Doctors' Book of Home Remedies.* Emmaus, Pa.: Rodale, 1990.

Elwood, Ann, Carol Orsag, and Sidney Solomon. *Macmillan Illustrated Almanac for Kids.* New York: Macmillan, 1981.

Elwood, Ann, and Carol Orsag Madigan. *Life's Big Instruction Book.* New York: Warner Books, 1995.

Erickson, Judith B. *Directory of American Youth Organizations.* Minneapolis: Free Spirit, 1994.

Essoe, Gabe. *The TV Book of Lists.* New York: Carol Publishing Group, 1981.

Fiffer, Steve, and Sharon Sloan. *50 Ways to Help Your Community.* New York: Doubleday, 1993.

Ford, Clyde. *We Can All Get Along.* New York: Dell, 1994.

Galbraith, Judy. *The Gifted Kids Survival Guide.* Minneapolis: Free Spirit, 1994.

Gootman, Marilyn. *When a Friend Dies.* Minneapolis: Free Spirit, 1994.

Howard, Tracy Apple, with Sage Howard. *Kids Ending Hunger: What Can We Do?* Kansas City, Mo.: Andrews and McMeel, 1992.

Johnson, Stancil. *Frisbee.* New York: Workman, 1981.

Kadrey, Richard. *Covert Culture Sourcebook.* New York: St. Martin's Press, 1993.

Karaoke Scene Magazine

Kincher, Jonni. *Psychology for Kids.* Minneapolis: Free Spirit, 1990.

Krantz, Les. *America by the Numbers.* Boston: Houghton Mifflin, 1993.

Kroloff, Charles A. *Fifty-four Ways You Can Help the Homeless.* Southport, Conn.: H. L. Levin, 1993.

Levine, Michael. *The Kids' Address Book.* New York: Perigree, 1994.

Lewis, Barbara. *The Kids' Guide to Social Action*. Minneapolis: Free Spirit, 1991.

Lindsell-Roberts, Sheryl. *Loony Laws and Silly Statutes*. New York: Sterling, 1994.

Logan, Suzanne. *The Kids Can Help Book*. New York: Perigree, 1992.

Lucaire, Ed. *Celebrity Setbacks*. Englewood Cliffs, N.J.: Prentice Hall, 1993.

McLoone-Basta, Margo, and Alice Siegel. *The Kids' Book of Lists*. Austin, Tex.: Holt, Rinehart and Winston, 1980.

McLoone-Basta, Margo, Alice Siegel, and the editors of the World Almanac. *The Second Kids' World Almanac of Records and Facts*. Mahwah, N.J.: World Almanac, 1987.

Marsh, Dave, and James Bernard. *The New Book of Rock Lists*. St. Louis, Mo.: Fireside, 1994.

Moore, Lawrence. *Lightning Never Strikes Twice and Other False Facts*. New York: Avon, 1994.

Neary, Kevin, and Dave Smith. *The Ultimate Disney Trivia Book*. New York: Hyperion, 1992.

Reiser, Howard. *Skateboarding*. New York: Ventura, 1989.

Rosenberg, Ellen. *Growing Up Feeling Good*. Beaufort, S.C.: Beaufort, 1992.

Shannon, Jaqueline. *Why It's Great to Be a Girl*. New York: Warner Books, 1994.

Siegel, Alice, and Margo Basta. *The Information Please Kids' Almanac*. Boston: Houghton Mifflin, 1992.

Stang, Ivan. *High Weirdness by Mail: A Directory of the Fringe*. Taft, Tex.: S&S, 1988.

Wallace, Amy, David Wallechinsky, and Irving Wallace. *The Book of Lists 3*. New York: Morrow, 1983.

Weston, Carol. *Girltalk*. New York: HarperCollins, 1992.

Windeler, Robert. *The Films of Shirley Temple*. New York: Citadel Press, 1978.

Index

Ben & Jerry's ice cream flavors, 201–2
Benefit4Kids, 97
Benitez, Wilfredo, 163
Better Business Bureau, 51
Bicycles
  safety on, 176–77
  young riders of, 163
Big Brothers/Big Sisters of America, 88
Big Whopper Liar's Contest, 128
Biography Today (magazine), 240
Blob, The (movie monster), 291
Blume, Judy, 219
Boodle: By Kids, for Kids (magazine), 246
Books
  advice on, 208–9
  about African-Americans, 211–12, 223–25
  about Asians, 226–27
  banned and challenged, 218–20, 230–31
  like *Harry Potter,* 233–34
  to help kids with tough issues, 215–16
  about Jews, 221–23
  kids who published, 217–18
  about Latinos, 212–13, 220–21
  about legendary places, 231–34
  about Native Americans, 225–26
  prize-winning, 209–13
  tips for writing, 238–40
  Wizard of Oz sequels, 227–30
  writers' favorite, 213–14
Boston cream pie (largest), 192
Bowling
  etiquette of, 177–78
  young champions of, 164
Boxing
  girls in, 163
  youngest champions in, 163

Boy Scouts of America, 88
Boys Clubs of America, 88
Boys' Life (magazine), 240–41
Braces (names for kids who wear), 378
Brorsen, Metha, 164
Brothers and sisters. *See also* Families
  children without, 123
  twin, 124–25
  younger, 122–23
Budgeting, 60
Bugs Bunny and friends, 313–14
Bullfighter (youngest), 162
Bullies (how to handle), 9, 106–7, 216
Burger King restaurants, 204
Business (starting your own), 54–56
Business Kids (magazine), 241

C

Calaveras County Fair and Jumping Frog Jubilee, 128
Calliope (magazine), 246–47
Camp Fire, 89
Campaign Against Workplace Bullying, 106
Cancer Kids, 89
Candies
  best-selling, 195–97
  candy bars, 205
  facts about, 197–98
  Life Savers, 190
  M&Ms, 191, 195
Candy bars, 205
Capp, Al, 7
Card collecting, 180–81
Carsickness (avoiding), 26
Carnival games, 131–32
Castro, Margaret, 163
Celebrities (writing letters to), 152–54

Gardner, Randy, 163
Gereson, Gary, 164
Gestring, Marjorie, 162
Ghidrah (movie monster), 292
Ghosts (in the White House),
    344–45
G.I. Joe, 150–51
Gifts (free or inexpensive), 157–59
Girl Scouts of the USA, 90
Girls
    Bill of Rights for, 68–69, 330–31
    as boxers, 163
    facts about, 356
    as Little League Baseball players,
        164
    softball championship teams of,
        340–41
    Web sites for, 266–67
Girls Clubs of America, 90
Girls Incorporated, 68–69
Glenn, John, 34–35
Godzilla (movie monster), 292
Goldberg (pro wrestler), 25
Golfers, 164, 167–68
Good deeds, 84–86
Good luck signs, 382–84
Gootman, Marilyn E., 112, 216
Gould, Shane, 164
Government office addresses,
    64–67
Grammer, Kelsey, 283
Grant-A-Wish, 98
Great American Bathtub Race,
    128–29
Gregory, Thomas, 164
Guardian Angels, 90
Guns, 89, 334
Gymnastics performers, 162, 163

H

Häagen-Dazs ice cream flavors, 202
Halloween
    safety tips for, 19
    trick-or-treating for UNICEF on,
        73
Handler, Elliot and Ruth, 178
"Happy Birthday" (on the tele-
    phone), 159, 376
Harry Potter series (Rowling)
    books like, 233–34
    characters in, 235–36
    collectibles relating to, 237–38
Hasbro, 140
Hawkins, Francis, 217
Health problems. *See* Illness
Hearts and Minds, 90
Heifer Project International, 71–72
Hemingway, Ernest, 208
Hiccups (stopping), 30
Highlights for Children (magazine),
    248
Hingis, Martina, 163
Hinton, S. E., 217
Hippies (words used by), 385–86
Hitchhiking, 10
Holidays (little-known), 387–88
Holmes, Andrea, 165
Home Education (magazine), 242
Home schooling, 96–97, 242
Homeless people, 74–75. *See also*
    Runaways
Homework
    excuses for not doing, 46–47
    help with, on Internet, 261–63,
        267–68
Hot dogs, 191
How on Earth! (magazine), 248
Hug-A-Tree and Survive, 90
Hula hoops, 134
Hunger (how to end), 71–74, 79, 91
Hunt, Amber, 163

I

i (magazine), 241
Ice cream
    cones, 191

fear of, 12
in movies, 290–96
Mothra (movie monster), 293–94
Motion sickness (avoiding), 26
Mountain climbers (youngest),
162–63
Movies
"cheating" by, 296–97
child actors in, 313, 316, 317
children's top-grossing, 285–86
children who have won awards
for, 313
classic, 300–305
dinosaur, 299–300
Disney characters in, 286–90
King Kong's dimensions in, 312
mistakes in, 297–98
monsters in, 290–96, 298–300
snacks at, 204–5
space, 317–20
vegetable monsters in, 296
Web sites about, 265
MTV, 325–27
Muggers, 9
Muir, Karen, 164
Mummy, The (movie monster),
294
Murphy, Eddie, 283
Muse (magazine), 252
Music. *See also* Culture; Musical
instruments
age at which classical musicians
began to play, 324
to be played on push-button telephones, 159, 375–76
on MTV, 325–27
operas that kids like, 321–23
rock songs with sound effects for
titles, 320–21
titles by Weird Al Yankovic,
324–25
Web sites for, 264–65
Musical instruments

age at which classical artists began
playing, 324
why it's important to play, 327
Musical instruments you can make,
381

N

Names
for kids who wear braces, 378
for Santa Claus, 349
of Santa's reindeer, 348
of the Seven Dwarfs, 348
ways to sign your, 386–87
weird city, 345–46
Nathan's Famous Hot Dog Eating
Contest, 129
National Association for the Deaf,
107
National Association of Elementary
School Principals, 87
National Beta Club, 92
National Coalition Against Domes-
tic Violence, 92
National Council on Child Abuse
and Family Violence, 92
National Crime Prevention Coun-
cil, 92
National Fence-Painting Contest,
129
National Geographic World (maga-
zine), 242
National Information Center for
Children and Youth with Dis-
abilities, 92–93
National Jewish Council for the
Disabled, 93
National School Safety Center, 93
National Wildlife (magazine), 242
Native Americans (books about),
225–26
Nausea (avoiding), 12–13, 26
New Moon (magazine), 250
Newbery Medal books, 209–11

911, 10
Nintendo Power (magazine), 242
Nosferatu (movie monster), 294
Noyes, Alfred, 208
Nuclear war, 3
Nuxhall, Joe, 162

O

O'Donnell, Rosie, 7–8
Odyssey (magazine), 242
Older people. *See* Senior citizens
Olive Oyl, 255
Olympic sports, 162–64. *See also*
    Special Olympics
Onassis, Jacqueline Kennedy, 208–9
Only children, 123
Operas, 321–23
Organizations (working for and
    with children), 86–95
Orr, Coby, 164
Osment, Haley Joel, 317
Outdoor jobs, 58–59
Owl (magazine), 243
Oxfam America, 73

P

Parents. *See also* Punishments
    divorcing, 118–19
    lies told by, 15–16
    people to talk with instead of,
        16–17, 20, 21
    rude things done by, 15
    things that are hard to tell to,
        113–15
    who fight, 117, 119
Parker Brothers, 134, 140
Pasta, 191
Paul, Wesley, 164
PC video games, 147–48
Peeing (words for), 336
Peer pressure (how to identify),
    99–101. *See also* Cliques;
    Friends

People for the American Way, 230
Perfectionism, 215
Pets
    death of, 13–14
    jobs involving, 56–57
Phantom of the Opera (movie
    monster), 294–95
Phobias. *See* Fears
Pimples (avoiding), 26–27
Pinball history, 141–43
Pizza Hut restaurants, 204
Pizza(s)
    facts about, 202–4
    largest, 193
Play (importance of), 90–91
Play-Doh, 181–83
Plays (magazine), 243
Poe, Edgar Allan, 208
Poetry, 208, 218
Poets at Work (magazine), 250
Poisonous plants, 29–30
Poitier, Sidney, 7
Pokémon, 314–15
Police. *See also* 911
    reporting bullies to, 9
    reporting child abuse to, 21
    reporting strangers to, 11, 31
Politics. *See* Changing the world
Pollution prevention, 77–79
Popcorn
    flavors of, 196
    at movies, 204–5
Popeye, 255
Popsicle, 191
Potato chips, 190
Predictions
    about the future, 332–33
    that didn't come true, 343–44
Project Wild, 70
Protecting yourself. *See* Safety
Public speaking tips, 40–41
Publishing your writing, 246–52
Pumpkin (largest), 193